# The Accredited
# Counter Fraud
# Specialist Handbook

# The Accredited Counter Fraud Specialist Handbook

MARTIN TUNLEY
ANDREW WHITTAKER
JIM GEE
MARK BUTTON

WILEY

This edition first published 2015
© 2015 Martin Tunley, Andrew Whittaker, Jim Gee, and Mark Button

*Registered office*
John Wiley & Sons Ltd, The Atrium, Southern Gate, Chichester, West Sussex, PO19 8SQ, United Kingdom

For details of our global editorial offices, for customer services and for information about how to apply for permission to reuse the copyright material in this book please visit our website at www.wiley.com.

Wiley publishes in a variety of print and electronic formats and by print-on-demand. Some material included with standard print versions of this book may not be included in e-books or in print-on-demand. If this book refers to media such as a CD or DVD that is not included in the version you purchased, you may download this material at http://booksupport.wiley.com. For more information about Wiley products, visit www.wiley.com.

**Library of Congress Cataloging-in-Publication Data**

Tunley, Martin.
　The accredited counter fraud specialist handbook / Martin Tunley, Andrew Whittaker, Jim Gee and Mark Button.
　　pages cm
　Includes bibliographical references and index.
　ISBN 978-1-118-79880-5 (pbk.)
　1. Fraud.　2. Fraud–Prevention.　3. Fraud investigation.　I. Title.
　HV6691.T86 2015
　658.4'73–dc23　　　　　　　　　　　　　　　　　　　　　　　2014035523

A catalogue record for this book is available from the British Library.

ISBN 978-1-118-79880-5 (pbk) ISBN 978-1-119-01725-7 (ebk)
ISBN 978-1-118-79879-9 (ebk) ISBN 978-1-118-79878-2 (ebk)

Cover Design: Wiley
Cover Illustration: TK
Set in 10/13 Photina MT Std by Aptara
Printed in Great Britain by TJ International Ltd, Padstow, Cornwall, UK

# Contents

CHAPTER ONE

# How the counter fraud profession developed and what the counter fraud professional should be

## CHAPTER **SUMMARY**

This chapter will consider the professionalisation of counter fraud investigation, including how the Accredited Counter Fraud Specialist has evolved. The development of a professional infrastructure and the essence of the counter fraud professional will then be outlined. Finally, the chapter will redefine the counter fraud professional and the lexicon of countering fraud.

## INTRODUCTION

This chapter will consider the importance for an organisation – whatever the size – of employing a counter fraud professional and developments over the last

15 years to establish a new Counter Fraud Specialist profession. This may seem like an extravagant expense, but there are a variety of economical models which can be used to achieve this aim. For example small organisations can contract in the services of a professional for a selected number of days depending upon their needs or they can train a member of staff to take on these responsibilities. For medium to larger organisations the risks of fraud are likely to warrant much more investment in the resource, ultimately culminating in a full-time position or multiple positions. There is no one size fits all and clearly the size, complexity and nature of fraud risks vary significantly between organisations. This chapter will consider what counter fraud professionals look like; it will also examine the professional infrastructure and consider some of the changes required to enhance this. It will also analyse what the skill-set of the counter fraud professional should be.

##  COUNTER FRAUD PROFESSIONAL INFRASTRUCTURE

A wide range of strategies have been advocated to create the best solutions to counter fraud and lead ultimately to competitive advantage for the organisation. Underpinning all of this is having (whether employed direct or via a contract) an appropriate counter fraud professional (or professionals – depending upon the size of the organisation) to lead the fight against fraud. In most organisations the focus of counter fraud activity usually centres on reactive investigations and developing controls. These are only part of what is required, as the chapters of this book will show. Most commonly counter fraud responsibilities are allocated to one or more of the following depending upon the size and nature of the organisation: auditors, investigators or security managers. In the more enlightened organisations these more general staff develop a fraud expertise and secure specialist fraud qualifications. In some organisations, such is the size and/or the fraud risk that they employ specialist staff dedicated to combating fraud such as Counter Fraud Specialists or fraud examiners.

Whichever model an organisation uses, what is important is for the person responsible to be a 'counter fraud professional'. 'Professional' has many connotations in both mainstream and academic debate. Central to the definition is the idea of a profession. Avoiding some of the extensive academic debates on what constitutes a profession the central traits are:

- standards and a code of ethics;
- a body of knowledge disseminated by professional journals, conferences etc.;

- a recognised association covering all aspects of the industry;
- institutions capable of training and evaluating personnel and awarding certification of competence;
- an educational discipline that is able to prepare students in the specific functions and philosophies (Larson, 1977; Manunta, 1996; Simonsen, 1996).

Elements of these in relation to fraud professionals exist to varying degrees in different countries. For example in the USA there is the Association of Certified Fraud Examiners (ACFE) which has a standard of ethics, a knowledge base with dissemination structures (but no academic journal), a recognised training programme (Certified Fraud Examiner) and some degree-level programmes at universities. In the UK ACFE also has a presence, but there is in addition to the Institute of Counter Fraud Specialists (ICFS), recognised certification by the Counter Fraud Professional Accreditation Board (CFPAB) through the Accredited Counter Fraud Specialist award (ACFS) and degree programmes. However, even amongst those who have achieved ACFS, surveys of these professionals in the UK revealed substantial gaps in a professional infrastructure:

- Only around a quarter are educated to at least graduate level (only around 13% going on to achieve one of the higher awards of the CFPAB, such as CCFS);
- Low levels of additional accredited training are undertaken;
- Around three-quarters are not a member of any professional association (Button et al, 2007).

 ## THE HISTORY OF THE COUNTER FRAUD PROFESSION

It is now more than 16 years since the UK Government Minister, the Right Honourable Frank Field MP's ground-breaking Government Green Paper 'Beating Fraud is Everyone's Business' (Department of Social Security, 1998). Field, then Minister of State for Welfare Reform, gave the very first UK Government commitment to creating a counter fraud profession. Jim Gee (one of the authors of this Handbook) was the Minister's Fraud Advisor, having previously performed the same role when Field was Chair of the House of Commons Social Security Select Committee. He was also Head of the London Borough of Lambeth Corporate Anti-Fraud Team, brought in by its Chief Executive Heather Rabbatts, in

1996, shortly after Lambeth was described as 'the most corrupt local authority' in the UK.

Gee remembers working with Field on the Green Paper and being asked to read and comment on the passage about a counter fraud profession. He remembers suggesting that the phrase 'the creation of a counter fraud profession' be inserted as a commitment, and providing background information about the need for 'specialist professional training and education'.

These comments were drawn from the experience of establishing professional training and education in London. As early as 1997, work had been commenced involving the Association of London Government, the London Boroughs Fraud Investigators Group, the University of Portsmouth and Thames Valley Police Force's Training Department, to create a professional training course for Counter Fraud Specialists, along with a Professional Accreditation Board to accredit those who successfully completed the training. These developments were consciously modelled on the arrangements to be found in other areas of work where professional skills are predominant. Avoiding unhelpful pretensions, the initial analogies were the social work and teaching professions.

In these areas, you typically find:

- Prescribed professional training which develops technical skills;
- A common ethical framework for the deployment of those skills
- A Professional Accreditation Board to regulate those who are accredited as a result of successfully completing the professional training;
- A Centre of Excellence to innovate and to highlight emerging best practice.

The particular experience of the London Borough of Lambeth highlighted the need for new standards of professionalism. In the early 1990s work to counter fraud and corruption was very weak, with a deficiency of both skills and resources. The new Chief Executive, Heather Rabbatts, liberated Lambeth from the tyranny of historic poor performance and brought with her a real understanding of the importance of protecting public funds and maintaining the trust and confidence of those living in the area. Having little worthwhile to defend, Lambeth could start afresh, designing counter fraud arrangements fit for the time.

So the commitment in Frank Field's Green Paper naturally followed this initial work – a model had been set up which had been shown to work. There followed a period during which Department of Work and Pensions (DWP) officials such as Janet Bestwick, Peter Darby and Lillian Buchanan worked with Jim

Gee and other local authority representatives to establish a professional training course for Counter Fraud Specialists in the benefits fraud area. This training subsequently became known as Professionalism IN Security (PINS) training and the process was overseen by a DWP/Local Authority Accreditation Board administered by the University of Portsmouth.

In 1998 Alan Milburn, then Minister of State at the Department of Health, decided, with very helpful advice from his advisor on governance, John Flook (then Chair of the Healthcare Financial Management Association), to radically upgrade the NHS's work to protect itself against fraud. A new position of Director of Counter Fraud Services was advertised and Jim Gee was appointed to fill it. This led to the creation of a Directorate of Counter Fraud Services and then the NHS Counter Fraud Service (NHS CFS), as well as an obligation being placed on all NHS organisations (in secondary legislation) to appoint a Local Counter Fraud Specialist.

This was followed, in December 1998, by a commitment from the Department of Health, on behalf of the NHS, in the strategy document 'Countering Fraud in the NHS', to ensure that professionally accredited counter fraud officers were in place in every part of the NHS.

Recognising the need to provide professional training to the (now) hundreds of people appointed to undertake this work, the NHS CFS established a strong, well-resourced training department under the leadership of David Snell (formerly a trainer with Thames Valley Police), Jenny Davidson and Andy Whittaker (one of the authors of this book) who had been involved in the original Association of London Government training.

A Foundation Level Accredited Counter Fraud Specialist training syllabus was designed, focusing on providing much needed technical skills in how to detect, investigate and seek to apply sanctions in respect of fraud. The training also contained an ethical module designed to make sure that Counter Fraud Specialists understood the meaning of key concepts such as fairness, objectivity, professionalism, propriety, vision and expertise. There was a requirement to successfully complete the ethical module before being accredited.

The related NHS Professional Accreditation Board was, again, administered by the University of Portsmouth and its then Reader, now Professor Mark Button (one of the authors of this Handbook). It also had representatives from NHS organisations, the Department of Health and other stakeholders.

Between 1999 and 2001, the Department of Work and Pensions (DWP) and the NHS had separate professional accreditation boards, but these were brought together with the encouragement of Professor Steve Savage at the University of

Portsmouth. A single Counter Fraud Professional Accreditation Board (CFPAB) was launched by Malcolm Wicks, then Minister at the DWP, and Lord Phillip Hunt, a Minister at the Department of Health, in October 2001.

The new CFPAB had six sectors representing Counter Fraud Specialists from across the economy – the Department of Health, the Department of Work and Pensions, the Inland Revenue, Local Government, Consignia (formerly the Post Office) and the Abbey National – and by the date of the launch 2821 Accredited Counter Fraud Specialists had already completed the first level of their professional training.

Since then the counter fraud profession has grown very substantially, with around 14,000 Counter Fraud Specialists accredited at Foundation, Advanced, Degree and MSc levels at the end of 2013. The board itself now has members drawn from the police, Department for Work and Pensions, NHS, local authorities, HM Passport Office, HM Revenue and Customs, KPMG and Questgates.

There are further weaknesses in professional infrastructures which will now be explored. The next section will also set out a route map to the creation of a professional infrastructure, drawing upon the transformation of personnel management to Human Resource Management (HRM) in the UK.

 ## DEVELOPING A PROFESSIONAL INFRASTRUCTURE

This section offers a 'route map' to how a profession was created for those working in counter fraud. The first and easiest step is for there to be one dominant professional association in a country. In the UK the picture is very fragmented, with a number of bodies which could emerge into this role. In the USA ACFE is in the prime place to achieve this position.

The dominant association then needs to create a suite of memberships which are linked to higher study and/or the equivalent. ACFE has the entry level CFE, but no higher awards. In the UK the Counter Fraud Professional Accreditation Board, which is not a professional association, but does accredit and recognise training, has a learning route linked to higher education. This route is set out in Table 1.1.

Any professional infrastructure should build upon the experience of the CFPAB and other professional bodies and have a structure such as the following:

- Entry Award – Equivalent to first year of bachelor's degree.
- Established award achieved after at least three years' study/experience – Equivalent to bachelor's degree.
- Higher award based upon higher study or outstanding contribution to profession – Equivalent to master's level study.

**TABLE 1.1** CFPAB progression of awards

| CFPAB Award | Level |
| --- | --- |
| Accredited Counter Fraud Technician | Various training providers provide and must be accredited by a higher education establishment to the equivalent of one twelfth of a first year of a bachelor's degree. |
| Accredited Counter Fraud Specialist, Accredited Counter Fraud Manager, Accredited Counter Fraud Intelligence Specialist | Various training providers provide and must be accredited by a higher education establishment to the equivalent of a third of a first year of a bachelor's degree. |
| Certified Counter Fraud Specialist | Completion of first year of recognised bachelor's degree. |
| Graduate Counter Fraud Specialist | Completion of recognised bachelor's or master's degree. |

In the UK context many professional associations link the above to categories of membership such as Student, Graduate, Member, Fellow etc. Such categories encourage increased professionalism because ultimately most people want to progress up the ladder to enhance their own status and financial rewards.

It is not enough, however, to create such a framework. The next step is to market and enforce it. All counter fraud professionals should be encouraged to join and those in positions of power recruiting new counter fraud staff should specify the appropriate level of membership as an essential requirement.

The new merged body should also learn from other representative associations and offer a range of services that further enhance professionalism. Assessing different bodies some of the functions that should be provided are listed below:

- Hold an annual conference
- Hold seminars on appropriate subjects
- Provide training
- Create a branch structure for knowledge transfer/networking
- Provide accreditation of training and academic courses
- Publish a professional magazine
- Publish a professional journal
- Conduct, commission and disseminate research
- Develop online resources

- Develop best practice and guides to specific security functions
- Sell publications at discount
- Publicise job opportunities
- Provide e-mail alerts on latest information.

Many of these already exist and they could be provided to members as part of membership packages. For example the *Journal of Financial Crime*, which is the closest the fraud world has to a professional academic journal, could be supplied as part of membership (as many medical professional associations supply academic journals as part of their fees). A clear priority will be the need for an annual conference of counter fraud professionals which provides opportunities to share knowledge on the latest developments in countering fraud. Again there are already many fraud related conferences that do this, but it is important for all to attend one dedicated conference.

There is another area where such an association could have a very important role to play in enhancing the fight against fraud and that is to create structures where counter fraud professionals can safely discuss their experience – including their failures. Learning from experience (or isomorphic learning) is central to enhancing the fight against fraud. Counter fraud staff should be able to openly discuss fraud, 'behind the wire', amongst their peers under so-called 'Chatham House Rules' (what is discussed is not discussed outside the room). The development of such networks will greatly enhance isomorphic learning and overall the improvement of the fight against fraud.

It is important to link such developments to codes of ethics and enforce the 'Chatham House Rules' in relation to the Code of Conduct. This, however, is just one aspect of what the Code should cover. Other aspects should include: exercising functions with honesty and integrity; adhering to appropriate laws and regulations; abiding by the rules of the association; commitments to develop professionally; respecting the rights of minority groups and emphasising the importance of human rights, to name but some. The new association should set out such a code, publicise it to members and actively enforce it.

Most established professions have Centres of Excellence in some form which conduct research, identify best practice and have established networks for disseminating that best practice. The counter fraud world is lacking in this. The Centre for Counter Fraud Studies is one of the few dedicated centres in academia focused upon fraud. It also hosts the Fraud and Corruption Hub which is a resource with links to the most significant research and publications on fraud. More of these need to be created around the world.

## THE ESSENCE OF THE COUNTER FRAUD PROFESSIONAL

This chapter has set out much of the professional infrastructure required. Ultimately professionalism boils down to the operative who is employed to deal with fraud. As has previously been mentioned, the focus of counter fraud staff is often on reactive investigations. There needs to be more than this. The holistic approach, as set out throughout this book, means focusing upon proactive measures too. Therefore the counter fraud professional should focus upon:

- Monitoring fraud metrics and tailoring the strategy accordingly
- Preventative measures
- Developing an anti-fraud culture
- Detecting fraud as quickly as possible
- Investigating fraud
- Pursuing sanctions against those who have been caught
- Pursuing redress where possible.

In some organisations such is the size of a counter fraud department that there may be staff focused specifically upon some of these. Nevertheless it is important for the counter fraud professional to have a grounding in all of these areas. The above list comprises the broad set of knowledge required. There are other important traits which are also required and will now be examined.

### The Enlightened Professional

Central to the expertise of a counter fraud professional is the need to be appropriately trained, educated and informed in the latest research and thinking relating to fraud. This can involve undertaking short training courses or enrolling upon a counter fraud related degree or master's programme. It can also mean attending conferences and seminars as well as reading professional magazines and journals. It is also important that these activities are pursued on a regular basis, or what is more commonly known as continuing professional development (CPD). Underpinning this is the need – where there is evidence – to pursue evidence based solutions to the problems faced by the organisation. This chapter now outlines some of the key sources of knowledge and training/education to support CPD.

## Information on Latest Research

The Fraud and Corruption Hub – http://www.port.ac.uk/ccfs
Wiley – http://eu.wiley.com/WileyCDA/
Gower – http://www.ashgate.com/
Journal of Financial Crime – http://www.emeraldinsight.com/products/journals/journals.htm?id=jfc

## Fraud News

ACFE Fraud Magazine – http://www.fraud-magazine.com/
Fraud Intelligence – http://www.informaprofessional.com/publications/newsletter/fraud_intelligence

## Fraud Courses

ACFE – http://www.acfe.com/
Centre for Counter Fraud Studies – http://www.port.ac.uk/ccfs
Fraud degrees and higher training courses – http://www.larry-adams.com/university_fraud_courses.htm

## Professional Associations

ACFE – http://www.acfe.com/
ICFS – http://www.icfs.org.uk/

### The 'Reflective' Professional

Based upon the original ideas of Schön (1983) who advocated 'reflective practice' where professionals are expected to regularly reflect on their work and learning, there is much of use for the counter fraud professional. Schön argues that professionals face two sets of problems at the high and low ground. On the high ground, it is argued, problems are well defined as are the strategies to deal with them, frequently based upon extensive research. Take for example the principles of building a bridge; there are many factors to bear in mind with guidance based upon much research. On the 'swampy lowlands', however, there are also many problems which are messy with no simple solutions and it is here where the most significant threats exist according to Schön. To use the bridge analogy again, however, when the decision about whether to build a bridge or what type of bridge to build is considered the technological knowledge is lost in the political, financial, environmental and various other factors that confuse the issue. It is here that reflective practice (and the related action research) can help solve these problems. This approach has gained favour amongst some healthcare professions. Nurses, clinical educators, physiotherapists, occupational therapists, radiographers as well as managers are some of the occupations that have been encouraged to combine the theory aspects of their course with reflection on their professional practice (Palfrey et al, 2004). By its very nature it is difficult to specify an approach to pursuing 'reflective practice', but Palfrey et al, drawing upon the work of Kember et al (2001), set out the following:

- The need to reflect critically on what one does as a practitioner (as a counter fraud professional) and on what happens as a result of one's practice.
- A regular re-examination of one's experience, beliefs, and conceptual knowledge.
- The generation of new perspectives and knowledge arising from reflections on action (reflecting after one's actions) and reflection in action (reflecting during one's actions).
- The welcoming of challenges to one's standard way of thinking about and acting on problems.

(Palfrey et al, 2004: 37)

Given the unique challenges faced by counter fraud professionals which are often in the 'swampy lowlands' the 'Reflective Practice' model would seem well suited to the counter fraud professional. Nevertheless in an organisation dominated by practice based upon evidence from research the difficulty of applying reflective approaches does pose problems.

## The Counter Fraud Leader

Not all counter fraud professionals will need to be leaders, but many will. Leadership is to be distinguished from management. Sperry (2003) argues that typically management is distinguished by the functioning of individuals under conditions of stability focused upon tasks such as meeting objectives, assessing compliance and co-ordinating staff and work patterns. By contrast leadership is aligned to more unstable conditions and times of change and focused upon inspiring and/or galvanising the commitment of staff. However he goes on to argue that this distinction does not reflect the research and that 'effective management and leadership cannot be separated' (Sperry, 2003: 2). The contrasting aspects of management and leadership are required for success and the theme of his book is that they are complementary. Underpinning this debate is the basic problem that there has been much research on leadership but little agreement on what leadership and management are (Bryman, 1986). Nevertheless the distinction above, if accepted, does raise scenarios where the two sets of skills conflict. As Villiers and Adlam (2003: xii) argue:

> The cautious, artful, consensus-seeking manager – who knows the cost of everything and upsets no-one, and whose quota is always fulfilled – may be quite incapable of swift and dynamic leadership when the situation requires it.

Before we begin to discuss what makes an effective manager/leader it would be useful to clarify some of the terms used in such debates:

**Skills:** How to's of a function which are transferable from person to person
**Knowledge:** what a person knows
**Talents:** Natural abilities in a person
**Competencies:** expected behaviours.

Let us use an analogy faced by some counter fraud professionals, such as dealing with a potentially violent situation when a fraudster has just been identified. The knowledge component would be to recognise certain non-verbal behaviours in a person, skills would be the appropriate strategies applied to the person to calm them down. There may, however, be certain people who have a natural talent for coping with an aggressive person because of their character. The competency is to be able to calm an aggressive person without using force – for some this might be based upon skills and knowledge learnt while in others it might be down to talent.

However, when competencies are examined they often reveal conflicts. A skill may be identified which is actually a talent. For example being able to make effective decisions in a pressured situation might be a talent rather than a skill that can be learned. And if competencies are based on talents the expected behaviour might be very difficult to achieve. Sperry (2003) argues that competencies should be purely skill based and the most effective leaders are those who can identify the people with the appropriate talents and who then develop the missing skills and knowledge in them. These leadership and management skills are the most important determinant of an organisation's success, '. . . more important than industry, environment, competition and economic factors combined' according to Whetten and Cameron (2002: 5). Sperry (2003) goes on to outline 12 essential skills that underpin the effective leader. These are:

**Operational**

1. Galvanising commitment and motivation
2. Maximising team performance
3. Delegating to maximise team performance
4. Managing stress and time effectively

**Relational**

5. Communicating effectively and strategically
6. Negotiating and managing conflict and difficult people
7. Coaching for maximum performance and development
8. Counselling and interviews for maximum performance and development

**Analytic**

9. Thinking and deciding strategically
10. Mastering the budget process
11. Mastering and monitoring financial and human resources
12. Assessing corporate and personal resources.

Source: Adapted from Sperry (2003: 7–8).

 ## REDEFINING THE COUNTER FRAUD PROFESSIONAL

How counter fraud work can deliver real, positive financial benefits is central to the redefinition of the counter fraud professional. They must speak the language of business such that what they advocate will produce a reward to the organisation in reduced fraud losses, which mean either increased profitability or, in the public sector context, reduced taxation or more resources to spend on essential services. The counter fraud professional needs to influence a change from the perception that countering fraud is an additional cost on the bottom line to it being a benefit to the bottom line. The following are central to achieving this: accurate measurement of fraud losses, a strategy tailored to the risks, appropriate investment in prevention and the development of an anti-fraud culture, quick detection of fraud, professional investigation of fraud, the pursuit of the full range of sanctions and redress and the development of appropriate metrics.

 ## REDEFINING THE LEXICON OF COUNTERING FRAUD

The counter fraud professional also needs to use the appropriate lexicon of the modern business world and deliverers of public services. This is increasingly preoccupied with reducing costs, increasing efficiency, improving profitability etc. The counter fraud professional needs to know what fraud and the response to it are costing the organisation and what can be done to reduce this. Knowledge of metrics, return-on-investment and financial costing models are all central. It is also important to be attuned to the objectives of the organisation and how countering fraud can enhance it. The contrast between the old and new lexicons is set out below:

> **Old:** limited knowledge of impact of fraud (detected at best), a service for the organisation that is a cost, focus upon detection and investigation.
> **New:** accurate knowledge of costs of fraud, financial benefit to the organisation, integrated, holistic approach.

### Communicating the Rewards of Successfully Countering Fraud to the Wider Organisation and Particularly the Leaders

It is also important for the counter fraud professional to evangelise the benefits of the modern approach across the organisation. This, as well as adding to the effort to create an anti-fraud culture, makes clear the positive impact countering fraud is having on the organisation. Not to do so risks questions arising over what is the benefit of spending large sums of money on countering fraud. This invariably makes counter fraud resources more vulnerable when the organisation faces financial difficulties as it is often seen as an easy area to cut. Therefore communicating to all levels of the organisation the work of counter fraud professionals is very important.

### Securing Positions of Influence within the Organisation

Linked to effective communication is the importance of securing positions in the most influential committees, forums etc. of an organisation and if this is not possible, direct reports to those who are. In the related field of security management there has been much written on the lack of influence in the boardroom. This is also the case for many counter fraud professionals. In most organisations a place on the board is unlikely for a counter fraud professional, but a direct report to someone who is should be achievable. The board itself should periodically be exposed to reports on fraud and the progress in dealing with it. Other influential forums within the organisation should also where possible have a counter fraud presence. This ensures that decisions are not made which might unintentionally increase the level of fraud.

 ## REVIEW

This chapter has explored the person of central importance in an organisation in countering fraud: the counter fraud professional. It began by examining who are the counter fraud professionals before highlighting some of the weaknesses in a professional approach. The broader professional infrastructure was then examined and this showed a number of weaknesses. A number of potential reforms were then examined. The chapter then ended with a consideration of the counter fraud professional at an individual level and some of the traits and orientations that are required for them to become professionals.

This book aims to play its part in ensuring that counter fraud professionals are effective, by strengthening the knowledge base of those involved.

 ## FURTHER READING

Bryman, A. (1986) *Leadership and Organizations*. London: Routledge and Kegan Paul.

Button, M. (2008) *Doing Security: Critical Reflections and an Agenda for Change*. Basingstoke: Palgrave.

Monks, R.A.G. and Minow N. (2010) *Corporate Governance*. Chichester: John Wiley & Sons.

Schön, D. (1983) *The Reflective Practitioner: How Professionals Think in Action*. New York: Basic Books.

CHAPTER TWO

# The Fraud Act 2006 and fraud related legislation

## CHAPTER **SUMMARY**

This chapter will explore legislation relating to fraud and associated offences that an ACFS needs to be aware of. The statutes discussed in detail include the Fraud Act 2006, Criminal Law Act 1977, Theft Acts of 1968 and 1978, Theft Amendment Act 1996, Bribery Act 2010 and Computer Misuse Act 1990 (including the relevant sections of the Police and Justice Act 2006). Where applicable, the chapter will include relevant case law that is applicable to the ACFS role and offences under investigation. The chapter will conclude with an inventory of additional legislation that an ACFS needs to be aware of depending upon their organisation's primary function.

 **INTRODUCTION**

Prior to the Fraud Act 2006 there was no criminal offence of fraud within English legislation. When attempting to prosecute what we now refer to as fraud, an array of deception offences were utilised, including 'obtaining property by deception', 'obtaining a money transfer by deception', 'obtaining a pecuniary advantage by deception', 'procuring the execution of a valuable security by deception', 'obtaining services by deception' and 'evasion of liability by deception', all of which have been repealed following the enactment of the Fraud Act 2006. This range of highly specific offences resulted in a number of difficulties when attempting to apply the law, principally because behaviour which could be regarded as dishonest or fraudulent did not always fit neatly into these categories. The Fraud Act 2006 was therefore enacted to simplify the law and increase the prospect of securing a successful prosecution. What the Act actually does therefore, is enshrine in law the ways in which fraud can be committed. This chapter will outline the relevant sections of this statute, before moving on to discuss other legislation relating to fraud and associated offences that an ACFS needs to be aware of.

 ## THE FRAUD ACT 2006

The stated objective of the Fraud Act 'is to make the law of fraud more simple and readily understandable' (Farrell, Yeo, and Ladenberg, 2007: 11). Accordingly, this statute 'makes a number of fundamental alterations to the general understanding of fraud' (Johnson and Rogers, 2007: 296). The legislation offers a clear definition of how fraud is committed, although it does not offer a definition of what actually constitutes fraud. The legislation came into effect on 15 January 2007 and replaced many of the existing offences relating to deception. However, the Act cannot be applied retrospectively; therefore any offences committed prior to the aforementioned date must be dealt with by way of one of the Theft Acts or other relevant legislation. When it is uncertain when the offence may actually have occurred, and it may have happened prior to, on or after 15 January 2007 the ACFS should try and obtain as much information as possible to assist in establishing the exact date on which any relevant activity occurred to assist the prosecuting team.

The significant change brought about by the Act is that it removes the element of deception from the offence, and focuses more on the behaviour of the suspect rather than their intention. Accordingly, an offence under this Act is based upon fraudulent behaviour combined with dishonesty. That is to say, an assessment of the suspect's fraudulent intent based upon the intended outcome as a result of their behaviour.

The main advantages of this legislation are therefore:

- It is easier for jurors to understand the principles of the case and related offences.
- It provides an effective framework for the Crown Prosecution Service to prosecute fraud offences.
- It provides the public with a clear understanding of the ways in which fraud can be committed, thus improving fraud awareness and the likelihood of offences being reported.
- New technologies are included in the single offence of fraud, thus removing the anomalies within previous legislation relating to devices such as cashpoint machines.
- The single offence also removes the requirement to create additional legislation.

## Offences Repealed

Schedule 3 of the Fraud Act 2006 lists the offences which were repealed by this statute:

Theft Act 1968:

- Obtaining property by deception (s. 15)
- Obtaining a money transfer by deception (s. 15A)
- Obtaining a pecuniary advantage by deception (s. 16)
- Procuring the execution of a valuable security by deception (s. 20(2)).

Theft Act 1978:

- Obtaining services by deception (s.1)
- Evasion of liability by deception (s.1).

## Overview

The Fraud Act introduces provision for a general offence of fraud. This is broken into three key sections:

- s. 2    Fraud by false representation
- s. 3    Fraud by failing to disclose information
- s. 4    Fraud by abuse of position.

A person will be guilty of fraud if they are in breach of any of these sections. The Act also creates new offences of:

> s. 6 Possession of articles for use in frauds
> s. 7 Making or supplying articles for use in frauds
> s. 9 Participating in fraudulent trading
> s. 11 Obtaining services dishonestly.

Each of the above will now be considered individually.

Section 2 – Fraud by false representation
(1) A person is in breach of this section if he—
   (a) dishonestly makes a false representation, and
   (b) intends, by making the representation—
     (i) to make a gain for himself or another, or
     (ii) to cause loss to another or to expose another to a risk of loss.
(2) A representation is false if—
   (a) it is untrue or misleading, and
   (b) the person making it knows that it is, or might be, untrue or misleading.
(3) 'Representation' means any representation as to fact or law, including a representation as to the state of mind of—
   (a) the person making the representation, or
   (b) any other person.
(4) A representation may be express or implied.
(5) For the purposes of this section a representation may be regarded as made if it (or anything implying it) is submitted in any form to any system or device designed to receive, convey or respond to communications (with or without human intervention).

This section sets out the offence of committing fraud by false representation. It makes it clear that the representation must be made dishonestly and that it is made with the intention of making a gain, or causing a loss, or risk of loss to another. Examples of fraud by false representation would include a person selling goods claiming they were genuine items whilst knowing them to be cheap replicas. It would also apply to someone who sends an e-mail falsely representing that the message has been sent by a legitimate financial institution and thereby extracting banking information from the recipient (known as 'phishing'). We will now explore the key elements of fraud by false representation.

## Dishonestly

The current definition of dishonesty is set in case law *R v Ghosh* [1982]. A two-stage test to determine dishonesty was established by the Court of Appeal in the judgment for this case. The first consideration is to question whether a defendant's behaviour would be regarded as dishonest by the ordinary standards of reasonable and honest people. If the answer is 'no', then the accused must be acquitted. If the answer is 'yes' the second consideration must then be applied. This is whether the defendant was aware that their conduct would be regarded as dishonest by reasonable and honest people.

## False representation

A representation is considered to be false if it is either untrue or misleading, and the person making such a representation knows that it is, or might be, untrue or misleading. The phrase *might be* is broad and allows an ACFS to adopt a style of questioning that should establish guilty knowledge or belief.

## Representation

A representation can be made by words or communicated by conduct. There is nothing which specifically indicates the format the words must take, therefore they could be written, spoken or be by electronic means, for example something posted on a website.

## Representation by conduct

If a person dishonestly misuses a credit card or bank card by using it to pay for goods, knowing they have no authorisation to use the card, a representation by conduct has been made. The representation they are making to the cashier is that they are authorised to use the card. This definition is not restricted to payment cards; for example, someone holding a charity collecting tin but intending to use the money collected for their own purposes is making a false representation by conduct.

## Gain or loss

The terms apply to the gain or loss of money or other property. Actual gain or loss does not have to occur, it only requires that the individual intends this to happen, and it can be either temporary or permanent.

Gain is defined as *keeping what one has as well as getting what one does not have* (s. 5(3)).

*Loss includes a loss by not getting what one might get, as well as a loss by parting with what one has* (s. 5(4)).

### Property

Property is defined as all types of property, real or personal and includes intellectual property.

It also includes things in action and tangible property (Farrell, Yeo and Ladenburg, 2003: 17–18).

Examples of things in action are things which have a value but are of no physical substance, for example a copyright.

## Basingstoke drug cheat prosecuted

A patient prosecuted following an investigation by the Local Counter Fraud Specialist.

On two separate occasions Mr X altered a number of prescriptions which he had obtained from the Health Centre. These were taken to the local Pharmacy, where he obtained additional drugs that he was not entitled to. On the first occasion the forgeries were successful and extra drugs were obtained, including controlled drugs. On the second occasion the pharmacy checked with his doctor and the deception was uncovered. Upon his arrest Mr X was also found to be in possession of heroin and cannabis. On 19th August he pleaded guilty in the Magistrates Court to four charges of fraud by false representation and one charge of possession of class A and B drugs. He was sentenced to a six months' supervision order and was ordered to forfeit the drugs which were destroyed.

(Hampshire and Isle of Wight Counter Fraud Service, 2010: 1)

Section 3 – Fraud by failing to disclose information
A person is in breach of this section if he—
(a) dishonestly fails to disclose to another person information which he is under a legal duty to disclose, and
(b) intends, by failing to disclose the information—
    (i) to make a gain for himself or another, or
    (ii) to cause loss to another or to expose another to a risk of loss.

Similar to fraud by false representation, there is a requirement that the defendant acts dishonestly and intends to make a gain for him or herself, or to cause a loss to another, or to expose another to a risk of loss.

*Legal duty of disclosure*

This reflects the fact that when entering into a formal relationship, for example a contract, there is a legal duty to correctly declare circumstances. It further explains that a failure to disclose information gives the victim a reason to seek damages. It also reflects that a victim could set aside any change in his or her legal position arising as a result of consenting to an action involving a false or failed declaration (Law Commission, 2002: paras 7.28 and 7.29). Examples might be failing to declare savings when making a claim to a means tested welfare benefit, or failing to disclose a health condition when applying for life insurance.

## Sisters jailed for £123k  NHS fraud at University

Two sisters who lived in the UK illegally for many years, and committed almost identical frauds against the NHS, have each been sentenced to ten months' imprisonment.

Miss X and Miss Y pleaded guilty to seven and six charges respectively. Both used false documents to gain NHS bursaries and nursing places at a University, defrauding nearly £123,000 between them. They had planned to move to Australia and work there as nurses after qualifying but were arrested on 15th April 2010, with the assistance of the UK Border Agency. Miss X defrauded £73,376.90. Her three year nursing diploma, which she completed, cost the East of England Strategic Health Authority (SHA) £18,544.25. She also obtained an NHS Student Bursary of £49,432.65 covering three years, plus £5,400 from the University HE Access to Learning Fund. Her younger sister Miss Y defrauded £49,146.56. She completed two years of the same course, which cost the East of England SHA around £15,997. She obtained an NHS Student Bursary of £29,954.56, covering two years, plus £3,195 from the University HE Access to Learning Fund.

Miss X pleaded guilty to seven counts: three of Possession of Identity Documents with Intent (contrary to the Identity Cards Act 2006); three of Fraud by Failing to Disclose Information (contrary to the Fraud Act 2006); and one of False Accounting (contrary to the Theft Act 1968). Miss Y pleaded guilty to six counts: two of Possession of Identity Documents with Intent (contrary to the Identity Cards Act 2006); three of Fraud by Failing to Disclose Information (contrary to the Fraud Act 2006); and one of Fraud by False Representation (contrary to the Fraud Act 2006).

Section 4 – Fraud by abuse of position
(1) A person is in breach of this section if he—
    (a) occupies a position in which he is expected to safeguard, or not to act against, the financial interests of another person,
    (b) dishonestly abuses that position, and
    (c) intends, by means of the abuse of that position—
        (i) to make a gain for himself or another, or
        (ii) to cause loss to another or to expose another to a risk of loss.
(2) A person may be regarded as having abused his position even though his conduct consisted of an omission rather than an act.

This section sets out the offence of committing fraud by abuse of position. It requires a person in a privileged position to act dishonestly by abusing the position held. Furthermore, the dishonest act must be with the intention of making a gain for themselves or another person. Alternatively, it may be with the intention of causing a loss or risk of loss to another (the loss not having actually to occur). The offence may also be committed by failing to do something that they should do (omission) as well as by an act (commission).

An example could be where a carer or even a relative has power of attorney over another individual's finances and takes money from that person's bank account for their own use.

## Woman was sentenced to 27 months' imprisonment for Fraud by Abuse of Position

Ms X attended Crown Court on 26th June after nearly a two year investigation by detectives

Police were contacted by a travel company who had become aware of some irregularities regarding the flight bookings and transactions made by Ms X. Concerns grew within management after a number of clients claimed to have been given fictitious flight tickets. Management approached police with their concerns and an investigation was carried out, which highlighted Ms X as a suspect.

It was explained to officers that following the ash cloud, that had occurred at the beginning of 2010 causing a number of flights to be cancelled, a number of customers had complained. When the flights were cancelled the seats were reallocated and these customers had not received their new tickets. Following further complaints and irregularities, the travel company looked into the matter and found all of the complaints had been generated by bookings made by Ms X. Management at the company found about 140 transactions had irregularities and seemed to have been paid into the wrong account. Officers attended and arrested Ms X, she was later charged with Fraud by Abuse of Position.

A detailed investigation was carried out to determine the extent of Ms X's fraudulent actions and her method. It was found that she had taken a number of cash payments, which was against company protocol; these had been deposited into her bank account. Her method for card payments is explained.

Customer A makes a flight booking to Ms X and pays with a Credit Card. Ms X allegedly made the booking and issued a fictitious document confirming the flight details for customer A.

She would then use the Credit Card details from customer A to pay off an outstanding 'cash invoice' and await customer B's booking. Ms X would then use customer B's credit card to pay for customer A's ticket if the flight was imminent or use the Credit Card to pay off another cash invoice. Ms X would charge the card of B using a web-based (virtual) payment system where the name of the cardholder and address needs to be entered. She would then await a further customer C so she could issue a ticket/invoice for Customer A and then B.

It is estimated that Ms X gained between £110,000 and £140,000; however, the loss to the company was substantially greater of at least £250,000 and their reputation was severely damaged

(Metropolitan Police, 2012).

Section 6 – Possession etc. of articles for use in frauds
1. A person is guilty of an offence if he has in his possession or under his control any article for use in the course of or in connection with any fraud.

It is an offence for a person to possess, or have under their control any article for use in the course of or in connection with any fraud. There is no requirement for a specific intention, general intent is sufficient. A person does not need to have physical possession of an article, having the article under their control is sufficient, for example having false documents hidden in their loft. An article for the purpose of this section of the Act includes, but is not restricted to, any computer program or data held in electronic form. For example, a computer program containing templates for producing blank documents such as utility bills or bank statements. Other examples of an article include possession of a list of national insurance numbers intended for use in making fraudulent benefit claims, a device to be attached to a cashpoint machine to copy data from bank or credit cards, a stolen or counterfeit stamp that is used to authorise payment, or a draft letter to be used for advance fee fraud which would result in the victim handing over money.

## Cyber crime gang behind major bank fraud jailed

Nine members of a gang which carried out a sophisticated cyber attack on the UK banking industry, stealing just over £1.25 million by remotely controlling bank accounts, have been sentenced to a total of 24 years and nine months' imprisonment. The organised crime group also used bank and credit cards obtained from around one million intercepted or stolen letters to fraudulently purchase Rolex watches, designer jewellery and other high-value items, worth over £1 million.

The gang used a device known as a Keyboard, Video, Mouse (KVM) switch to access and control bank accounts remotely on three occasions. On 4 April 2013, Mr X entered the bank's back office, allowing the group to access the IT system of one of the bank's branches. The group used the KVM device from a nearby hotel to make 128 transfers worth £1,252,490 to a network of mule accounts set up to launder the stolen cash. The bank reported the cyber attack that day and recovered over £600,000 of the money. On 17 July 2013, Mr Y entered another branch and was able to unlawfully gain access to the bank's computers where £90,000 was stolen. The bank reported the matter to the Metropolitan Police who quickly attended and recovered the KVM device. On 12 September 2013, the group made another attempt to unlawfully gain access to another bank's IT system by fitting another KVM device. This time, Mr Y gained access to a branch, where he fitted the KVM switch onto the bank's computers in an effort to access the accounts. Meanwhile, Mr Z and Mr A attempted to gain access to the Santander banking system in order to transfer what police believe would have been substantial funds.

Metropolitan Police detectives supported by Territorial Support Group officers raided an address in Kingsley Avenue, Hounslow where Mr Z and Mr A and eight others were arrested. Police recovered computers that were logged into Santander bank accounts, but no money was stolen. Mr Z was also arrested having left the bank.

(Metropolitan Police, 2014)

Section 7 – Making or supplying articles for use in frauds
(1)  A person is guilty of an offence if he makes, adapts, supplies or offers to supply any article—
    (a)  knowing that it is designed or adapted for use in the course of or in connection with fraud, or
    (b)  intending it to be used to commit, or assist in the commission of, fraud.

A person is guilty if they make, adapt, supply or offer to supply any article by two separate means, knowing that the article has been adapted for use, or supplying the article with the intention of it being used for the commission of fraud. 'Offences of this type involve an element of planning (whether by the offender or by another person); the planning of an offence has been identified . . . as a

## Bent registrar jailed for five years over birth certificate scam

A crooked registrar has been jailed for five years after being found guilty of issuing five false birth certificates to a gang of African fraudsters.

Former Newham registrar Mr X created five fake certificates which were used by the ringleader of the gang who went on to create false identities for children to milk the benefits system. The gang stole at least £4 million from taxpayers over 20 years. Mr X was found guilty of one charge of misconduct in public office and jailed for five years. He was also found guilty of a further five counts of supplying articles for use in fraud for which he was jailed for a total of four years. Last week, Mr X's role in the scam was exposed as the prosecutor told the jury: 'This case revolves around the making of false identities for children and Mr X as a registrar was at the centre of helping make those identities.'

The court heard how Mr X started to work for Newham Council in 2004 before becoming a registrar in 2006 and a senior registrar a year later. The evidence suggested that he was later introduced to Ms Z and her gang and began providing false birth certificates for use in their long-running conspiracy. Ms Z controlled the identities of the mothers named on the certificates. Mr X had a duty to confirm all births had taken place that he had to register. Typically, registrars find an NHS number already assigned to the child when registering the birth as hospitals feed information into the system when a child is born. Instead, he simply manually filled out birth certificates, after seemingly being given names by the gang.

In May 2011, the General Registry Office (GRO) contacted the Register Office. It was concerned about Mr X's registration of a set of twins, and also another single child. These births had actually never taken place. An internal disciplinary investigation was carried out by the Council and Mr X was sacked in 2011. A criminal investigation was also started.

The Council's Executive Member for Crime and Anti-Social Behaviour, said: 'Mr X systematically abused his position and in-depth knowledge of the system. We employed him in good faith and he abused that trust. He betrayed us and many other people'.

(Newham London, 2013)

factor indicating a higher level of culpability and the proposed starting points incorporate this aggravating factor' (Crown Prosecution Service, 2012). Examples might include a device to be attached to a cashpoint machine to copy card details or a device to be attached to a utility meter to cause a malfunction and thus show a lower consumption reading.

Section 9 – Participating in fraudulent business carried on by sole trader etc.
(1)  A person is guilty of an offence if he is knowingly a party to the carrying on of a business to which this section applies.
(2)  This section applies to a business which is carried on—
    (a)  by a person who is outside the reach of [section 993 of the Companies Act 2006] (offence of fraudulent trading), and
    (b)  with intent to defraud creditors of any person or for any other fraudulent purpose.

This section of the Act makes it an offence for a person knowingly to be a party to the carrying on of fraudulent business where this business is not a company or corporate body. This includes sole traders, partnerships and trusts. This offence is committed when a person is a knowing party to a fraudulent business either with the intent to defraud creditors, or for any other fraudulent purpose.

## 'Professional fraudster' jailed for Britain's biggest Ponzi scheme

Mr X has been jailed for 14 years and six months for masterminding what was described as being 'by some way' Britain's worst-ever Ponzi scheme that saw celebrities and other victims conned out of £115 million.

Sports stars and entertainers were among hundreds of others who lost their life savings to the businessman, described in court as a 'professional fraudster'.

Mr X was jailed after pleading guilty to four specimen counts of obtaining money transfers by deception; one count of participating in fraudulent business; one count of unauthorised regulated activity; and one count of converting and removing criminal property.

'You are an extremely intelligent, articulate, sophisticated and plausible liar. In short, a professional fraudster,' the Judge said. 'You set up and masterminded what may well be the largest and longest-running Ponzi fraud to come before the courts in this country'.

(Metro, 2012)

Example offences include cheating investors and defrauding other businesses by ordering goods and then failing to settle the invoices (long firm fraud).

Section 11 – Obtaining services dishonestly
(1) A person is guilty of an offence under this section if he obtains services for himself or another—
   (a) by a dishonest act, and
   (b) in breach of subsection (2).
(2) A person obtains services in breach of this subsection if—
   (a) they are made available on the basis that payment has been, is being or will be made for or in respect of them,
   (b) he obtains them without any payment having been made for or in respect of them or without payment having been made in full, and
   (c) when he obtains them, he knows—
      (i) that they are being made available on the basis described in paragraph (a), or
      (ii) that they might be,
   but intends that payment will not be made, or will not be made in full.

This offence replaces the s. 1 Theft Act 1978 offence of obtaining services by deception. However unlike the aforementioned statute, there is no deception

## Man faces court over alleged £17k fraud

A businessman has been charged with a string of offences over an alleged £17,000 fraud.

Company director Mr X has been charged with 14 counts of fraud by false representation, and obtaining services dishonestly.

Mr X was charged following an investigation by Sussex detectives at Hastings after complaints from 12 different organisations who had employed him to carry out telemarketing work for them between June 2010 and January this year.

The 12 complaints were made by the companies via the national Action Fraud website.

It is alleged that Mr X obtained a total of £17,000, working as a sales company based at his then home. Two separate complaints were also made by two private schools. It is alleged Mr X avoided payment for education for his children at one school and attempted the same offence at the second school.

(Rye and Battle Observer, 2012)

element to this new offence. It is an offence under this section, however, if a person obtains services for themselves or another, by any dishonest act and seeks to obtain these services for which payment is required, with the intention to avoid payment. It is necessary that the person knows the services are made available on the basis they are chargeable, or may be chargeable, and evidence must be offered to show this. The offence will not be committed simply by failing to pay for services. The 'dishonest' and 'intent' elements must be present before or at the time of obtaining the service. This offence would apply to a person who dishonestly used false credit card details to obtain a service from the internet, for example, a music site requiring a subscription to access songs. Another example is the connecting of a decoder to allow access to additional television channels with no intention of actually paying for these.

## Criticism of the Fraud Act 2006

The major criticism of the Fraud Act 2006 is that out of three main new categories of fraud, two are offences of intent or conduct, rather than of outcome. Thus, where the deception Acts made it necessary for there to be proof that the actions of person 'A' caused person(s) 'B' to do whatever was being charged (for example, to transfer property), now it is sufficient to prove that person 'A' intended to make a gain or cause a loss by their actions. According to Ormerod (2007: 2), this represents a significant widening of the scope of fraud as an offence, such that, for example, it could be said that s. 2 of the Act criminalises lying. In such circumstances, a number of practical problems potentially arise. For example, how do courts distinguish in sentencing an act that potentially may have made millions of pounds from thousands of people, from one that was dismissed as spam or an irritant (p. 3)? More generally, by focusing on intent and conduct, ss 2, 4, 6 and 7 rely on criminal liability being decided on the basis of the *Ghosh* test on dishonesty (*R v Ghosh* [1982] 75 Cr App R 154), something that the Law Commission were not in favour of (Law Commission, 2002: para. 5).

##  CRIMINAL LAW ACT 1977

The Criminal Law Act 1977 concerns the offence of conspiracy, and this specific offence has been the subject of much debate in relation to fraud. When reviewing fraud, the Law Commission (2002: 1.7) recommended that the common law offence of conspiracy to defraud should be abolished along with the eight offences of deception created by the Theft Acts 1968–96 and both should be replaced with two new statutory offences of fraud and secondly of obtaining services dishonestly. However, even after the enactment of the Fraud Act 2006, the common law offence of conspiracy to defraud was retained, and continues to be placed on a statutory footing, courtesy of the Criminal Law Act 1977 (as amended by the Criminal Justice Act 1987).

Accordingly, conspiracy to defraud does have some overlap with statutory conspiracy as detailed within the statute:

Section 1(1) – Criminal Law Act 1977
If a person agrees with any other person or persons that a course of con-duct shall be pursued which, if the agreement is carried out in accordance with their intentions either
(a) Will necessarily amount to or involve the commission of any offence or offences by one or more of the parties to the agreement; or
(b) Would do so but for the existence of facts which render the commis-sion of the offence impossible, he is guilty of conspiracy to commit the offence or offences in question.

This section of the legislation fully outlines the offence of conspiracy and replaced the common law offence of conspiracy, with the exception of conspir-acy to engage in conduct that tends to corrupt public morals or outrages public decency (s. 5(3)) and conspiracy to defraud (s. 5(2)). This common law offence has wider application than Theft Act offences. Statutory conspiracy to commit a substantive offence occurs if the alleged agreement satisfies the definition in s. 1 of the Criminal Law Act 1977 as outlined above. To charge a suspect with conspiracy to defraud, the proposed activity must have the potential to result in a fraud being perpetrated against another person. The agreement element also takes varying forms, the simplest being that two or more persons reach an agreement to commit a fraudulent act collectively. The second form of con-spiracy can be where two or more individuals reach an agreement to commit multiple frauds, with each member committing an offence individually. This may be co-ordinated by one central facilitator, and it is possible that the indi-vidual conspirators may not know each other. In terms of points to prove, if it can be established that the conspirators know others are involved in the plan-ning process, even if their identity is unknown, then they are all conspiring.

The offence of conspiracy to defraud is indictable and carries a maximum of ten years' imprisonment. Examples of offences under this statute might include agreements to dishonestly deprive a person of something which belongs to that person or something they might have been entitled to, such as dishonestly obtaining land or other property that cannot be stolen (such as intellectual property) or other confidential information.

## CRIMINAL ATTEMPTS ACT 1981

The Criminal Attempts Act 1981 broadens the scope of conspiracy further by introducing an amendment to the Criminal Law Act as follows:

Section 5 – Extension of definition of the offence of conspiracy
(1) For subsection (1) of section 1 of the Criminal Law Act 1977 (definition of the offence of conspiracy) there shall be substituted the following sub-section–
(1)   Subject to the following provisions of this Part of this Act, if a person agrees with any other person or persons that a course of conduct shall be pursued which, if the agreement is carried out in accordance with their intentions, either—
   (a) will necessarily amount to or involve the commission of any offence or offences by one or more of the parties to the agreement, or
   (b) would do so but for the existence of facts which render the commission of the offence or any of the offences impossible,
he is guilty of conspiracy to commit the offence or offences in question.

However, the overall offence of conspiracy continues to be covered by s. 1(1) of the Criminal Law Act 1977.

## THEFT ACT 1968

The Theft Act 1968 came about as a result of the eighth report by the Criminal Law Review Commission which examined theft and related offences. The resultant statute offers a definition of theft; however a decision was taken by those drafting the legislation not to include a specific offence of fraud. The legislation was given Royal assent on 26 July 1968 and became effective on 1 January 1969. It is essential that an ACFS develops a thorough understanding of the principles of this legislation as it still has relevance to this role, even post Fraud Act 2006. The statutory definition of theft is essential knowledge to an ACFS in both the public and private sectors and can be found in s. 1 of the Theft Act 1968:

Section 1 – Basic definition of theft

(1) A person is guilty of theft if he dishonestly appropriates property belonging to another with the intention of permanently depriving the other of it; and 'thief' and 'steal' shall be construed accordingly.
(2) It is immaterial whether the appropriation is made with a view to gain, or is made for the thief's own benefit.
(3) The five following sections of this Act shall have effect as regards the interpretation and operation of this section (and, except as otherwise provided by this Act, shall apply only for purposes of this section).

There are five core components to theft as detailed below:

1. Dishonestly
2. Appropriates
3. Property
4. Belonging to another
5. Intention of permanently depriving the other of it

The absence of any one of the above components will nullify the offence. This is useful to the ACFS when considering the points to prove when seeking to establish if an offence has been committed. The five points offer direction to the ACFS in terms of the investigative trail to be followed and the specific enquiries to be conducted. These five components are then covered in detail within the next five sections of the Act.

## Section 2 – Dishonesty

The concept of dishonesty underpins the offence of theft and related offences; however the Act does not offer a definition of dishonesty. Therefore, applying case law, the subjective test for dishonesty is provided by *R v Ghosh* [1982] 75 Cr App R 154, which has been discussed earlier in this chapter within the section on the Fraud Act 2006.

Sometimes when trying to establish what something is, a good starting point is to attempt to define what it is not. This certainly applies when attempting to establish what constitutes dishonesty, and direction is offered by s. 2 of the Act as follows:

Section 2 – 'Dishonestly'
(1) A person's appropriation of property belonging to another is not to be regarded as dishonest—
  (a) if he appropriates the property in the belief that he has in law the right to deprive the other of it, on behalf of himself or of a third person; or
  (b) if he appropriates the property in the belief that he would have the other's consent if the other knew of the appropriation and the circumstances of it; or
  (c) (except where the property came to him as trustee or personal representative) if he appropriates the property in the belief that the person to whom the property belongs cannot be discovered by taking reasonable steps.
(2) A person's appropriation of property belonging to another may be dishonest notwithstanding that he is willing to pay for the property.

An example of (a) *a right in law* would be if a garage owner retained possession of a customer's car because they had not paid the bill for a service.

A simple example of (b) *the belief that he would have the other's consent if the other knew of the appropriation and the circumstances of it* would be if two people living in communal accommodation shared a fridge and one of them (A) took some food from the fridge belonging to the other person (B), without B's permission. There would be no dishonest appropriation if A could reasonably demonstrate that B would have consented to the taking of the food. However, the situation would be different if there was a notice on the fridge forbidding the taking of foodstuffs belonging to others without express permission.

Finally, an example of (c) *appropriates the property in the belief that the person to whom the property belongs cannot be discovered by taking reasonable steps* would be if A finds a £20 note in the street and keeps it. This would not be dishonest appropriation as it would be commonly held that it would be too onerous, if not impossible, to discover the original owner of the note. However, the situation would be different if the amount found was £200 as there would be every prospect of the loser reporting the matter to the police as property lost in the street. Therefore, the owner could be reasonably discovered without too much effort.

It is also important to consider s. 2(2) of the Act: *appropriation of property belonging to another may be dishonest notwithstanding that he is willing to pay for the property*. A good example would be if A came across a £50 theatre ticket lying on a table belonging to B and A took the ticket while leaving behind the £50 face value of the ticket for B. A would then have committed a dishonest appropriation if B objects. This would also be the case even if A left £200.

## Section 3 – Appropriates

Section 3 – 'Appropriates'
(1) Any assumption by a person of the rights of an owner amounts to an appropriation, and this includes, where he has come by the property (innocently or not) without stealing it, any later assumption of a right to it by keeping or dealing with it as owner.
(2) Where property or a right or interest in property is or purports to be transferred for value to a person acting in good faith, no later assumption by him of rights which he believed himself to be acquiring shall, by reason of any defect in the transferor's title, amount to theft of the property.

A simple explanation for appropriates is where an individual assumes the rights of the owner of the property. An example might be where somebody borrows some tools from their neighbour, but instead of returning them they sell them on as their own to a third party. In this instance, the person selling the tools has assumed the rights of the owner, simply because the tools are not theirs to sell.

## Section 4 – Property

Section 4 – Property
(1) 'Property' includes money and all other property, real or personal, including things in action and other intangible property.

The Act is relatively clear when it comes to property, this includes money and most property, be it real or personal. Accordingly, everyday possessions would be considered to be property. The one exception is land, although wild flowers on land would be considered to be property if picked for reward or sale. Things in action are something that a person may not have physical possession of, but a right to, which in some instances would be a legal right. An example would be having the right to recover monies owed on a signed contract through legal proceedings. Intangible property would be items that have value but no substance, such as trademarks, copyright or patents.

## Section 5 – Belonging to Another

Section 5 – 'Belonging to another'
(1)  Property shall be regarded as belonging to any person having posses-
     sion or control of it, or having in it any proprietary right or interest (not
     being an equitable interest arising only from an agreement to transfer
     or grant an interest).

Belonging to another refers to whoever has legitimate control or possession over
the property, or having any right or interest in it. This is easy for an ACFS to
interpret in the case of direct ownership or possession, however belonging to
another also applies in cases where someone having control over some property
is not necessarily the owner. A rented van is an example of this, in that the driver
does not own the van, but has complete control over it. The same would apply to
company laptop or mobile phone. Think also of situations regarding someone to
whom personal property is entrusted, for example a motor vehicle repair work-
shop. If a customer's car is stolen, then the offence will have also been committed
against the proprietor who has a 'proprietary right or interest', especially if repair
work has been carried out to the car, which will have incurred a cost unlikely to
be recovered from the customer. It should also be noted that abandoned property
cannot be stolen, although the appropriator should make a reasonable attempt to
try and identify any potential owner, or be able to persuade any interested party
that it was reasonable to assume that the owner could not be located.

## Section 6 – Intention to Permanently Deprive

Section 6 – With the intention of permanently depriving the other of it
(1)  A person appropriating property belonging to another without mean-
     ing the other permanently to lose the thing itself is nevertheless to be
     regarded as having the intention of permanently depriving the other of
     it if his intention is to treat the thing as his own to dispose of regardless
     of the other's rights; and a borrowing or lending of it may amount to so
     treating it if, but only if, the borrowing or lending is for a period and in
     circumstances making it equivalent to an outright taking or disposal.

The appropriation of another person's property must be accompanied by the
intention to permanently deprive the other person of that property. Unless it
can be demonstrated that this was the intention when the property was appro-
priated, no theft has occurred. This must be decided on a case-by-case basis
because the term is relative; however in most cases the position is reasonably

clear. Taking property without permission and keeping it indefinitely is a straightforward act of permanently depriving. Borrowing an item and returning it in an unserviceable condition might be considered theft as the owner has been permanently deprived of the value of the property. From the perspective of the ACFS, all the facts of the case and any evidence must be considered and sufficient *mens rea* (guilty mind) determined.

 ## FRAUD RELATED OFFENCES

The following offences within the Theft Act 1968 are of relevance to an ACFS conducting a fraud investigation, and may be selected by the Crown Prosecution Service when bringing a case before the court.

- s. 16 – Obtaining a Pecuniary Advantage by Deception (repealed)
- s. 17 – False Accounting
- s. 24a – Dishonestly Retain a Wrongful Credit.

### Section 16 – Obtaining Pecuniary Advantage by Deception (repealed by the Fraud Act 2006)

Because the Fraud Act 2006 cannot be applied retrospectively, should an ACFS come across a protracted fraud that commenced prior to 15 January 2007 when this statute was enacted, this offence may still be relevant to the investigation.
s. 16 of the Theft Act 1968 states:

Section 16 – Obtaining pecuniary advantage by deception
A person who, by any deception, dishonestly obtains for himself or another any pecuniary advantage.

There are four ways in which a pecuniary advantage may be obtained:

- Borrowing by way of an overdraft when no authorised overdraft facility exists or exceeding an agreed overdraft.
- Being given the opportunity to gain remuneration or greater remuneration, for example by making false claims on a CV.
- Winning money by placing bets under false pretences.
- Taking out any policy of insurance or annuity contract and dishonestly representing material facts.

This offence requires an act of deception, and that someone is deceived. There does not have to be any specific gain or loss, either temporarily or permanently, merely the opportunity to obtain a pecuniary advantage.

Because deception is a key element of the aforementioned offence, it is worth exploring the act of deceiving as laid down within the statute. This is covered by s. 15 of the Theft Act 1968, which has also been repealed as a result of the Fraud Act 2006. Section 15(4) actually defines deception as:

> any deception (whether deliberate or reckless) by words or con-
> duct as to fact or as to law, including a deception as to the present
> intentions of the person using the deception or any other person.

Deception can be made in a number of different ways, what the suspect says, the way they behave or a combination of the two, it may also be deliberate or reckless. The key points of criminal deception are as follows:

- Someone must be genuinely deceived.
- A machine cannot be deceived (*R v Goodwin* [1996]).[1]
- Property must change hands because of the deception.
- The objective must be to permanently deprive.
- Deceptions committed abroad can be prosecuted if planned in the UK.

## Section 17 – False Accounting

False accounting is concerned with the falsifying, altering or hiding of any account or document necessary to carry out a deception. Section 17 of the Act defines the offence as follows:

Section 17 – False accounting
(1) Where a person dishonestly, with a view to gain for himself or another or with intent to cause loss to another—
   (a) destroys, defaces, conceals or falsifies any account or any record or document made or required for any accounting purpose; or
   (b) in furnishing information for any purpose produces or makes use of any account, or any such record or document as aforesaid, which to his knowledge is or may be misleading, false or deceptive in a material particular;

---

[1] A significant flaw in the Theft Act 1968, whereas the Fraud Act 2006 includes 'chip and pin' and cashpoint machines.

he shall, on conviction on indictment, be liable to imprisonment for a term not exceeding seven years.

(2) For purposes of this section a person who makes or concurs in making in an account or other document an entry which is or may be misleading, false or deceptive in a material particular, or who omits or concurs in omitting a material particular from an account or other document, is to be treated as falsifying the account or document.

What constitutes 'any account, record or document made or required for an accounting purpose', can be interpreted in a number of different ways. In simple terms it means accounting in a financial sense, as it is generally understood, but would also mean an account produced by mechanical means. It doesn't matter whether the information in the document or record is furnished for another purpose in addition to accounting; what is important is that it is false in some respect.

It is also essential for the completion of the offence that the false account or record is created with a view to gain or to cause loss to another.

## MPs' Expenses Scandal

You may recall that following the MPs' expenses scandal, some members of parliament were charged and successfully prosecuted for false accounting in connection with the parliamentary expense claims they submitted.

Section 34 of the Theft Act 1968 defines gain and loss as follows:

Section 34 – Interpretation
(2) For purposes of this Act—
   (a) 'gain' and 'loss' are to be construed as extending only to gain or loss in money or other property, but as extending to any such gain or loss whether temporary or permanent; and—
     (i) 'gain' includes a gain by keeping what one has, as well as a gain by getting what one has not; and
     (ii) 'loss' includes a loss by not getting what one might get, as well as a loss by parting with what one has . . .

The gain must be monetary or some other form of property and can be temporary or permanent. Loss is determined by the end result of an action that has an adverse effect on another through lost money or property which may be temporary or permanent.

An ACFS also needs to be fully conversant with what is meant by a false account. Here are some practical examples:

- **Insurance claim form (*R v Robinson* [1915])** – the defendant was originally charged with attempting to obtain property by deception by way of a
fraudulent insurance claim. Just before the commencement of the court case,
the defendant indicated he was willing to plead to the lesser charge of false
accounting on the basis that the claim form, which contained a schedule
of loss detailing the property allegedly stolen, adjacent to which was the
'amount of claim' column containing the individual values of the items, represented a false account. The reasoning was that in order to determine the
total value of the claim, the individual value of the items required adding up.
This adding up constituted an accounting exercise and the claim form was,
therefore, deemed to be a document required for an accounting purpose.
- **Insurance cover note (*R v Manning* [1998])** – in this case the insured
driver had given false information relating to the value and age of a vehicle
he wished to insure. This information was instrumental in calculating the
policy premium, which is an accounting process. Therefore, the insured
was convicted of false accounting.
- **Mechanical turnstile (*Edwards v Toombs* [1983])** – the defendant
allowed known associates to vault a mechanical turnstile at the entrance
to a football ground. The turnstile recorded the number of people entering
the ground which in turn led to the calculation of gate receipts. Given the
defendant's actions, the turnstile ceased to provide an accurate account
of the number of people passing through it. The defendant was therefore
convicted of false accounting.
- **False invoice** – invoices are documents that can be used for an accounting process. Therefore, the submission or tendering of a false invoice could
amount to false accounting, though other offences may also be considered,
such as forgery and/or deception, depending on the individual circumstances of the case. Best practice dictates that if the evidence exists, the
most serious offence should be considered in the first instance.
- **Company accounts** – concealing, altering or distorting company accounts
also constitutes false accounting. While the offence would occur at the point
of the dishonest act being carried out, practically, care must be taken to
ensure that the accounts have been firstly submitted to auditors for 'signing
off'. Knowledge of the business's auditing cycle would, therefore, be required.

- **Benefit claim form** – the information contained in a benefit claim form is used to calculate the level of benefit, and providing false information could, therefore, constitute false accounting.

## Section 24a – Dishonestly Retaining a Wrongful Credit

This section is actually an amendment to the original 1968 Act, having been enacted as part of the Theft Act 1978. It has been further amended by the Theft (Amendment) Act 1996 and the Fraud Act 2006. The origins of this revised offence can be traced back to 1995, when a case came before the courts that involved the obtaining of mortgages by deception. The defendant, John Crawford Preddy, had given false information on mortgage applications with the money being electronically transferred from the banks to the solicitor organising the applications. Preddy was charged with obtaining money by deception under s. 15 of the Theft Act 1968 and was convicted. However, on appeal it was successfully argued that crediting a bank account did not amount to obtaining property belonging to another because no identifiable property had changed hands. Preddy was acquitted (*R v Preddy* [1996] AC 815). This led to an urgent revision of the law and resulted in the enactment of the Theft (Amendment) Act 1996.

The offence of dishonestly retaining a wrongful credit is as follows:

Section 24A – Dishonestly retaining a wrongful credit
(1) A person is guilty of an offence if—
    (a) a wrongful credit has been made to an account kept by him or in respect of which he has any right or interest;
    (b) he knows or believes that the credit is wrongful; and
    (c) he dishonestly fails to take such steps as are reasonable in the circumstances to secure that the credit is cancelled.
(2) References to a credit are to a credit of an amount of money.
[(2A) A credit to an account is wrongful to the extent that it derives from—
    (a) theft;
    (b) blackmail;
    (c) fraud (contrary to section 1 of the Fraud Act 2006); or
    (d) stolen goods.]

According to s. 24A(2A) a credit is only wrongful if it derives from a dishonest source. Therefore, the underlying elements of this offence focus on the source of the funds received, the ownership of the account into which the funds were deposited, and the knowledge of the account holder as to the origin of those funds. That is to say, did the account holder know that they were not entitled

## Lichfield woman ordered to pay back £50,000 given to her by mistake

A Lichfield woman has been ordered to pay back more than £50,000 put in her bank account by mistake. The money – which totalled £51,821.34 – was meant to be paid to a Housing Association by the District Council but an error meant it went to Ms X instead.

Stafford Crown Court was told that in just two days the 23-year-old spent £5,000 on Gucci, Louis Vuitton, Ralph Lauren and Dior goods, while another £1,000 went on paying off court fines and the same amount was given to her family. She also transferred the remaining £40,000 to a newly-opened savings account. Ms X was arrested on April 25 for theft and charged on September 15 with dishonestly retaining a wrongful credit.

Police recovered all but two of the designer items she bought, while the cash gift was recovered and a freeze was put on her bank accounts. A Staffordshire Police spokesperson added: 'Enquiries were then made with HM Courts and Tribunal Service and the monies paid to cover her court fines were recovered, too. Unfortunately the designer goods could not be returned to the retailers because the debit card used to purchase them was not recovered.'

Ms X was convicted of dishonestly retaining a wrongful credit on January 10 2014 and on March 28 was sentenced to a 12 month supervision order with 150 hours' unpaid work. And the confiscation hearing at Stafford Crown Court yesterday (June 24) ordered her to pay £51,006.55 – the total of the recovered funds and the retail value of the clothing. 'The clothing and accessories will now be sold at auction in order to help pay the Confiscation Order,' a police spokesperson added. 'Ms X was given six months to satisfy the Order or serve a default sentence of 20 months.'

(Lichfield Live, 2014)

to those monies? For the offence to be proven, the holder of the account or one who has a right or interest in the account must either know or believe the credit to be wrongful and dishonestly fail to cancel the credit.

 ## BRIBERY ACT 2010

The Bribery Act 2010 was enacted in April 2010 and came into force on 1 July 2011. The legislation has redefined the existing offences of receiving and paying bribes. The legislation provides a new consolidated scheme of bribery offences which has been described by Vivian Robinson QC, General Counsel, Serious Fraud Office, as 'one of the most draconian anti-corruption measures in the world'. The Act covers bribery in the UK and abroad in respect of individuals and businesses that have a connection to the UK (O'Shea, 2011: 1). The legislation resulted in the repeal of common law offences, the Public Bodies Corrupt Practices Act 1889, Prevention of Corruption Act 1906, and Prevention of Corruption Act 1916 (pp. 8–15). The Bribery Act 2010 created two general offences. The first covers the offering, promising or giving of an advantage (offences of bribing another person). The second deals with the requesting, agreeing to receive or accepting of an advantage (offences of being bribed). The formulation of these two offences abandons the agent/principal relationship on which the previous law was based in favour of a model based on an intention to induce improper conduct. The Act also creates the offence of bribery of a foreign public official and a new offence where a commercial organisation fails to prevent bribery. The Act also removes the requirement for the Attorney General's consent to prosecute; this now falls to the Director of Public Prosecutions, the Director of the Serious Fraud Office or the Director of Revenue and Customs Prosecutions (p. 214).

There is a maximum penalty of 10 years' imprisonment for all the offences, except the offence relating to commercial organisations, which will carry an unlimited fine. Extra-territorial jurisdiction has been provided to prosecute bribery committed abroad by persons ordinarily resident in the UK, as well as UK nationals and UK corporate bodies.

The Act also offers examples of how the offence is committed within the definition.

Section 1 of the Act outlines the offences of bribing another person:

Section 1 – Offences of bribing another person
(1) A person ('P') is guilty of an offence if either of the following cases applies.
(2) Case 1 is where—
    (a) P offers, promises or gives a financial or other advantage to another person, and
    (b) P intends the advantage—
        (i) to induce a person to perform improperly a relevant function or activity, or
        (ii) to reward a person for the improper performance of such a function or activity.

(3)  Case 2 is where—
  (a)  P offers, promises or gives a financial or other advantage to another person, and
  (b)  P knows or believes that the acceptance of the advantage would itself constitute the improper performance of a relevant function or activity.
(4)  In case 1 it does not matter whether the person to whom the advantage is offered, promised or given is the same person as the person who is to perform, or has performed, the function or activity concerned.
(5)  In cases 1 and 2 it does not matter whether the advantage is offered, promised or given by P directly or through a third party.

The offence of bribery as it applies to the recipient or potential recipient of the bribe and four case scenarios to illustrate the offence are outlined in s. 2:

Section 2 – Offences relating to being bribed
(1)  A person ('R') is guilty of an offence if any of the following cases applies.
(2)  Case 3 is where R requests, agrees to receive or accepts a financial or other advantage intending that, in consequence, a relevant function or activity should be performed improperly (whether by R or another person).
(3)  Case 4 is where—
  (a)  R requests, agrees to receive or accepts a financial or other advantage, and
  (b)  the request, agreement or acceptance itself constitutes the improper performance by R of a relevant function or activity.
(4)  Case 5 is where R requests, agrees to receive or accepts a financial or other advantage as a reward for the improper performance (whether by R or another person) of a relevant function or activity.
(5)  Case 6 is where, in anticipation of or in consequence of R requesting, agreeing to receive or accepting a financial or other advantage, a relevant function or activity is performed improperly—
  (a)  by R, or
  (b)  by another person at R's request or with R's assent or acquiescence.

In Cases 3 and 5, it does not matter whether the improper performance is by R or by another person. In Case 4, it must be R's requesting, agreeing to receive or acceptance of the advantage which amounts to improper performance, subject to subsection *(6)*. In Case 6 (*subsection*

*(5))* what is required is improper performance by R (or another person, where R requests it, assents to or acquiesces in it). This performance must be in anticipation or in consequence of a request, agreement to receive or acceptance of an advantage. *Subsection (6)* is concerned with the role of R in requesting, agreeing to receive or accepting advantages, or in benefiting from them, in Cases 3 to 6. First, this subsection makes it clear that in Cases 3 to 6 it does not matter whether it is R, or someone else through whom R acts, who requests, agrees to receive or accepts the advantage *(subsection (6)(a))*. Secondly, *subsection (6)* indicates that the advantage can be for the benefit of R, or of another person *(subsection (6)(b))*. *Subsection (7)* makes it clear that in Cases 4 to 6, it is immaterial whether R knows or believes that the performance of the function is improper. Additionally, by *subsection (8)*, in Case 6 where the function or activity is performed by another person, it is immaterial whether that person knew or believed that the performance of the function is improper.

(House of Lords, 2009)

## Bribery Act 2010 – First Conviction

A former court administrative officer, Mr X, suggested that he could 'get rid' of a speeding charge. He pleaded guilty to accepting a £500 bribe in exchange for omitting to record a traffic offence on a court database and was convicted under the Bribery Act of requesting and receiving a bribe intending to improperly perform his functions as well as misconduct in a public office. Mr X was sentenced to 3 years' imprisonment for bribery and to 6 years' imprisonment for misconduct in a public office.

The decision, and the severity of the sentence, emphasises that the Courts will take any instances of bribery or corruption seriously and any person who is prosecuted under the Bribery Act may expect serious consequences

(Mackinnons, 2011)

The remaining offences within the Act that an ACFS needs to be aware of are:

s. 6 Bribery of foreign public officials – Unlike the general bribery offences in sections 1 and 2, the offence of bribery of a foreign public official only covers the offering, promising or giving of bribes, and not the acceptance of them. The person giving the bribe must intend to influence the recipient in the performance of his or her functions as a public official, and must intend to obtain or retain business or a business advantage.

(legislation.gov.uk)

s. 7 Failure of commercial organisations to prevent bribery – The offence is committed where a person (A) who is associated with the commercial organisation (C) bribes another person with the intention of obtaining or retaining business or an advantage in the conduct of business for C. *Subsection (2)* provides that it is a defence for the commercial organisation to show it had adequate procedures in place to prevent persons associated with C from committing bribery offences. Although not explicit on the face of the Act, in accordance with established case law, the standard of proof the defendant would need to discharge in order to prove the defence is the balance of probabilities.

(legislation.gov.uk)

Relevant commercial organisation is defined at subsection (5) as:

- a body incorporated under the law of any part of the UK and which carries on business whether there or elsewhere,
- a partnership that is formed under the law of any part of the UK and which carries on business there or elsewhere, or
- any other body corporate or partnership wherever incorporated or formed which carries on business in any part of the UK.

(legislation.gov.uk)

 ## COMPUTER MISUSE ACT 1990

The Computer Misuse Act 1990 (CMA) received Royal assent on 29 June 1990, legislating to protect computer material against unauthorised access and modification. The CMA creates three offences, unauthorised access to a computer (s. 1), unauthorised access with intent to commit or facilitate commission of further offences (s. 2) and unauthorised acts with intent to impair, or with recklessness as to impairing, operation of computer, etc. (s. 3). The Act was amended by the Police and Justice Act 2006 which created an additional offence of making, supplying or obtaining articles for use in offences under s. 1 or s. 3 (s. 3A). Offences under this statute can be committed from anywhere in the world and

British citizenship is immaterial. The Act covers both employees and external third parties. This discussion will be limited to those offences relevant to an ACFS when undertaking counter fraud investigations.

## Section 1 – Unauthorised Access to Computer Material

Section 1 – Unauthorised access to computer material
(1) A person is guilty of an offence if—
   (a) he causes a computer to perform any function with intent to secure access to any program or data held in any computer [or to enable any such access to be secured];
   (b) the access he intends to secure [or to enable to be secured,] is unauthorised; and
   (c) he knows at the time when he causes the computer to perform the function that that is the case.
(2) The intent a person has to have to commit an offence under this section need not be directed at—
   (a) any particular program or data;
   (b) a program or data of any particular kind; or
   (c) a program or data held in any particular computer.

In terms of points to prove, there are specific *mens rea* elements, as specified in s. 1(2) CMA:

(1) there must be knowledge that the intended access was unauthorised; and
(2) there must have been an intention to obtain information about a program or data held in a computer.

(Crown Prosecution Service, nda)

There has to be knowledge on the part of the offender that the access is unauthorised; mere recklessness is not sufficient. This covers not only hackers but also employees who deliberately exceed their authority and access parts of a system officially denied to them (CPS, nda). Unauthorised access is defined in s. 17(5) as occurring when an individual gains access to a program or data to which they are not entitled as no permission has been given by those with authority to give consent. Accordingly, this could include a member of staff who has legitimate access to certain areas within a program but then goes on to access other data which they have no authority to view. Relevant case law is found within *R v Bow Street Magistrates Court and Allison (AP) Ex parte Government of the United States of America (Allison)* [2002] 2 AC 216 where their

Lordships determined that an offence had occurred when an employee viewed data which they knew they had no authority from their employer to access.

## Section 2 – Unauthorised Access with Intent to Commit or Facilitate Commission of Further Offences

This section creates a further offence of using the data unlawfully accessed in s. 1 of the Act to commit or facilitate a further criminal offence as detailed below:

Section 2 – Unauthorised access with intent to commit etc.
(1) A person is guilty of an offence under this section if he commits an offence under section 1 above ('the unauthorised access offence') with intent—
 (a) to commit an offence to which this section applies; or
 (b) to facilitate the commission of such an offence (whether by himself or by any other person);
 and the offence he intends to commit or facilitate is referred to below in this section as the further offence.

The Act does not differentiate between whether the intent to commit an offence occurs at the time of unauthorised access under s. 1, or on a future date. A person can still be found guilty under this section of the Act even if it is not actually possible to commit further offences using the material unlawfully accessed. A person can still be convicted of a s. 1 offence even if found not guilty of an offence under s. 2 (s. 12 CMA refers).

## Section 3 – Unauthorised Acts with Intent to Impair, or with Recklessness as to Impairing, Operation of Computer, etc.

The section was amended by s. 36 of the Police and Justice Act 2006. Therefore any offence under this section of the CMA must have taken place on or after the date the former mentioned legislation came into force. The offence relates to altering and amending the data or program unlawfully accessed, as follows:

Section 3 – Unauthorised acts with intent to impair etc.
(1) A person is guilty of an offence if—
 (a) he does any unauthorised act in relation to a computer;
 (b) at the time when he does the act he knows that it is unauthorised; and
 (c) either subsection (2) or subsection (3) below applies.

(2) This subsection applies if the person intends by doing the act—
- (a) to impair the operation of any computer;
- (b) to prevent or hinder access to any program or data held in any computer;
- (c) to impair the operation of any such program or the reliability of any such data; or
- (d) to enable any of the things mentioned in paragraphs (a) to (c) above to be done.

The intention referred to does not have to be directed at any specific computer, program or data of any particular kind. This offence may be considered when investigating denial of service attacks (Crown Prosecution Service, nda).

## Section 3A – Making, Supplying or Obtaining Articles for Use in Offence under Section 1 or 3

This section was inserted by s. 37 of the Police and Justice Act 2006. If the article was supplied in connection with a fraud, then offences under s. 6 and/or s. 7 of the Fraud Act 2006 may be applicable. The Act outlines the specific offences as follows:

Section 3A – Making, supplying or obtaining articles etc.
- (1) A person is guilty of an offence if he makes, adapts, supplies or offers to supply any article intending it to be used to commit, or to assist in the commission of, an offence under section 1 or 3.
- (2) A person is guilty of an offence if he supplies or offers to supply any article believing that it is likely to be used to commit, or to assist in the commission of, an offence under section 1 or 3.
- (3) A person is guilty of an offence if he obtains any article with a view to its being supplied for use to commit, or to assist in the commission of, an offence under section 1 or 3.
- (4) In this section 'article' includes any program or data held in electronic form.

In determining the likelihood of an article being used (or misused) to commit a criminal offence, the following should be considered:

- Has the article been developed primarily, deliberately and for the sole purpose of committing a CMA offence (i.e. unauthorised access to computer material)?

- Is the article available on a wide scale commercial basis and sold through legitimate channels?
- Is the article widely used for legitimate purposes?
- Does it have a substantial installation base?
- What was the context in which the article was used to commit the offence compared with its original intended purpose?

(Crown Prosecution Service, nda)

## INVENTORY OF ADDITIONAL LEGISLATION

The following list contains legislation and regulation that an ACFS may need to be aware of, depending upon the primary function of their organisation:

- Companies Act 2006
- Forgery and Counterfeiting Act 1981
- Identity Documents Act 2010
- Money Laundering Regulations 2003 and 2007
- Proceeds of Crime Act 2002
- Rehabilitation of Offenders Act 1974
- Serious Crime Act 2007.

## REVIEW

This chapter has outlined legislation relating to fraud and associated offences relevant to the ACFS role. Initially the Fraud Act 2006 was explained, detailing the key offences and the points to prove. Offences under the Theft Acts 1968 and 1978, and the Theft Amendment Act 1996 that an ACFS needs to consider when conducting a counter fraud investigation were then explored. The chapter also introduced relevant case law that has shaped this legislation in terms of applicability and interpretation. Offences under the Computer Misuse Act 1990 that an ACFS must be aware of were then presented. Finally, the chapter offered an inventory of additional legislation that may be relevant to an ACFS depending upon whether they are undertaking criminal or civil investigations.

## ■ FURTHER READING

Farrell, S., Yeo, N. and Ladenberg, G. (2007) *Blackstone's Guide to the Fraud Act 2006*. Oxford: Oxford University Press.

Johnson, M. and Rogers, K. M. (2007) The Fraud Act 2006: The E-Crime Prosecutor's Champion or the Creator of a New Inchoate Offence? *International Review of Law Computers*, 21(3), 295–304.

O'Shea, E. (2011) *The Bribery Act 2010: A Practical Guide*. Bristol: Jordan Publishing.

CHAPTER THREE

# Governing legislation

## CHAPTER **SUMMARY**

This chapter will explore compliance legislation that governs counter fraud investigation procedures commencing with the Criminal Procedure and Investigations Act 1996, before moving on to the Data Protection Act 1998, Human Rights Act 1998, Regulation of Investigatory Powers Act 2000, and Telecommunications (Lawful Business Practice) (Interception of Communications) Regulations 2000. Police station processes for arrested persons, search and seizure, the application of the Police and Criminal Evidence Act 1984 and associated codes of practice will be explained. Additional legislation that is relevant to the ACFS will also be discussed, including the Public Interest Disclosure Act 1998 and Freedom of Information Act 2000.

 **INTRODUCTION**

There is a legal framework that prescribes mandatory requirements when conducting an investigation. It is imperative that these are adhered to, thus ensuring that the investigation is legal, professional and ethical. Additionally, should the case file be referred to the Crown Prosecution Service, conducting the investigation in strict accordance with these statutory requirements will prevent this being rejected on the grounds of abuse of process, which would result in time and valuable resources being wasted. The matter may be even more embarrassing should the case reach court and this comes out during the course of proceedings. Thus, each stage of the investigation should involve careful consideration of these governing statutes and it is the responsibility of the ACFS to be compliant. It should also be noted that these procedures should also be followed by the ACFS, even if it is not anticipated that the case will find its way to the criminal courts. In this way it will be possible to defend any suggestions of unfairness or impropriety. Remember, the civil courts and tribunals must take account of the principles of the European Convention of Human Rights.

All aspects of the investigation are regulated by governing legislation, also known as compliance legislation. The Criminal Procedure and Investigations Act 1996 lays down mandatory requirement throughout all stages of the investigation including a duty to record and retain material gathered during a criminal investigation, and reciprocal pre-trial disclosure of material in relation to the investigation should the case reach court. The Data Protection Act 1998 specifies how investigative data should be gathered, retained, stored, reviewed and disclosed. The Human Rights Act prescribes when the right to privacy may be breached, whilst also granting each individual rights that impact upon the prosecution and trial process. Surveillance and the use of covert human intelligence sources are governed by the Regulation of Investigatory Powers Act 2000. Any interception of telephone traffic must strictly comply with the Telecommunications (Lawful Business Practice) (Interception of Communications) Regulations 2000. Police station procedures for arrested persons and rules governing search and seizure are laid down within the Police and Criminal Evidence Act 1984. Further legislation that the ACFS must be aware of during the investigation include the Public Interest Disclosure Act 1998 which affords protection to whistleblowers and the Freedom of Information Act 2000 within which there are certain exemptions from the requirement to disclose information that are relevant to an ACFS.

**CRIMINAL PROCEDURE AND INVESTIGATIONS ACT 1996**

## Introduction

The Criminal Procedure and Investigations Act 1996 (CPIA) was created as a consequence of a number of historical issues relating to how investigations were carried out. These include inability to catch criminals, miscarriages of justice, lack of transparency, minimal accountability and the abuse of power (Maguire, 2008: 444). All of which raised questions about the overall integrity of investigations and suggested there was an urgent need to govern the investigative process.

Before moving on to discuss the Act itself, it is first worth explaining what constitutes a criminal investigation. This may be defined as 'cracking unsolved crime, identifying perpetrators, launching prosecutions, proving guilt at trial and bringing offenders to justice' (Roberts, 2007: 95). Similarly, Stelfox (2009: 17) suggests that a criminal investigation is not just about bringing 'offenders to justice', but also incorporates 'victim and witness care, community reassurance, intelligence gathering, crime reduction, disruption of criminal networks and asset recovery'. All the aforementioned are integral components of criminal and civil law based fraud investigations conducted by an ACFS.

From a legal perspective, s. 1(4) of the Criminal Procedure and Investigations Act 1996 defines a criminal investigation as:

an investigation which police officers or other persons have a duty to conduct with a view to it being ascertained–

(a)  Whether a person should be charged with an offence, or

(b)  Whether a person charged with an offence is guilty of it.

From a private sector ACFS perspective (a) is more relevant than (b), as commercial and corporate ACFSs have no powers to charge or summons persons in relation to offences committed. However, some investigations undertaken could be to explore whether a suspect may ultimately be charged with a criminal offence, for example in cases of internal employee fraud. Furthermore, on occasions the police do contract out enquiries to a civil ACFS in complex fraud enquiries.

So, what does this mean operationally?

The result is that fraud related criminal investigations may be broken down into three types:

- **Investigations into crimes committed** – e.g. someone has stolen benefit cheques in transit through the mail system and laundered these through bank accounts opened using counterfeit identity documents resulting in the loss of thousands of pounds.
- **Investigations whose purpose is to ascertain whether a crime has been committed** – e.g. Ms Prosser's clothing factory was subject to an arson attack the day after she doubled her stock sum insured on her business insurance policy and she is refusing to deal with anyone other than through her solicitor.
- **Investigations begun in belief that a crime may be committed** – e.g. intelligence-led investigations, such as organised staged road traffic accident fraud ('cash for crash').

The example given for the first investigation typology would be investigated by the DWP's counter fraud investigation service, whereas the latter two scenarios offered are examples of investigations that any ACFS involved in the field of commercial or corporate investigations might become involved in, and should this result in a positive investigation outcome, could result in the matter being reported to the police. Criminal investigation, especially in the area of fraud and theft, is not the sole province of law enforcement. Therefore, it is easy to see the relevance and applicability of the CPIA to the private sector investigative environment.

## The Role of the ACFS

Section 2.1 of the CPIA Code of Practice (COP) introduces two specific investigatory roles relevant to the ACFS. According to Roberts (2007: 95–96) 'It is the job of the investigator to unearth, recover, procure, amass, sort, compile, test, evaluate and arrange this evidence as compelling proof of the offender's guilt.' There are legal requirements laid down in CPIA 1996 concerning the handling, treatment and recording of evidence which are all underpinned by ethical principles. The Code of Practice contained in Part II of the Act also clearly defines who an investigator is and what their role is within an investigation. ACPO (2005a) guidance advises that 'an investigator is any . . . officer involved in the conduct of a criminal investigation. All investigators have a responsibility for carrying out the duties imposed on them under this code, including in particular recording information and retaining records of information and other material' (p. 14).

The essential theme of the Act is a duty to maintain and retain accurate records in relation to a criminal investigation, for the purposes of disclosure in the event of a prosecution taking place at Crown Court (the provisions of the Act are diluted in relation to summary trial). This duty is much more onerous for law-enforcement officers than it is for corporate ACFSs. Nevertheless, an understanding of the general requirements of CPIA is necessary, if only from the perspective of best practice and to ensure that commercial sector investigation procedures, wherever possible and appropriate, emulate those of law enforcement, the result being that the police are likely to look much more favourably on cases presented to them that comply with this statute. There is also a better likelihood of success at court, should a case proceed to that stage.

The CPIA places specific duties on the ACFS during the course of the investigation to record, retain and review all material relating to the investigation. Details of all relevant investigation material should be recorded at the time or as soon as practicable afterwards and should be in a durable or retrievable form.

The CPIA Code of Practice describes relevant investigation material as:

- material of any kind that has some bearing on any offence or person under investigation, or
- on surrounding circumstances of the case unless incapable of impacting on the case.

Examples of relevant materials include:

- **Incident reports (claim forms or written referrals)** – this could also include telephone tape recordings to a whistleblowers hotline or e-mails.
- **Field notes and photographs** – any writing or scribbling jotted down in the field and any photographs taken legally.
- **File and case review notes** – this would include telephone file notes and post interview or visit evaluations.
- **Memos** – internal or external including e-mails.
- **Investigation plans and decision logs** – evidencing investigation strategies, even thought processes on a case file are an important part of the investigative process.
- **Witness statements (including drafts)** – also includes statements not used as part of the evidence.

- **Interview records (taped or written)** – almost certainly the most important area for disclosure given the majority of information gathered during an investigation is through some sort of interview.
- **Reports and correspondence to clients and third parties (non-privileged)** – unless corresponding with client lawyers, all reports and correspondence are disclosable.
- **Expert reports** – for example a report from a handwriting expert. These are disclosable unless privileged.
- **Evidential packages from non-prosecuting agencies** – handed to the police who in turn must disclose the contents to the defence.
- **Physical objects and documentary exhibits** – of any description, whether used in evidence or not.
- **Incriminating evidence and evidence favourable to the defendant (exculpatory evidence)** – investigations are a search for the truth and the evidence must be more evenly weighed. All aspects have to be considered and no material must be deliberately suppressed. Unquestionably this is the main ethical component of CPIA.

Section 3.5 of the CPIA Code of Practice stipulates that in conducting an investigation, the ACFS should pursue all reasonable lines of enquiry, whether these point towards or away from the suspect. This is an example of how the CPIA mandates ethical decision making by the ACFS when conducting any counter fraud investigation.

## Disclosure

The CPIA places the duty of disclosure on a statutory footing in England and Wales, introduces the specific role of disclosure officer and mandates significant changes to the disclosure process, specifically reciprocal pre-trial disclosure which comprises of three main stages:

- **Prosecution advising defence of information intended for use at trial (Primary Disclosure)** – when the police charge a suspect they will advise the CPS of the relevant investigation information and evidence. At this point, the ACFS must bring to the CPS's attention any material which might reasonably be considered capable of undermining the prosecution case. The CPS, or the prosecution, will, in turn, inform the defence of the information they intend to use at trial as well as any information that might assist the defence. A technical point to bear in mind is that the prosecution must also advise the defence of certain categories of information they do not intend to use at trial, whether it is deemed irrelevant or of a 'sensitive' nature. This will give the defence the opportunity to challenge this assumption if they wish.

■ **Defence to advise prosecution of case they intend to present at trial (Defence Disclosure and Statement)** – after Primary Disclosure; the defence team has a duty to inform the prosecution of the case (defence) they intend to present at trial. The intention is to have everyone 'lay their cards on the table' at an early stage. However, police officers complain that in some cases a defence statement merely amounts to the defendant saying 'I didn't do it!', which is not particularly helpful and hardly within the spirit of the Act. Also, the defence may make an application to the court if they think the prosecution is holding back material or have incorrectly categorised it as irrelevant. Note that defence disclosure is only voluntary at summary trial.

■ **Defence disclosure triggers off the duty of the prosecutor to present any further material to defence (Secondary Prosecution Disclosure)** – after the prosecution has received the defence's disclosure and statement, they then have a duty to re-evaluate the situation and present any further material that may be deemed relevant or helpful to the defendant's case in the light of the defence's disclosure.

Since its enactment in 1997, there has been an amendment and modification to the disclosure process within the CPIA via the Criminal Justice Act 2003. Now the duty of disclosure upon the prosecution is a general one and the mandatory secondary disclosure requirement has been rescinded. Currently, rather than going through a formal routine of secondary disclosure, the prosecutor now has a general duty to regularly review the case and only disclose additional material as and when appropriate, and not as an automatic response to the serving of the defence statement. Furthermore, the Criminal Justice Act 2003 (CJA) amendment places a greater onus on defence counsel to provide a more detailed statement of the circumstances surrounding the defence or suffer sanctions should they fail to do so.

The consequences of non-disclosure by the ACFS on the case include the following:

■ The accused may raise a successful abuse of process argument at the trial.
■ The prosecutor may be unable to argue for an extension of the custody time limits.
■ The accused may be released from the duty to make defence disclosure.

- Costs may be awarded against the prosecution for any time wasted if prosecution disclosure is delayed.
- The court may decide to exclude evidence because of a breach of the CPIA 1996 or Code of Practice, and the accused may be acquitted as a result.
- The appellate courts may find that a conviction is unsafe on account of a breach of the CPIA 1996 or Code of Practice.
- Disciplinary proceedings may be instituted against the prosecutor or the ACFS.

It is worth noting that since the enactment of CPIA some defence lawyers have gone to unreasonable lengths to obtain material they consider might have some bearing on their client's innocence when, in reality, this is just a fishing expedition or an attempt to delay the prosecution process. The situation is further exacerbated in serious and complex fraud trials when large quantities of documents need to be evaluated by the ACFS responsible for determining what is disclosable. However, the defence is still likely to exercise their right to see for themselves, because potentially any material may have a significant impact on the case. While the CPIA mandates that such tests are objective, because of the adversarial system of law in the UK, there is a fine line between objectivity and subjectivity. On the other hand, given the heavy and complex bureaucratic burden imposed, there might be a temptation for the ACFS to omit material simply to shorten the disclosure process and make life easier. However, this is totally unethical and lacking in professionalism. Furthermore, if discovered this could result in the case being dismissed.

## Sensitive Material

Certain material, in addition to privileged material (legal source), does not have to be disclosed to the defence in the first instance, or even at all in some cases. This type of material is defined within the legislation as sensitive material. It should be noted that when an ACFS is referring a case to the police, it is recommended that all material be disclosed. However should the case be referred for prosecution, it is the police, in conjunction with the Crown Prosecution Service, that make the final decision on what is disclosed. Sensitive material may be withheld under the provision of Public Interest Immunity (PII), the specifics and mechanics of which are beyond the scope of this book as the decision-making process is undertaken by the prosecuting authorities. Nevertheless, an ACFS should be aware of PII in order to understand what constitutes sensitive material and whether the prosecuting authorities should be made aware of its existence.

Examples of 'sensitive material' are:

- Information relating to national security or from intelligence services.
- Information given in confidence (considered on a case-by-case basis).
- Intelligence only information, particularly that which might reveal intelligence gathering methods.
- Identities or specific activities of any informant.
- The location and/or occupants of premises used for surveillance purposes during the investigation.
- Investigation tactics and processes (e.g. covert surveillance or forensics).
- Material that might lead to or result in further crime or hinder prevention or detection of crime.
- Information from child witnesses or other vulnerable persons.
- Information which if disclosed might lead to loss of life or threaten national security.

 ## DATA PROTECTION ACT 1998

The Data Protection Act 1998 (DPA) is compliance legislation that was designed to protect the rights of individuals against the inappropriate exercise of power or excessive intrusiveness by either the state or organisations. The statute provides the regime by which personal data are held by organisations and individuals, and requires anyone who handles personal information to comply with a number of important principles. Non-compliance with the DPA can result in criminal sanction. The DPA is enforced by the Information Commissioner using the Information Commissioner's Investigation Unit which holds statutory powers to investigate breaches and enforce compliance.

The legislation affords certain rights to individuals (data subjects) including access, prevention, rectification, eradication and a grievance process (Mullock and Leigh-Pollitt, 1999). The DPA was first enacted in 1984, largely for data contained on computer systems; the 1998 statute includes paper records, whilst also establishing the post of Data Protection Registrar. This legislation may also be considered to be enabling legislation as it permits organisations to lawfully disclose data to law enforcement agencies for the prevention and detection of crime.

The DPA was enacted with several aims in mind, the most important being:

- To implement European Directive 95/46/EC on the protection of individuals with regard to the processing of personal data and of the free movement of such data (the Directive), and thereby harmonise the law in this area throughout Europe.

▪ To provide consumer protection in the area of personal privacy.
▪ To provide individuals with certain rights and powers over the way in which their personal information is dealt with by third parties.

(Biondi, 2004: 1)

When the Freedom of Information Act (FOIA) was enacted in 2000, there was a need to amend the DPA as the FOIA contained sections which changed the way in which public bodies were required to handle and process information. Also, rather than create a separate role of Freedom of Information Registrar, the Government sensibly decided to combine this with the duties already being performed by the Data Protection Registrar. The FOIA abolished the Registrar's job and established the post of Information Commissioner who heads the Information Commissioner's Office (ICO). The FOIA will be discussed in more detail later in this chapter.

## DPA Terminology

▪ Data:
  (i)  Information that is being processed by automated equipment
  (ii)  Information that is recorded as part of a relevant filing system.
▪ A 'relevant filing system' is defined in s. 1(1) as:

> any set of information relating to individuals to the extent that, although the information is not processed by means of equipment operating automatically in response to instructions given for that purpose, the set is structured by reference to the individual or to criteria relating to individuals, in such a way that specific information relating to a particular individual is readily accessible.

▪ *Personal data*: Information relating to an identified or identifiable living individual. Not being limited to factual information it may also include expressions of opinion or attention.
▪ *Sensitive personal data:* Data relating to criminal offences and records, ethnic origin, race or religious beliefs; explicit consent from the subject of the data is required to hold such data.
▪ *Data subject:* A person who is the subject of personal data.
▪ *Data controller:* A person or organisation with the power to control the purpose or manner of processing of personal data.

- *Data processor:* A person or organisation that processes information on behalf of a data controller.
- *Data subject:* A person who is the subject of personal data.
- *Relevant filing system:* A highly structured filing system.

(Room, 2007)

## Data Protection Principles

If information is personal or sensitive personal data, under the terms of the DPA, it must be managed in accordance with the eight data protection principles. These specify that data must be:

1. Processed fairly and lawfully

    All laws must be complied with and sensitive data only to be held with the data subject's permission.

2. Processed for specified purposes

    The data controller must specify the purpose for which personal data is obtained. Data held must be compatible with the purpose for which it was obtained.

3. Adequate, relevant and not excessive

    Data processors should identify the minimum amount of data required and be aware that any changes in circumstances may render the data held inadequate.

4. Accurate

    Personal data must not be inaccurate or misleading as to any matter of fact.

5. Not kept for longer than is necessary

    Personal data should be reviewed regularly and obsolete data should be deleted.

6. Processed in line with your rights

    Individuals have the right to be told if information about them is being processed, what it is, its source and the purposes for which it is being processed.

7. Secure

    Appropriate measures must be taken to prevent unauthorised or unlawful processing of personal data and against accidental loss/destruction or damage.

8. Not be transferred outside European Economic Area

    There must be no transfer unless permission of the data subject is given or the country ensures an adequate level of protection of subject's rights.

These principles are another example of how legislation ensures that ethical considerations are always foremost when an ACFS is undertaking criminal investigation activities.

It is important to bear in mind that the DPA also stipulates that under s. 7 of the DPA the subject of information has the right to access personal data that a data controller may hold on them and be advised why it is being held or if it has changed at any point. Requests for this information must be made in writing and may be subject to a nominal fee. The person requesting the data must also be able to satisfy the controller of their identity before the data is released, and any such data must be communicated in an intelligible form and exclude data relating to any other data subject.

*Durant v Financial Services Authority* [2003] is a case that has had a significant impact on section 7 requests, because it provides judicial precedent in relation to what is considered personal data and the meaning of the term 'relevant filing system' with regard to manual filing systems. Prior to this ruling it was generally considered that a section 7 request would mean disclosure of all data to which the subject was linked. Lord Justice Auld has changed the position somewhat by declaring:

> Section 7 of the Data Protection Act is not an automatic key to any information, readily accessible or not, of matters in which the party making the request for information may be named or involved.

In this instance, the Court of Appeal paid specific attention to the interpretation of 'relate to', with 'identifiable' not being the issue. The Court concluded that data will relate to an individual if it:

> Is information that affects [a person's] privacy, whether in his personal or family life, business or professional capacity.

In consequence, the Commissioner has suggested that in cases where it is not clear whether information relates to an individual, consideration should be given to whether or not the information in question is capable of having an adverse impact on the individual.

There are some exceptions within DPA under which personal data will not be released:

s. 28  National security
s. 33  Research and statistics
s. 35  Legal proceedings.

## Criminal Offences

Section 55(1) of the Data Protection Act specifies that:

Section 55 – Unlawful obtaining etc. of personal data
(1) A person must not knowingly or recklessly, without the consent of the data controller,
    (a) Obtain or disclose personal data or information contained in personal data or,
    (b) Procure the disclosure to another person of the information contained in personal data.

It is therefore an offence for an ACFS to ask a police officer to divulge whether a suspect under investigation has any criminal convictions. It would also be an offence for the officer to impart such data. Subject to the standard exemptions, personal information should not be disclosed to external individuals or organisations, so care must be taken about what is discussed when conducting enquiries. Breach of s. 55 is not an imprisonable offence, however the fines imposed can go up to the statutory maximum, and internal disciplinary action could be taken by an employer. Organisational embarrassment and reputational damage are also distinct possibilities.

Additional offences are:

s. 55(4) A person who sells personal data is guilty of an offence if he has obtained the data in contravention of subsection (1).
s. 55(5) A person who offers to sell personal data is guilty of an offence if:
    (a) He has obtained the data in contravention of (1), or
    (b) He subsequently obtains the data in contravention of that subsection – this prevents passing data onto third parties to sell on.

At this stage it is also appropriate to draw attention to s. 56 of the Act which at the time of writing has not yet been enacted but is due for imminent introduction. Under this section of the Act it is an offence for an organisation to require an individual to obtain via a subject access request details from the Police National Computer of criminal convictions (or confirmation that no record is held), for the purpose of employment vetting or insurance claim validation. This is not an area that would normally fall under the remit of most ACFSs, however it is something that those employed within the insurance industry need to be aware of.

## Statutory Exclusions

The following sections of the Act provide exemption for data controllers from the requirement to comply with the non-disclosure provisions. It is important to note that the exemptions do not impose an obligation on data controllers to disclose data that they hold.

- **Section 28 – National security** – Certificate of exemption required – The security services must obtain a certificate of exemption from the Secretary of State if they need to contravene any of the eight DPA principles.
- **Section 29 – Crime and taxation** – Prevention and detection of crime; apprehension or prosecution of offenders; Assessment or collection of any tax or duty – The exemption of most relevance to the ACFS and probably the most widely used. The exclusion is available to anyone working in either the public or private sector as long as it can be justified as being applied for the above reasons.

Of course, the best way to access data held by a data controller is with the data subject's consent. This may have been given at the time that they initially provided their data to the organisation and it is always worth reviewing the privacy notice that was signed at the time that the data were provided. Further guidance on privacy notices may be found in the Information Commissioner's documents 'Privacy Notices: Code of Practice' and 'The Guide to Data Protection'.

Nevertheless, it can still be difficult to persuade organisations to impart information, even though the exemption exists. It is best practice, therefore, to serve a s. 29 notice on whoever an attempt is being made to obtain information from. On occasions this may not be necessary if it is information held by an ACFS's own organisation. However this will only apply if the information has previously been supplied by the data subject in respect of what is currently under investigation. It should also be noted that 'sensitive data' will not be disclosed under s. 29.

Some private sector industries have formal protocols with the police for obtaining personal data under s. 29. For example, the insurance industry has such a protocol under a Memorandum of Understanding (MOU) between the Association of Chief Police Officers (ACPO) and the Association of British Insurers (ABI). It is important for an ACFS to remember that there must be a genuine consideration of criminal action at the time of the request. An ACFS should not routinely use s. 29 when there is absolutely no prospect of a criminal investigation and the information is being requested purely to help establish liability in a civil matter. Furthermore, if an individual requests access to their data and they are the subject of a fraud investigation, then s. 29 can be relied upon to decline their request.

- **Schedule 7, Section 10 – Legal professional privilege** – with the exception of money laundering legislation, data or information arising from legal privilege is sacrosanct in its own right and not subject to the DPA.
- **Section 35 – Legal proceedings** – personal data are exempt from the non-disclosure provisions where the data are required by the order of a court or in connection with any legal proceedings, including prospective legal proceedings, or for the purpose of obtaining legal advice, or are otherwise necessary for the purposes of establishing, exercising or defending legal rights. This exemption is often used during civil proceedings involving fraud.

## Best Practice to be DPA Compliant

Here are some general compliance tips for an ACFS, given the sensitive nature of counter fraud investigations. Remember that any failure to adhere to compliance legislation will result in abuse of process and irrespective of how strong the evidence is, or how well an investigation has been conducted, a successful outcome will not be achieved.

- Record information in the appropriate format.
- Record information in compliance with the recording and data quality principles.
- Ensure links are made to existing records (thus creating 'intelligence').
- Never record any offensive comments on a file or other database.
- Ensure all recorded information is accurate.
- Never disclose information to a third party without permission from the data subject unless exclusions or exemptions apply.
- Be aware of 'social engineering'.[1]
- Never leave personal data accessible to unauthorised personnel.
- Keep your computer password confidential and lock workstation when absent.
- Maintain a clear desk policy.
- Dispose of unwanted personal data by shredding or official confidential waste procedures.

---

[1] This technique is often used by fraudsters to obtain information which they are not entitled to. Always call back through the caller's central switchboard and never release information until you are completely satisfied with the caller's credentials and have received written confirmation of their request (fax or e-mail).

▪ If in doubt consult your Accredited Counter Fraud Manager or Security/ Compliance Department. Alternatively, refer to the Information Commissioner's website.

Accurate recording of information is important because it ensures all information is held in accordance with the law, provides an auditable decision-making process and ensures that records comply with the data quality principles of being accurate, adequate, relevant and timely. Failure to record information correctly can prevent organisations from being able to adequately manage risk. Ethically it is important that all information is auditable so that when the case goes to court all data can be accounted for, thus avoiding the risk of abuse of process.

It is also essential that data are regularly reviewed because this determines their adequacy and continuing necessity for an investigatory purpose. Equally, the review process also ensures compliance with the DPA. Review procedures should be practical, risk focused and able to identify information which is valuable to the investigating organisation's purpose. Failure to review and retain information appropriately may be unlawful and undermine public confidence in the investigating agency. When reviewing data, the following should be considered:

▪ There is a continuing need to hold these data
▪ The record is adequate, up to date and not excessive
▪ That all personal records comply with the principles of the DPA
▪ The assessment as to the level of risk the data subject perceived to present is correct.

An example of an application form requesting information under s. 29 of the DPA can be found in Chapter 10.

##  HUMAN RIGHTS ACT 1998

The observation offered by Wadham and Mountfield (1999) that the Human Rights Act 1998 (HRA) will 'have a momentous impact on our legal system' has certainly proved to be well founded. The UK signed the European Convention on Human Rights (ECHR) in 1951, but it was not incorporated into law because it was argued that the common law already provided such rights. After the 1997 election and the arrival of New Labour in government, the Human Rights Act 1998 was enacted as the conduit to incorporate the ECHR into UK law. Essentially, the ECHR and HRA are one and the same and are terms which can be used interchangeably. One major effect of enactment of the HRA was that the European Court of Human Rights has supremacy over the UK courts. As a consequence:

- All laws passed by Parliament must be compatible with ECHR/HRA – if not, the law must be returned back to Parliament and made so, though Secretaries of State retain the power to enable this by statutory decree.
- All 'public bodies' must ensure that everything they do is compatible with ECHR/HRA – this affects all policy implemented by public bodies.
- The main aim of HRA is to instil public confidence in the state – the aim is to reinforce the principle that the state is the servant of the citizen, rather than the opposite.

While the Act does not define what constitutes a public body or authority, they are generally held to be bodies carrying out a governmental or public function. For example:

- Police.
- Courts – includes the civil and criminal courts as well as tribunals. This has an impact on a private sector ACFS who may have to justify their part in an investigation to any of these public bodies who will want to be certain that HRA principles have been observed, given that they are bound by its requirements.
- National Health Service.
- Government departments.
- Local authorities.
- Private utility companies – where the body is exercising a function in the public interest.
- Companies doing government work – these types of organisations are called 'hybrid' companies and are becoming increasingly more common with the arrival of Private Finance Initiatives and Public Private Partnerships, both of which involve the public and private sectors coming together to work jointly on various projects.

## How Does the HRA Work?

- It makes it unlawful for a public authority (this includes the Welsh Assembly) to act in any way that is incompatible with the ECHR.
- Courts in England and Wales have to interpret legislation in a way that is compatible with the Convention.

- Individuals whose rights have been violated by a public authority are able to take action in court. This can be done by way of judicial review, or by using the ECHR as a defence in a criminal or civil case.

The HRA has also had a significant impact on the investigative arena by increasing the rights of individuals under investigation and making those conducting investigations more accountable, both in the public and private sectors. Therefore, a thorough understanding of the HRA from an investigative perspective is crucial for an ACFS.

## Convention Rights (the Articles)

There are three different types of Convention rights:

1. **Absolute rights** – such as the protection from torture, inhuman and degrading treatment and punishment; the prohibition of slavery and enforced labour and protection from retrospective criminal penalties. There is little or no scope for interference with these rights.
2. **Limited rights** – for example, the right to life and the right to liberty. These rights are limited only under very specific circumstances which are laid down within the ECHR itself. For example the right to liberty can be interfered with if an individual is sentenced to imprisonment.
3. **Qualified rights** – which include the right to respect for private and family life, religion and belief, freedom of expression, assembly and association. Interference with these rights is only permissible if what is done:
   - Has some form of basis in law;
   - Is done to secure a permissible aim detailed within the relevant article, for example, the prevention of crime; and
   - Is necessary in a democratic society, and fulfils what is defined as a pressing social need (*Handyside v UK* (1976) 1 EHRR 737), for example public health, or pursues a legitimate aim, counter-terrorism activity or countering crime being such examples. However, any interference must always be proportionate to the aim being pursued.

As previously mentioned, proportionality is of crucial importance to the above criteria. Accordingly, even if the interference is to pursue a legitimate aim, such as the prevention of crime, this will not be justifiable if the means used are excessive in the circumstances. In sum, interference must be carefully designed to meet the objective in question and *must not be arbitrary or unfair*.

There are 18 Articles in Part 1 of the HRA, these being:

1. Obligation to respect human rights
2. Right to life
3. Prohibition of torture
4. Prohibition of slavery and forced labour
5. Right to liberty and security
6. Right to a fair trial
7. No punishment without lawful authority
8. Right to respect for private and family life
9. Freedom of thought, conscience and religion
10. Freedom of expression
11. Freedom of assembly and association
12. Right to marry
13. Right to an effective remedy
14. Prohibition of discrimination
15. Derogation in time of emergency
16. Restrictions on political activity of aliens
17. Prohibition of abuse of rights
18. Limitation on use of restrictions on rights.

Those which the authors deem applicable to an ACFS are:

- Article 3 – Freedom from torture, inhumane and degrading treatment.
- Article 5 – Right to liberty.
- Article 6 – Right to a fair trial.
- Article 8 – Right to privacy and a family life.

Examining these in order:

**Article 3 – Freedom from torture, inhumane and degrading treatment** – from the perspective of an ACFS, Article 3 arises in the context of questioning suspects/witnesses during investigations. For example: excessively long interviews; denial or deprivation of basic needs during questioning, which can include food and drink and 'comfort breaks'; unnecessary coercion or duress, such as bullying or oppression; discrimination based on race or religion. All of these could be deemed to be relevant to Article 3, whilst also being in contravention of the Police and Criminal Evidence Act 1984, which will be discussed later in this chapter.

**Article 5 – Right to liberty** – it is worth remembering that other than those conferred to every citizen by law, an ACFS (unless a police officer) has no powers of arrest or detention. Witnesses or suspects cannot be compelled to remain at a location to be interviewed and any attempt to prevent them from leaving could be seen not only as coercive but also as an attempt to deprive them of their liberty. Even the creation of the interview environment needs to be considered. For example, if an interviewee cannot easily exit the room because of the need to physically negotiate a route around the interviewer(s), then it might be construed that the interviewee's right to liberty was being interfered with. Therefore, it is always worth reminding interviewees at the outset that they are free to leave whenever they like.

**Article 6 – Right to a fair trial** – 'In the determination of his civil rights and obligations or of any criminal charge against him, everyone is entitled to a fair and public hearing within a reasonable time by an independent and impartial tribunal established by law.' Accordingly, everyone charged with a criminal offence shall be presumed innocent until proved guilty according to law and has the following minimum rights:

(a)  to be informed promptly, in a language which he understands and in detail, of the nature and cause of the accusation against him;
(b)  to have adequate time and facilities for the preparation of his defence;
(c)  to defend himself in person or through legal assistance of his own choosing or, if he has not sufficient means to pay for legal assistance, to be given it free when the interests of justice so require;
(d)  to examine or have examined witnesses against him and to obtain the attendance and examination of witnesses on his behalf under the same conditions as witnesses against him;
(e)  to have the free assistance of an interpreter if he cannot understand or speak the language used in court.

Article 6 can be considered in the context of evidential admissibility, self-incrimination and duty of disclosure. Therefore, any evidence obtained inappropriately or illegally may render a trial unfair under Article 6. For example, abuse of process (unnecessary delays in investigation or entrapment, PACE exclusionary rules), non-disclosure contrary to the CPIA, breach of the DPA or employment law, and any breaches of Article 3.

**Article 8 – Right to privacy and a family life** – specifies that:

Everyone has the right to respect for his private and family life, his home and correspondence.

This can be considered particularly in the context of covert investigations involving surveillance, human intelligence sources and interference with or interception of communications or correspondence.

*Home* – is defined as a private dwelling, private motor vehicle and, in some cases, commercial premises.

*Correspondence* – is defined as written communications, telephone calls and other electronic communication, such as faxes and e-mails that are considered private. This does not include such correspondence sent or received by an employee using their works communications systems, including the post service, the use of which is governed by the Telecommunications (Lawful Business Practice) (Interception of Communications) Regulations 2000 which is covered later in this chapter.

Examples of infringements of Article 8 are:

▪ Covert surveillance – the rules of which, insofar as public bodies are concerned, are governed by the Regulation of Investigatory Powers Act 2000 (RIPA).
▪ Interception of communications – also governed by RIPA but mitigated by the Telecommunications (Lawful Business Practice) (Interception of Communications) Regulations 2000 for the conduct of business.
▪ Photographing suspects in non-public places.
▪ Searches of private motor vehicles.
▪ Searches of 'private property' at work, seizure of personal documents or property.
▪ Disclosure of confidential information about the medical condition of a witness or suspect.
▪ Access and misuse of personal data.

The above list is not exhaustive.

Article 8 is a qualified right, therefore lawful interference is allowed, but only if it is in the interests of:

▪ National security.
▪ Public safety or economic well-being of the UK – fraud and theft is obviously contrary to the economic well-being of the UK.
▪ Prevention of disorder or crime – fraud and theft are obviously crimes.
▪ Protection of health or morals.
▪ Protection of rights and freedoms of others.

The HRA principally impacts upon investigations by providing a set of standards which must be met in order to permit interference in the rights of privacy of an individual (Article 8). As a consequence, an ACFS must be able to demonstrate that their activities:

▪ Observe the rule of law
▪ Have legitimate aims
▪ Are reasonable and proportionate.

 ## REGULATION OF INVESTIGATORY POWERS ACT 2000

The Regulation of Investigatory Powers Act 2000 (RIPA) is a statute that was enacted quickly to comply with the 'in accordance with the law' element of Article 8(2) of the ECHR, following its adoption into domestic law through the Human Rights Act 1998. RIPA therefore provides statutory authority to public bodies when interfering with an individual's right to privacy as laid down in Article 8(1) of the ECHR. The Act regulates covert investigations undertaken by the police and other public bodies which include surveillance, the interception of communications and the use of informants, all of which have to be authorised. The overall effect of RIPA is that it strikes a balance between the need to conduct covert investigations and the protection of an individual's right to privacy. Furthermore, by embedding this in legislation, members of the public can see exactly what the state's powers are to conduct surveillance (Lennon, 2009: 30).

The legislation impacts on an ACFS working in both the public and private sectors. This is because civil courts and tribunals are public bodies from a human rights perspective, and thus have a statutory duty to ensure that due regard has been given to the principles of human rights in the evidence that is presented to them. Additionally, with the increased use of the private sector by government departments, the legislation can also apply to certain commercial organisations which undertake a vast range of government contracts as well as private sector work and thus may be considered to be a public body hybrid. By providing a definition of 'the circumstances in which the acquisition of communications data and surveillance can take place, and putting a regulatory framework around it, RIPA has significantly shaped investigative practice in this area' (Stelfox, 2009: 69). The statute provides a framework under which an ACFS must consider in each individual case whether the use of surveillance is reasonable, necessary and proportionate. It is therefore imperative that an ACFS is aware of their statutory obligations as outlined by this legislation.

RIPA is overseen by the Office of Surveillance Commissioners (OSC) and regulates four specific elements within the investigation process:

- Covert surveillance, which includes the use of Covert Human Intelligence Sources (CHIS)
- Interception of communications
- The acquisition of communications data
- Access to encrypted data.

There are five parts to the Act that provide powers and guidelines in relation to specific investigative techniques and the establishing of a system of scrutiny, as follows:

**Part I – Interception of communications and acquisition and disclosure of data** – includes unlawful and authorised interception, warrants and restrictions on use of intercepted material which are of relevance to an ACFS.

**Part II – Use of covert surveillance, agents, informants and undercover officers/ACFSs** – this is the most relevant part of the Act for an ACFS.

**Part III – Investigation of electronic data protected by encryption** – of relevance to an ACFS based within some public sector organisations, but of more interest to the security services.

**Part IV – Independent oversight of powers in the Act (Commissioners)** – they only have powers in relation to public bodies so have no legal impact as such on a corporate ACFS, apart from any private sector organisation performing contracted work from the Government. However, the manner in which Commissioners exercise their powers does provide a useful framework for audit, maintaining ethics and developing professional standards.

**Part V – Miscellaneous and supplemental matters, repeals and interpretation** – an ACFS should have an awareness of this part of the Act.

## What is Surveillance?

Surveillance is defined as 'the collection, processing and analysis of personal information about individuals or populations in order to regulate, control, govern, manage or enable their activities' (Coleman and McCahill, 2011: 102). A similar interpretation is offered by Pepper and Pepper (2009: 105) who suggest it involves 'gathering information by a range of covert and overt methods ranging from photographic and CCTV images to the use of electronic listening devices in order to manage people, places or inanimate objects'.

In statutory terms, surveillance is defined by s. 48(2) of RIPA as:

**(a) monitoring, observing or listening to persons, their movements, their conversations or their other activities or communications** – including post, correspondence and e-mails.

**(b) recording anything monitored, observed or listened to in the course of surveillance** – recording can be as basic as pen and paper, such as surveillance logs.

**(c) surveillance by or with the assistance of a surveillance device** – most commonly a camera of some sort, though transmitters and trackers would also be classed as surveillance devices.

However, s. 48(3) of RIPA decrees that there are certain exceptions that do not fall within this definition, these being:

(a) any conduct of a covert human intelligence source for obtaining or recording (whether or not using a surveillance device) any information which is disclosed in the presence of the source;

(b) the use of a covert human intelligence source for so obtaining or recording information; or

(c) any such entry on or interference with property or with wireless telegraphy as would be unlawful unless authorised under—
    (i) section 5 of the Intelligence Services Act 1994 (warrants for the intelligence services); or
    (ii) part III of the Police Act 1997 (powers of the police and of officers of Revenue and Customs).

Surveillance techniques are used by an ACFS to progress a fraud investigation by obtaining information on a suspect including keeping observation on a specific location, a cashpoint machine for example, and also the movements of a suspect in terms of places visited and any associates met. It may also be used to keep observation on a particular property or business premises to record details of activities at that address.

## Covert Surveillance

RIPA does not cover 'ordinary' surveillance; it deals exclusively with covert surveillance. We therefore need to define covert surveillance and identify how it differs from overt surveillance. Section 26(9)(a) provides the definition for the purpose of the Act:

[S]urveillance is covert if, and only if, it is carried out in a manner that is calculated to ensure that persons who are subject to the surveillance are unaware that it is or may be taking place.

Using the aforementioned definition, below are examples of forms of surveillance that fall outside this classification:

- Closed Circuit Television (CCTV)
- Speed/Traffic monitoring cameras
- Public Order filming
- Police vehicle cameras – whether marked or unmarked, but must be in connection with general observations and patrols
- Photography in public places.

Covert surveillance is then categorised into two different types, the first being intrusive surveillance, which is defined in s. 26(3) of RIPA as being surveillance that:

(a) is carried out in relation to anything taking place on any residential premises or in any private vehicle; and
(b) involves the presence of an individual on the premises or in the vehicle or is carried out by means of a surveillance device.

Clarity is also needed on the definition of residential premises and a private vehicle.

For the purpose of surveillance, s. 48(1) of RIPA defines residential premises as:

any premises as is for the time being occupied or used by any person, however temporarily, for residential purposes or otherwise as living accommodation (including hotel or prison accommodation that is so occupied or used).

Examples of premises which would not be regarded as residential would include:

- A communal stairway in a block of flats (unless known to be used as a temporary place of abode by, for example, a homeless person)
- A prison canteen or police interview room

- A hotel reception area or dining room
- The front garden or driveway of premises readily visible to the public
- Residential premises occupied by a public authority for non-residential purposes, for example trading standards 'house of horrors' situations or undercover operational premises.

(Home Office, 2010a: 16)

Section 48(1) of RIPA also defines a private vehicle as:

any vehicle which is used primarily for the private purposes of the person who owns it or of a person otherwise having the right to use it.

This actually means 'any vehicle, including vessels, aircraft or hovercraft, which is used primarily for the private purposes of the person who owns it or a person otherwise having the right to use it. For example, a company car owned by a leasing company and used for business and pleasure by the employee of a company' (Home Office, 2010a: 17).

Further clarity is required as to what constitutes 'on' a premises and whether general observation constitutes covert surveillance. The determining factor is whether the subject under surveillance would ordinarily be out of view. If not, and the observation point is outside the curtilage of the premises or the vehicle, then it would probably not count as intrusive surveillance.

Intrusive surveillance is regarded as one of the most serious breaches of a person's rights under Article 8 of the Human Rights Act 1998, and is therefore used in moderation. Authorising officers are usually of Chief Constable or Commissioner rank status and intrusive surveillance should only be authorised:

- In the interests of national security
- For the prevention and detection of serious crime
- In the interests of the economic well-being of the UK.

(Home Office, 2010a: 52–53)

There will be few occasions when an ACFS will be involved in intrusive surveillance: only if involved in an investigation into serious organised fraud and this is the only option available to progress the investigation.

## Directed Surveillance

The second type of covert surveillance is directed surveillance and is defined within s. 26(2) of RIPA as being surveillance that is not intrusive and is undertaken:

(a) for the purposes of a specific investigation or a specific operation;
(b) in such a manner as is likely to result in the obtaining of private information about a person (whether or not one specifically identified for the purposes of the investigation or operation); and
(c) otherwise than by way of an immediate response to events or circumstances the nature of which is such that it would not be reasonably practicable for an authorisation under this Part to be sought for the carrying out of the surveillance.

Direct surveillance is the typology most likely to be carried out by an ACFS in both the public and private sectors. In the former, it could be when investigating benefit fraud or tax evasion, and in the latter, it could be to do with personal injury or sickness insurance claimants, or even occupational fraud in the workplace. While there still is an interference with an individual's right to privacy, it is less marked than intrusive surveillance as it is undertaken in public places or other similar locations. Accordingly, there are less severe restrictions on this type of surveillance activity.

Section 28(3) of RIPA outlines the authorised reasons for conducting directed surveillance, these being;

(a) in the interests of national security;
(b) for the purpose of preventing or detecting crime or of preventing disorder;
(c) in the interests of the economic well-being of the UK;
(d) in the interests of public safety;
(e) for the purpose of protecting public health;
(f) for the purpose of assessing or collecting any tax, duty, levy or other imposition, contribution or charge payable to a government department; or
(g) for any purpose (not falling within paragraphs (a) to (f)) which is specified for the purposes of this subsection by an order made by the Secretary of State.

Before undertaking directed surveillance authorisation is required, as follows:

- **Public body** – will have internal authorising officer to refer to – which will be of a much lesser 'rank' than is the case with intrusive surveillance.
- **Non-public body** – authorising officer should be a manager – for larger organisations, it is best practice for the ACFS not to make the decision them-selves regarding surveillance, only the recommendation. RIPA is all about oversight and accountability. However, if the instruction for surveillance comes directly from a client, then it can be considered that the necessary authorisation has already been made and the private sector ACFS should act accordingly without any reference to a manager, unless there is some form of intrusive element involved or an instructing client has somehow got things wrong.

Requests for authorisation for directed surveillance should describe what surveillance is proposed, the nature of the investigation and include the following:

- The reasons why the authorisation is necessary in the particular case and on the grounds (e.g. for the purpose of preventing or detecting crime) listed in s. 28(3) of the 2000 Act.
- The nature of the surveillance.
- The identities, where known, of those to be the subject of the surveillance.
- A summary of the intelligence case and appropriate unique intelligence references where applicable.
- An explanation of the information which it is desired to obtain as a result of the surveillance.
- The details of any potential collateral intrusion and why the intrusion is justified.
- The details of any confidential information that is likely to be obtained as a consequence of the surveillance.
- The reasons why the surveillance is considered proportionate to what it seeks to achieve.
- The level of authority required (or recommended where that is different) for the surveillance.
- A subsequent record of whether authorisation was given or refused, by whom, and the time and date this happened.

(Home Office, 2010a: 47–48)

The duration of the surveillance also warrants consideration. In the public sector there are timescales that apply to covert surveillance to ensure that this type of activity does not carry on indefinitely. Similarly, it is an issue of proportionality. The initial deadline for covert surveillance is

- Three months in first instance – then:
- Regular reviews by the Authorising Officer during this period and records kept, especially in respect of any decision to extend a surveillance operation.
- Three-month renewals may be authorised if warranted, but consideration must be given as to whether there is any likelihood of gaining any useful evidence after this time. Any extension will likely only involve serious crime, and in the private sector, would be unaffordable in many instances.
- Surveillance must cease on the day of cessation of authorisation; to do otherwise under RIPA may render any subsequently obtained evidence inadmissible.

Within the private sector, in most instances covert surveillance conducted by an ACFS is likely to cease within a matter of days, but from a supervisory perspective a watching brief should be kept on this type of operation to ensure that both costs and continued necessity are kept under review.

Finally, an ACFS should be aware that there is a Code of Practice produced by the Home Office that provides instruction on the use of covert surveillance and property interference. This is a valuable guide that can be referred to when considering whether to use surveillance in an investigation as it offers detailed information on the application procedures and what factors warrant consideration when planning a surveillance operation.

## Human and Technical Surveillance

Surveillance using an individual is known as human surveillance and will involve an ACFS going to locations where they can directly witness the actions of offenders. It may also involve the use of an undercover ACFS. Human surveillance can then be divided into two further types:

- Static surveillance: ACFSs use an 'observation post' to carry out surveillance of a location associated with an offender or an offence.
- Mobile surveillance: ACFSs follow offenders with the intention of recording their movements, contacts and behaviour.

(Stelfox, 2009: 120)

An observation post may include a property (office, shop or private dwelling) or even a vehicle parked up. The use of a dwelling may involve ethical decision making as this may put the occupants at risk. For example, if a suspect is shown surveillance footage at interview the static observation post may be easily identifiable. Additionally, details of the static observation may be disclosed in court. Mobile surveillance is challenging and requires specialist training to ensure the surveillance team are not identified by the surveillance subject. Serious offenders often develop anti-surveillance strategies which an ACFS needs to address with their own counter-surveillance techniques. Mobile surveillance can also require ethical decision making particularly with regard to the safety of the public, the surveillance team members and even the target of the surveillance when trying to maintain observations.

Using a surveillance device is known as technical surveillance and involves the placing of covert cameras or microphones in locations where they will record the actions or speech of suspects. Specialist technicians are required to install and maintain the equipment and it may on occasions involve entering the premises covertly for installation purposes (Stelfox, 2009: 121). There are ethical considerations when deciding whether to deploy technical surveillance. One of the main considerations is that of collateral intrusion (which also applies with human surveillance). Collateral intrusion is defined as obtaining private information about an individual who is not the subject of the fraud investigation. It is imperative that the ACFS makes the authorising officer aware of the potential of collateral intrusion, and includes an evaluation of the level of risk that this may occur when conducting surveillance. This should also include details of what steps are proposed to avoid, or at least limit this, thus enabling the authorising officer to make an informed decision on the reasonableness and proportionality of the surveillance application.

## Covert Human Intelligence Source (CHIS)

This is what is frequently referred to as 'undercover', and may involve a police officer infiltrating an organised gang. On occasions an undercover officer may adopt a false identity and maintain a completely different lifestyle whilst 'in the field' for a protracted period of time. Alternatively an undercover operation may be short term, and more likely to involve an ACFS, for example making test purchases to check for possible fraudulent accounting, or to establish that an individual is trading fraudulently.

What was previously referred to as an informant is another form of CHIS. Informants will typically, but not always, be criminals wishing to trade off information for immunity from prosecution or for monetary gain. Occasionally, they might be a member of the public offering information about any matter they perceive to be a serious transgression of the law. More controversially, they may be a protected person under the Public Interest Disclosure Act 1998 when status can become confusing. However, this is the exception rather than the rule when the distinction is drawn between an informant and an informer.

The usefulness of CHIS can be summarised as follows, they:

- Provide access to criminals and criminal networks.
- Create a climate of mistrust and uncertainty within criminal enterprises.
- Provide investigative focus and best evidence – having inside information allows the ACFS to gain the initiative and plan their next move with some degree of certainty. It also narrows down the lines of enquiry, thus saving on investigative resource expenditure.
- Supply intelligence – most organisations have adopted an intelligence-led investigation approach, and the use of a CHIS can provide valuable intelligence, particularly in the case of serious organised fraud.

RIPA governs the use of informants and provides a legal framework in which they should be handled. It affords informants protection and establishes a duty of care towards them. It even confers a new nomenclature for informants: a CHIS. But what exactly is a CHIS? And what is the difference between a CHIS and an informer?

Section 26(8) of RIPA defines someone as a Covert Human Intelligence Source if:

(a) he establishes or maintains a personal or other relationship with a person for the covert purpose of facilitating the doing of anything falling within paragraph (b) or (c);
(b) he covertly uses such a relationship to obtain information or to provide access to any information to another person; or
(c) he covertly discloses information obtained by the use of such a relationship, or as a consequence of the existence of such a relationship.

The Home Office Code of Practice on the use or conduct of a CHIS advises that it can be a 'particularly intrusive and high risk covert technique, requiring dedicated and sufficient resources, oversight and management. This will include ensuring that all use or conduct is:

- necessary and proportionate to the intelligence dividend that it seeks to achieve;

- in compliance with relevant Articles of the European Convention on Human Rights, particularly Articles 6 and 8.'

(Home Office, 2010b: 9)

Under s. 29(3) of RIPA authorisation for the use of a CHIS can be granted when the authorising officer believes that the authorisation is necessary:

(a) in the interests of national security;
(b) for the purpose of preventing or detecting crime or of preventing disorder;
(c) in the interests of the economic well-being of the UK;
(d) in the interests of public safety;
(e) for the purpose of protecting public health;
(f) for the purpose of assessing or collecting any tax, duty, levy or other imposition, contribution or charge payable to a government department; or
(g) for any purpose (not falling within paragraphs (a) to (f)) which is specified for the purposes of this subsection by an order made by the Secretary of State.

An application for the use of a CHIS should include the following:

- The reasons why the authorisation is necessary in the particular case and on the grounds listed in s. 29(3) of the 2000 Act (e.g. for the purpose of preventing or detecting crime).
- The purpose for which the CHIS will be tasked or deployed (e.g. in relation to drug supply, stolen property, a series of racially motivated crimes etc.).
- Where a specific investigation or operation is involved, the nature of that investigation or operation.
- The nature of what the CHIS conduct will be.
- The details of any potential collateral intrusion and why the intrusion is justified.
- The details of any confidential information that is likely to be obtained as a consequence of the authorisation.
- The reasons why the authorisation is considered proportionate to what it seeks to achieve.
- The level of authorisation required (or recommended, where that is different).
- A subsequent record of whether authorisation was given or refused, by whom and the time and date.

(Home Office, 2010b: 34–35)

Other critical considerations when considering engaging with a CHIS include the following:

- Identify who you are dealing with – do not take it for granted that the name given is the correct one. A CHIS may be a criminal and might be using a false identity. Seek identification whenever possible and undertake some basic background checks to find out who you are dealing with.
- Identify motivation – money is often a motivation for a CHIS and if so, establish what their expectation is. However, there might be other motivating factors, in particular revenge. This is a high risk indicator because such individuals can be extremely unpredictable and volatile.
- Undertake a risk assessment – is there risk of collateral intrusion into the privacy of persons other than those who are directly the subject of the covert operation? Is the risk of harm to the CHIS too great? Always consider proportionality.
- Accurate and secure record keeping – concise, but detailed record keeping of any contact is essential, but great care must also be taken to keep details of a CHIS and any contact highly confidential. Consider unobtrusive secure filing cabinets not readily accessible to staff for storage of records. Use code names in communications to prevent identification. Keep things on a 'need to know' basis.
- Go accompanied wherever possible – it is always best practice to be accompanied by another ACFS when meeting a CHIS, both from a corroboration and a health and safety perspective.
- COP adherence – if you are unsure how to proceed, refer to the Home Office Code of Practice (Home Office, 2010b) which gives comprehensive guidelines and best practice for CHIS handling.

The maximum duration of the authorisation will be twelve months, and regular reviews should be conducted to evaluate whether it is still reasonable and proportionate to continue using a CHIS. The frequency of reviews is determined by the reviewing officer within the public authority, but should be as often as considered 'necessary and practicable'. The renewal will normally last for another twelve months and be given in writing, however in urgent cases renewals may be given orally and last for 72 hours (Home Office, 2010b: 36).

## Office of Surveillance Commissioner

The Office of Surveillance Commissioner comprises of a Chief Surveillance Commissioner and six Surveillance Commissioners, all of whom are retired judges. Their prior consent is required for certain types of surveillance that are considered particularly intrusive. They have powers to inspect police forces and other investigative agencies to ensure compliance with RIPA. Surveillance Commissioners have responsibilities under Parts I and II of RIPA, and are responsible for:

■ Scrutinising all notifications, renewals and cancellations of authorisations.
■ Giving prior approval for authorisations and renewals in certain specified cases.
■ Keeping under review the use of directed surveillance and covert human intelligence sources by law enforcement agencies.

## TELECOMMUNICATIONS (LAWFUL BUSINESS PRACTICE) (INTERCEPTION OF COMMUNICATIONS) REGULATIONS 2000

This piece of legislation came into force on 24 October 2000 as a result of pressure being put on the Government by businesses following enactment of RIPA. The legislation allows public bodies and private sector organisations to intercept communications on their own networks without having to obtain any consent. The Regulations cover all types of communication including telephone traffic, e-mails and faxes. The interception of communications in the form of recording or monitoring may be carried out for a number of purposes, but those relevant to an ACFS are to establish the existence of facts and prevent and detect crime. Any interception of employee communications must be reasonable and proportionate. Although there is an option for non-disclosure, employees and contractors should normally be notified that communications may be intercepted. The Regulations even cover monitoring of anonymous counselling and support services when provided free of charge.

## POLICE AND CRIMINAL EVIDENCE ACT 1984

The 1984 Police and Criminal Evidence Act (PACE) is considered to be 'the single most significant landmark in the modern development of police powers' (Reiner, 2000: 176). The measures attracted much comment, there being diverse opinions. The Chief Constable of Merseyside described them as tipping the balance too far in favour of the wrongdoers (Oxford, 1986: 68). An alternative view considered the very same measures as being 'a draconian increase in police powers' (Lea and Young, 1993: 254). However, there is no doubt that the legislation has been a major influence 'on the behaviour of the police and on the culture of policing' (Morgan and Newburn, 1997: 51–52).

The statute became law on 1 January 1986 and replaced the Judges' Rules. The Act placed police and other investigative agencies' powers in relation to the investigation of crime, in England and Wales, on a statutory footing for the first time. In addition to regulating police powers, the Act also concerns itself with the rights of suspects and the admissibility of evidence in a court of law. Due to the complexity of the legislation there are eight Codes of Practice all of which must be readily available to police officers and other criminal investigators (such as ACFSs), detained persons and members of the public. Of relevance to an ACFS in either the public or private sector, is that in all criminal and civil proceedings any code shall be admissible in evidence; and if any provision of a code appears to the court or tribunal conducting the proceedings to be relevant to any question arising in the proceedings it shall be taken into account in determining that question (PACE, s. 67(11)). The PACE Codes of Practice (COP) offer interpretation and guidance on stop and search, search and seizure, arrest, detention, investigation, identification and interviewing detainees.

In detail, the Codes of Practice cover:

- Code A – Stop and Search – the exercise by police officers of statutory powers of stop and search and requirements for them and other police staff to record public encounters.
- Code B – Searching of Premises and Seizure of Property – governs the exercise of powers in respect of searching of premises and the seizure of property found on persons or premises.
- Code C – Detention, Treatment and Questioning of Persons – ensures that persons suspected of involvement in crime are dealt with fairly and in accordance with the law.
- Code D – Identification of Persons Suspected of Crime – concerns the principal methods used for identifying persons in connection with the investigation of offences.
- Code E – Audio-recording of Interviews with Suspects – governs the way in which audio recordings of suspects are carried out.
- Code F – Video-recording of Interviews – should video-recording also be considered, for which there is no statutory requirement, this code sets out the necessary procedures
- Code G – Power of Arrest – sets out the criteria the police must consider when exercising their power of arrest under s. 24 of PACE as amended by s. 110 of the Serious Organised Crime and Police Act 2005.

- Code H – Detention, Treatment and Questioning of Terrorist Suspects – the most recent addition to the COP.

## Scope of PACE and the Codes of Practice

As for the scope and applicability of the Act, it:

- Applies throughout England, Wales and Northern Ireland – but not Scotland where comparable investigative powers are still, in the main, common law based.
- Is primarily directed at the police, but s. 67(9) is applicable to *persons other than police who are charged with the duty of investigating offences.* This is the part of the Act which causes the most controversy when considering whether it applies to an ACFS in the private sector or a non-police ACFS in the public sector. The issue turns on the question: What constitutes a duty to investigate offences? Unfortunately, neither the Act nor the Code of Practice gives any specific guidance on what the answer to the question is. Consequently, this is to be found in case law and precedent.

Failure to adhere to the PACE Codes of Practice may render some evidence obtained inadmissible in court due to abuse of process. Consequently, there may be criticism by the courts or adverse publicity in the media if a public sector organisation fails to adhere to these codes. It is also unprofessional, unethical and potentially could lead to internal disciplinary action.

There is also the question as to what extent PACE applies to an ACFS in the private sector, which, at times, creates debate, especially in sectors like the insurance industry where the argument tends to focus on the issue of cautioning, which is only a small, though very significant, part of PACE. Regardless of this, as with other investigative compliance legislation, to achieve common standards the methods and procedures used during an investigation by an ACFS in the private sector should, as far as is reasonably possible, mirror the standards used in the public sector. It is suggested, therefore, that an ACFS in the private sector should have a similar working knowledge of PACE as it will inevitably crop up as an issue at some point, whichever industry they might work in.

## Investigative Responsibilities

As previously discussed, s. 67(9) of PACE refers to persons other than police officers charged with the duty of investigating offences, yet fails to offer clarification on who this actually is, and the courts therefore consider this on a case-by-case basis. This can however include any form of legal duty imposed by legislation, common law or by employment regulations. In *R v Devani* [2008] 1 Cr App R 65(4) (CLW 08/01/02) the Court of Appeal considered a judge's refusal to exclude evidence which had been obtained by prison support officers and a prison officer questioning a solicitor without first administering a caution. Whilst prison support officers are not persons charged with the duty of investigating offences within s. 67(9) of PACE, prison officers are considered to be such persons, and they are therefore directly subject to the provisions of the PACE Codes of Practice. Accordingly, the judge in the case should have determined that the prison officer had breached Code C by failing to caution the solicitor.

An interview is defined as the questioning of a person regarding their involvement or suspected involvement in a criminal offence or offences (para 11.1A of PACE Code of Practice C (2012)) which, under PACE Code of Practice C (2012) 10.1, must be carried out under caution. Whenever a person is interviewed they must be informed of the nature of the offence, or further offence (Code of Practice C (2012) 11.1A). It is important that an ACFS knows exactly how and when to caution a suspect. PACE Code of Practice Code C (2012) 10.1 states:

> A person whom there are grounds to suspect of an offence must be cautioned before any questions about an offence, or further questions if the answers provide the grounds for suspicion, are put to them if either the suspect's answers or silence (i.e. failure or refusal to answer or answer satisfactorily), may be given in evidence to a court in a prosecution.

To answer the question when do I caution? Note 10A PACE Code of Practice C (2012) advises:

> There must be some reasonable, objective grounds for the suspicion, based on known facts or information which are relevant to the likelihood the offence has been committed and the person to be questioned committed it.

Once the ACFS has determined that the time is right, the caution should then be administered as in PACE Code of Practice C (2012):

> You do not have to say anything. But it may harm your defence if you do not mention when questioned something which you later rely on in Court. Anything you do say may be given in evidence.

Do not be concerned that as an ACFS you get the caution slightly wrong, or in the heat of the moment forget some of the words. PACE Code of Practice C (2012) 10.7 states that:

> [d]eviations from the wording are acceptable provided the sense of the caution is preserved.

A record should be made whenever a caution is given and any significant statements made by the suspect before the caution was administered should be put to the suspect after this has been given, and a response invited. A significant statement is defined as one which appears capable of being used in evidence against the suspect, for example an admission of guilt or incriminatory comments. A significant silence is considered to be a failure, or refusal, to answer a question or answer satisfactorily when under caution. Practically, this may relate to a situation where a previous interview, whether under caution or not, has elicited some information that, having been checked out, has proved to be false or inconsistent. If the previous interview was recorded in the form of a statement, then either any significant comments within the statement, or the statement in full, can be put to the suspect who should then be invited to make any further comment in the light of new information or evidence obtained. It is advisable not to give too much detail of this new information until the interview has commenced properly. Similarly, if in an earlier interview, or during previous questioning, under caution or otherwise, the suspect declined to answer a 'significant' question, they should be reminded of this and given the opportunity to offer a response in any subsequent interview.

It is also important that the ACFS ensures that the suspect being interviewed understands the caution. In fact Note 10D PACE Code of Practice C (2012) states:

> If it appears that a person does not understand the caution, the person giving it should explain it in their own words.

A further consideration is the suspect's right to legal advice as outlined within s. 58 of PACE. If the person is being interviewed at a police station they should be advised that they are entitled to free legal advice, however free legal advice does not have to be provided if being interviewed at any other location. If a suspect is invited to attend an interview they can be advised of the right to obtain legal advice when the interview is being arranged. Where a solicitor has been consulted and is available they must be allowed to be present at the interview if they request this. Additionally, if an ACFS is conducting an interview under caution at a location other than a police station, the suspect must be advised that they are not under arrest and are free to leave at any time.

It is also imperative that detailed record keeping should be maintained. PACE Code of Practice C (2012) 11.7 states that any interview with a suspect should be recorded accurately either on the relevant form or in the interviewer's pocket book and should detail:

- the venue of the interview
- the times of the beginning and end of the interview
- times of any breaks during the interview
- full details of all persons present.

PACE Code of Practice C (2012) 11.7 also states that:

- any written record must be made during the interview
- or as soon as practicable afterwards.

PACE is also very clear about the purpose of the interview, with PACE Code of Practice C (2012) Note 12A stating that it is:

> To obtain from the person concerned his explanation of the facts and not necessarily an admission.

## Right to Silence

Historically a person who had been arrested was not required to answer any subsequent questions put to them by a police officer. This was known as the right to silence. The Criminal Justice and Public Order Act 1994 enabled the courts to draw inferences from a suspect's refusal to answer questions, which covers:

- When a defendant used a defence in court that they had failed to mention previously when questioned.
- If a defendant aged 14 or over refused to give evidence at a trial.
- If a suspect was issued with a 'special warning' under the 1994 Act allowing inferences to be drawn from a suspect's failure to answer police questions in connection with incriminating circumstances.
- If a suspect failed to account for incriminating objects, marks or substances or failed to account for their presence at a particular place.

(Buckle and Brown, 1997: 34 and 37)

A special warning is an additional caution. Legislation does not offer the exact wording of a special warning, but for an inference to be drawn it must be given in language that the suspect is capable of understanding and should include the following:

- Details of the offence which is being investigated;
- Specific facts which the suspect is being asked to account for;
- Why the ACFS thinks these facts may link the suspect to the offence;
- Making the suspect aware that a court may draw an inference if the suspect fails to account for these facts;
- Stating that a record is being made of the interview and that it may be given in evidence if the suspect is brought to trial.

(PACE Code of Practice C (2012), 10.11 and Note 10D)

Changes to the right to silence were reflected in the caution that an arrested person receives before being questioned. The impact of this reform was to reduce the overall use of the right to silence by suspects (Buckle and Brown, 1997: 35–36).

## Unreliable Evidence

Section 76(1) of PACS states that 'confessions' shall be deemed inadmissible if obtained:

(a) by oppression
(b) in consequence of anything said or done which was likely, in the circumstances existing at the time, to render unreliable any confession.

The latter is often referred to as 'verballing' which is the putting of damaging remarks into a suspect's mouth during the interview and which is unethical and can render the interview as inadmissible in court.

Unfair evidence may also be excluded in court as per s. 78(1) of PACE which provides a discretion for the court to exclude evidence obtained during an interview which would otherwise be admissible against a defendant on the basis that it would be unfair to introduce it in court. Examples might be:

- Breach of a suspect's human rights
- Failure to follow rules of evidence/PACE or COP (e.g. failure to caution; abuse of process)

- Inadmissible evidence
- Poor recording of information.

## Entry, Search and Seizure

The powers to enter private property are outlined in ss 8, 17, 18 and 32 of PACE. Police enter private property either with a warrant issued by a magistrate (s. 8) or, under specified circumstances, without a warrant (ss 17, 18 and 32). PACE stipulates that a magistrate can issue a warrant granting an officer the power to enter premises if it is not possible to gain entry with consent.

- s. 17 permits entry for the purpose of executing a warrant.
- s. 18 grants powers to enter premises of any person arrested for an arrestable offence if it is believed that a search would reveal material related to that offence or one similar to it.
- s. 32 stipulates that, following an arrest, officers may enter and search the premises where the person was immediately before, or when they were arrested (if reasonably believed that evidence of the offence for which the arrest was made will be found).

Other powers of entry include:

- Misuse of Drugs Act 1971 (to enter business premises of someone who produces or supplies controlled drugs)
- Road Traffic Act 1988 (to enter premises to take a breath test following an accident that has led to personal injury)
- Theft Act 1968 (a warrant may be obtained to enter premises and search for stolen goods).

PACE also provides regulation concerning the seizure of items. Under s. 19 of PACE a constable may seize anything if he or she has reasonable grounds for believing that it constitutes evidence in relation to any offence, or that it has been obtained as a result of an offence being committed, and that it is necessary to seize such items to prevent them being concealed, lost, altered or destroyed. The general power of seizure only applies when a constable is on premises lawfully. Section 20 of PACE permits the seizure of computerised information in a form in which it can be taken away and is visible and legible. All seized materials may be retained for as long as is necessary (s. 22). For the purpose of search and seizure 'premises' is defined as any place and includes any vehicle, vessel, aircraft, hovercraft or offshore installation (s. 23).

As previously mentioned, a warrant to search premises may be obtained under s. 8 of PACE. An application is made to a magistrate using the form which can be found at Annex B in the Guidance Notes to PACE. A magistrate must consider that the use of this power is reasonable and proportionate and that there are reasonable grounds that an indictable offence (triable in the Crown Court only) has been committed. The types of warrant that can be obtained are:

- Single entry to one premises
- Multi premises – more than one location
- All premises – access to all premises occupied or controlled by an individual
- Repeated entry – allows for multiple entries.

An ACFS working in the private sector has no criminal law power of search, but may accompany police if deemed necessary (PACE Code of Practice B (2010) Note 3C). The Civil Procedure Act 1997 allows the High Court to grant search orders (civil search warrants which are referred to as Anton Pillar Orders). This enables a civil claimant to secure evidence in civil fraud cases where there is a likelihood of it being destroyed if the defendant is aware of the proceedings.

## Detention

Following arrest a person must be taken to a 'designated police station' and may be detained there under PACE as follows:

- Normally for 24 hours, although an officer of the rank of superintendent may add a further 12 hours (s. 42(1) of PACE).
- If further extension is required it has to be granted by a magistrate under s. 43 and s. 44 of PACE), and if permitted the total period of detention could total 96 hours.
- The Terrorism Act 2006 provides for a period of detention of up to 28 days for those suspected of having committed terrorist offences.

Two 'PACE clocks' run for the detained person. Clock one is for time in custody and commences once the suspect has arrived at the police station. Clock two commences once detention has been authorised. This is used to review the time spent in custody. This is carried out by the review officer (normally an inspector or above) and takes place after 6 hours, 15 hours and just before the 24 hours is up. Following the interview, there may be a need to obtain more information. If this cannot be done immediately, the suspect should be bailed or released. The Crown Prosecution Service (CPS) should be consulted as soon as practicable after the interview, and may give authorisation to charge the suspect. More time may be needed for the CPS to study the file and evidence. The suspect may therefore be bailed to return to the police station on a specified date (s. 37(7) PACE).

## Treatment in Custody

Changes to the way a person is held in custody were incorporated into PACE following reports by the Royal Commission on Criminal Procedure (1981) and the report by Lord Scarman on the Brixton Riots (Scarman, 1982). PACE introduced the tape recording (and subsequent visual recording) of interviews, also laying down guidelines on how these interviews should be conducted:

- PACE codes emphasise a suspect's rights to (free) legal advice.
- A new post of 'custody officer' was created; they are required to maintain a custody record.
- The custody officer has a legal responsibility for persons held in custody and must ensure that a suspect's rights are adhered to including determining whether there is sufficient evidence to charge a person who has been arrested (PACE Codes of Practice C (2012)).

The custody officer is responsible under PACE for the reception and treatment of prisoners at a police station, and acts independently from those conducting the investigation. It is the custody officer's decision whether or not to authorise the detention of a suspect based upon the evidence put before them.

PACE also provides the police with powers to take photographs, fingerprints and samples from persons arrested on suspicion of having committed a crime. These powers were developed in the 1984 Codes of Practice, and the revised 1995 Codes of Practice took into account developments that had taken place since the implementation of the Act. This included the taking of intimate and non-intimate body samples for forensic analysis, including redefining saliva and mouth swabs as non-intimate samples which could be taken even if a suspect refused consent. Non-intimate samples can now be taken for recordable offences, not just serious arrestable offences, thus expanding the range of offences for which samples could be taken (Buckle and Brown, 1997: 42). The Serious Organised Crime and Police Act 2005 amended a number of sections within PACE:

- Photographs of suspects may be taken at places other than police stations.
- Under specified circumstances fingerprints may be taken without a suspect's consent.

- The definition given to intimate samples was expanded to incorporate a swab taken from any part of a person's genitals (including pubic hair) or from a person's body orifice other than the mouth.

## PUBLIC INTEREST DISCLOSURE ACT 1998

The Public Interest Disclosure Act (1998) (PIDA) was enacted in July 1999 and forms part of the stock of employment related legislation. The legislation promotes accountability in the workplace and encourages employers to address malpractice. It does this by providing legitimate 'whistleblowers' with statutory protection from being disciplined or dismissed for their disclosures ('protected disclosures') concerning wrongdoing past, present or proposed within the workplace by their employer or others. For the purpose of this Act, protected disclosures are qualifying disclosures made to an appropriate recipient in accordance with the prescribed conditions that apply to each different type of recipient of the information. A protected disclosure has to pass the subjective test that the whistleblower has reasonable belief in the truthfulness of the information, it must be made in good faith, and there should be no personal gain.

A qualifying disclosure is therefore defined as any disclosure of information which, *in the reasonable belief of the worker making the disclosure*, tends to show one or more of the following:

- That a criminal offence has been committed, is being committed or is likely to be committed.
- That a person has failed, is failing or is likely to fail to comply with any legal obligation to which he is subject.
- That a miscarriage of justice has occurred, is occurring or is likely to occur.
- That information tending to show any matter falling within any one of the preceding paragraphs has been, or is likely to be deliberately concealed.

Other criteria include breach of health and safety and damage to the environment. Qualifying disclosures may concern the employer's activities anywhere in the world and may involve the breach of the law of any other country or territory as well as the UK. It should be noted, however, that any information obtained as a result of legal privilege is excluded.

If an ACFS is considering whistleblowing, as a general rule this should be done in accordance with their employer's whistleblowing policy. However, depending on individual circumstances this may not always be practicable. Accordingly disclosure can be made to any of the following:

- Your employer (including any representative of your employer, such as a senior manager)
- A legal advisor
- A Minister of the Crown
- A regulatory body (for example the Information Commissioner)
- A third party (for example a member of the media).

Employees, contractors, sub-contractors and home workers are all protected by PIDA. The Act, however, does not include anonymous whistleblowers, there is no retrospective protection and employees of the security services and armed forces are not protected.

## What Protection is Afforded to a Whistleblower?

The legislation provides the whistleblower with the right:

(a) not to be penalised or put at any disadvantage, short of dismissal, by your employer as a result of making a protected disclosure;
(b) to be automatically treated as having been unfairly dismissed if the reason for dismissal was that a protected disclosure had been made.

(Information Commissioner's Office, 2012)

 FREEDOM OF INFORMATION ACT 2000

The rationale behind the Freedom of Information Act 2000 (FOIA) is that it improves the democratic process by giving the public greater access to information about the workings of government through increased transparency, reduces the risk of whistleblowing leaks, ensures improved accuracy of government information and affords equal treatment of individuals when dealing with state institutions (Wadham and Griffiths, 2005: 1–3).

An individual's rights under the Act can be found at s. 1, which provides that:

Section 1 – General right of access to information held by public authorities

Any person making a request for information to a public authority is entitled

(a) to be informed in writing by the public authority whether it holds information of the description specified in the request, and
(b) if that is the case, to have that information communicated to him.

In terms of what information is considered to be held by a public body, s. 3(2) of the Act provides that information is held by a public authority if:

(a) it is held by the authority, otherwise than on behalf of another person, or
(b) it is held by another person on behalf of the authority.

Under the Act there is no need to establish who 'owns' the information. For example, certain information may be held by more than one public authority. Public authorities subject to the Act include:

- Part I: General: Core public authorities (Government Departments, House of Commons, House of Lords)
- Part II: Local Government
- Part III: The National Health Service
- Part IV: Schools and other Educational Institutions
- Part V: Policing.

There are however some exceptions, for example the security services, the Secret Intelligence Service and the Government Communication Headquarters.

To request information, s. 8(1) of PIDA states that the acceptable format for a request is that it:

(a) is in writing
(b) states the name of the applicant and an address for correspondence, and
(c) describes the information requested.

There are however certain absolute exemptions, three examples that an ACFS should be aware of being, information from, or relating to, certain security bodies (s. 23), information contained in court records (s. 32) and information disclosure that would breach parliamentary privilege (s. 34). There are also class based exemptions from disclosure under this legislation, these being all types of information that fall within a particular class. The one of relevance to an ACFS concerns information held by a public authority concerning investigations and proceedings (s. 30). Of equal interest to an ACFS is the prejudice based exemption for law enforcement at s. 31(1), which states that information that is not exempt under s. 30 of PIDA but is connected to a wide range of law enforcement functions and may still be exempt if disclosure under PIDA would, or would be likely to, prejudice:

(a) the prevention or detection of crime
(b) the apprehension or prosecution of offenders
(c) the administration of justice.

 ## REVIEW

This chapter has discussed the history, background and relevant provisions of all applicable governing legislation and what factors an ACFS in either the public or private sector needs to consider in order to remain legally compliant when investigating fraud, thus preventing an abuse of process and an unethical investigation. The legislation reviewed covers all aspects of the investigation an ACFS will be conducting, including surveillance; interviewing suspects; search and seizure; the requesting, retention and disclosure of data relevant to the investigation; human rights and disclosure should the investigation reach the prosecution stage. The chapter has also provided an awareness of the Public Interest Disclosure Act 1998 and the protection afforded to whistleblowers. The chapter closed with a discussion of the Freedom of Information Act 2000 and the exemptions relevant to law enforcement, investigation and proceedings that an ACFS should be aware of.

 ## FURTHER READING

Atkinson, D. and Moloney, T. (2011) *Blackstone's Guide to the Criminal Procedure Rules*. Oxford: Oxford University Press.
Coleman, R. and McCahill, M. (2011) *Surveillance and Crime*. London: Sage.
Ozey P., Norton, H. and Spivey, P. (2011) *PACE: A Practical Guide to the Police and Criminal Evidence Act 1984* (2nd edn). Oxford: Oxford University Press.

Prochaska, E. and Brown, C. (2011) *Blackstone's Guide to the Human Rights Act 1998.* Oxford: Oxford University Press.

Raphael, M., Swift, N. and Gokani, R. (2010) *Blackstone's Guide to the Bribery Act 2010.* Oxford: Oxford University Press.

Roberts, P. (2007) Law and Criminal Investigation. In T. Newburn, T. Williamson and A. Wright (eds) *Handbook of Criminal Investigation.* Cullompton: Willan Publishing, pp. 92–145.

## CHAPTER FOUR

# Organising and planning an investigation

## CHAPTER **SUMMARY**

This chapter will explain the structure of an investigation, the process of investigative decision making, and the significance of recording the decision-making process when progressing an investigation. Values, principles and the importance of maintaining an ethical investigation will be discussed whilst also exploring the antithesis of ethics in the form of corrupt practice. Intelligence and the intelligence cycle will be explained, including how intelligence is graded according to the National Intelligence Model.

 **INTRODUCTION**

A fraud investigation requires careful planning and management at each stage to ensure that it is efficient, legal and professional. Furthermore, it is imperative that it is underpinned throughout by ethical decision making, thus ensuring that the investigation embraces the suspect's human rights and alleviates the risk of any miscarriage of justice should the case reach the prosecution stage. This chapter will first explore what constitutes a criminal investigation, before moving on to explore the structure of an investigation and the process of investigative decision making. Throughout the investigation, it is essential that the ACFS should record the decision-making process when progressing the case. This chapter will therefore outline the importance of careful documentation of each stage of the investigation, so that it can withstand scrutiny from any third party, specifically defence counsel should the case reach court. The chapter will then explore the concept of an ethical investigation before introducing the concept of corruption, and what steps an ACFS should take if they suspect this activity is taking place within an investigation team.

 ## WHAT IS A CRIMINAL INVESTIGATION?

An ACFS needs to be aware of what constitutes a criminal investigation, and how this sits within the overall criminal justice process. The following definition encapsulates the fundamental principles of the purpose of an investigation, in both the criminal and civil law contexts. 'An investigation is the process undertaken to establish whether an act, intention to act or omission may have given rise to a civil or criminal liability and, if it has, the collection of evidence, or material to determine those responsible and how they will be dealt with in terms of redress and/or sanction' (Hampson, 2011: 9).

Another definition, relevant to conducting criminal fraud investigations is offered by Roberts (2007) who suggests that 'criminal investigations . . . are orientated towards cracking unsolved crime, identifying perpetrators, launching prosecutions, proving guilt at trial and bringing offenders to justice' (p. 95). When engaged in a criminal investigation, the objectives to be met are prescribed by the criminal law, which defines both the fundamental components of a crime and the criteria of criminal responsibility, thus dictating the 'points to prove' to be outlined within the investigation plan. It is important that the ACFS recognises the key elements of the alleged fraudulent offence(s) that need to be proved, whilst also considering any plausible denial that might be offered by the defence that needs to be disproved by evidence that is both admissible in court and stands up to scrutiny. The latter emphasises the importance of conducting both a legally compliant and ethical investigation. If it transpires that evidence has been gathered unethically, for example by an abuse of process, then there is a distinct possibility that the investigation will fail to achieve a positive outcome in court. Similarly, when engaged in a civil investigation, an ACFS should maintain the same ethical standards and ensure that all evidence is gathered using legally compliant means, thus again ensuring admissibility of this material should the case go to court.

 ## TYPES OF INVESTIGATION

There are three specific types of investigation that an ACFS may be involved in, these being 'reactive', 'proactive' and 'preventative intelligence gathering' (Clark, 2007: 426). A *reactive investigation* involves the 'search for evidence following an allegation of, or the discovery of circumstances which amount to, a crime' (p. 426). This type of investigation results from a civil or criminal offence already being committed, or information being received, possibly through a whistleblower's hotline, that an offence is due to be committed. The sequence of the reactive investigation process commences with crime scene preservation, which in the case of a fraud investigation may involve the preservation of materials and devices believed to have been used in the commission of the offence. There may then be a requirement to search for witnesses to corroborate the chain of events. These witnesses may also be victims of the fraud, and should therefore be treated accordingly. The ACFS may also need to search for additional investigative material (evidence) to substantiate that the alleged offence has been committed. Finally the ACFS will need to evaluate the evidence to determine whether this is sufficient to prove that the alleged offence has been committed, and that this evidence will stand up to scrutiny in court if the case is referred for proceedings. This type of investigation would be considered the traditional style of investigation, and the one which an ACFS will most frequently be involved in, unless they are assigned to a specialist team, for example a 'fraud drive team' conducting proactive investigations, which will now be discussed.

A *proactive investigation* 'should be intelligence led, making use of information gleaned from informants and from profiling techniques such as crime pattern analysis' (Clark, 2007: 426). This may focus upon the fraudster rather than the fraud, and is used when dealing with organised fraud. This typology of investigation includes gathering and exploitation of intelligence, subject pro-filing, and crime pattern analysis. Additionally, this type of investigation may also involve what is sometimes referred to as volume fraud, and draws upon data matching; for example, computerised matching of two different data strips, where one has a bearing on the other to identify potential frauds. This type of investigation technique is often employed by public sector organisations, the DWP being one example.

*Preventative intelligence gathering* involves the gathering of information that is then stored for public protection, 'and is a consequence of legislation that encourages multi-agency solutions to crime and disorder' (Clark, 2007: 426). The aim is to draw upon and exploit intelligence held and received to prevent an offence occurring (the intelligence cycle and National Intelligence Model will be discussed later in this chapter). This investigation typology came about as a result of some of the high profile investigations that failed from the outset, or, if an alleged offender was identified, resulted in a serious miscarriage of justice. The aim of this type of investigation is to design out fraud, and it may involve multi-agency working and the sharing of information and intelligence. Legislation such as the Crime and Disorder Act 1998 and the Sex Offenders Act 1997 promote multi-agency working, maximising the use of information that has been gathered.

 ## THE ROLE OF THE ACFS

During the course of the investigation, an ACFS will be required to perform a multitude of tasks, these being to 'unearth, recover, procure, amass, sort, compile, test, evaluate and arrange this evidence as compelling proof of the offender's guilt' (Roberts, 2007: 95–96). It is imperative that all of these tasks are conducted in an ethical manner to ensure that the criminal case stands up to scrutiny when reaching court. There are also legal requirements laid down in the CPIA Act 1996, discussed in Chapter 3, concerning the handling, treatment and recording of evidence in a criminal investigation which are all underpinned by ethical principles.

Managing an investigation requires careful thought, planning and execu-tion by the ACFS and involves 'bringing together the different processes and stages so as to construct a coherent and effective investigation which complies with the strictures of the law and with the extensive guidance and standard operating procedures which specify how an investigation should be managed' (Neyroud and Disley, 2007: 550). Accordingly, an ACFS needs to be fully skilled in all generic management functions to enable them to keep control over the process of investigation. These skills will include:

- Deciding on Priorities.
- Allocating time and resources to achieve them.
- Managing material gathered.
- Tasking others to carry out activities associated with the investigation.
- Integrating their work into the overall effort of the investigation.
- Keeping good records of what has been done and why.

(Stelfox, 2009: 46)

An ACFS will also need to bring together the various skills and knowledge that are covered throughout this book when managing an investigation. These include an understanding of what constitutes fraud and the points to prove; knowledge of the English legal system (criminal and civil); awareness of all governing legislation and the procedures that must be adhered to; managing suspects and witnesses; interviewing skills; evidence gathering and the rules of evidence; the gathering, retention and exploitation of intelligence; report writing and courtroom skills when required to give evidence on a case that has been investigated.

##  THE INVESTIGATION LIFE CYCLE

The Fraud Advisory Panel identifies what is known as the investigation life cycle, which involves five key stages that an ACFS needs to implement, these being:

1. Initial action
2. Objective setting and planning
3. Information gathering and interviews
4. Reporting
5. Taking action.

(Fraud Advisory Panel, 2012: 1)

Each stage will now be considered in turn, commencing with *initial action* which involves analysis and evaluation of the information relating to an alleged offence that has already occurred or that intelligence suggests may occur at some point in the not too distant future. This initial stage will require some investigative decision making by the ACFS, and will include initially an assessment of the source of the allegation, for example is it written and anonymous, does it originate from a whistleblower's hotline? Could the allegation be malicious or contrived? These considerations will have a bearing on the decision-making process at this initial stage. For example, if there is a strong suspicion and some evidence to suggest that the allegation is malicious, then it is possible that no further action will be taken. Having determined that the allegation is genuine and can be taken in good faith, the ACFS will need to evaluate all the information and intelligence to identify whether the behaviour in question justifies initiating either a criminal or civil investigation. Thirdly, from analysis of the material can a suspect be identified? If so, what information and intelligence is already held on them within any available fraud intelligence databases? When undertaking a corporate investigation, consideration must also be given to the client's and/or victim's expectations. For example, are they looking simply to recover losses? Or is there an expectation that the investigation will result in both sanction and redress? If there is an expectation that the case may be referred to the police, even though the investigation may be deemed to be civil, the ACFS needs to ensure that from this initial action stage onwards, the investigation is carried out to a criminal standard. Finally, if, following evaluation, it is decided that a criminal or civil law fraud investigation is justified, a decision should be taken on what additional information and intelligence is required. The latter will then be used to set objectives and formulate an investigation plan.

## Objective Setting and Planning

Having determined that the allegation warrants the initiation of an investigation, the ACFS now needs to formulate an investigation plan including specific objectives which should be time bound. The objectives will be determined by the nature of the allegation, the potential offences identified and information/intelligence gaps identified during the initial evaluation stage, and the intended investigation outcome in terms of whether it is intended to pursue a criminal prosecution or just seek civil recovery of all identified losses. Finally, consideration must be given to any budgetary and resource implications resulting from the activities necessary to achieve the objectives specified. Once these objectives have been formulated, they need to be agreed by all relevant members of the investigation team, but specifically senior management. The ACFS allocated to be the senior investigating officer will also be required to undertake a risk analysis of the prescribed objectives, firstly to determine their achievability, and secondly to consider any health and safety, human rights and equality issues that may arise as a result of the actions required to achieve these objectives. Some of the risks worthy of consideration include:

- reticence to punish employees or investigate them for internal fraud, preferring to permit their "quiet" resignation so as to avoid negative publicity (for fear of reputational damage, public perception, etc.);
- unqualified staff attempting to conduct investigations and compromising evidence (which ultimately means a case will not be prosecuted via the criminal justice system);
- failure to comply with relevant legislation resulting in evidence becoming inadmissible in court;
- failing to establish contacts and credibility with law enforcement;
- assuming the police will investigate the fraud once it has been reported to them – or expecting them to conduct the whole investigation on behalf of the organisation.

(Fraud Advisory Panel, 2012: 1)

Once these criteria have been examined and a decision taken to progress the investigation, the ACFS will then be required to formulate an investigation plan. A copy of an example investigation plan template can be found in Chapter 10. However, when developing the plan the following criteria are worthy of consideration:

- Is there a fraud response plan to refer to?
- Will the investigation follow the criminal, civil or internal disciplinary route?
- If criminal, should the police be notified immediately, or once relevant evidence has been gathered?
- If internal, does the suspect need to be suspended or have their security clearance restricted at this point?
- Who is the lead investigator?
- What are the potential offences identified?
- What is known and what needs to be known?
- What are the points to prove concerning the offences identified?
- What information and/or evidence are required to satisfy the points to prove?
- How will this evidence be obtained?
- Is there any existing evidence or materials relating to the fraud, particularly comport based evidence (evidence that supports the facts of the case) that needs to be preserved immediately?

- Do any existing evidential documents need to be referred for document or handwriting analysis?
- If there is any computer based evidence? Does this need to be referred to a specialist for forensic examination?
- Does any of the identified evidence to be gathered need prioritising?
- How many additional investigators will be required to form the investigation team?
- Is surveillance likely to be required as part of the evidence gathering process, and if so, what is the likely size of any surveillance team required and what specialist equipment might be needed?
- If the investigation concerns internal fraud, who within the organisation needs to be appraised of this?
- If the fraud impacts on other organisations should a joint investigation be considered?
- Is a memorandum of understanding required if a joint investigation is being considered?
- When evidence is gathered, how and where will this be securely stored?
- Does a dedicated disclosure officer need to be appointed?

## Information Gathering and Interviews

Having formulated the investigation plan, the ACFS will now need to embark on gathering the relevant information and evidence identified when determining the points to prove. Having already established what information is required, consideration will now need to be given to how that information will be obtained. Firstly, can anything be obtained using open source intelligence via the internet? If so, then either the officer in charge of the investigation or one of the investigation team can start to progress the investigation by sourcing this material. The second stage is to identify any information and evidence that can be obtained using any legal gateways that are in place between the investigating organisation and the relevant data holder. Finally, consideration should be given to making requests for information under s. 29 of the Data Protection Act 1998 if a criminal investigation is being pursued.

Once all the relevant information and evidence has been gathered this will need to be evaluated to ascertain whether it is sufficient to prove that any of the alleged offences have been committed. This will involve evaluating the overall strength of the case, determining if there is sufficient evidence for a conclusion to be arrived at or whether further enquiries are needed and if there is a need for additional evidence gathering. The ACFS should maintain a list of all potential evidence, which will assist the review process. If it is a complex case with multiple suspects, the use of an intelligence board may assist in keeping track of the investigation. Additionally, in a serious and organised fraud case it is worth engaging the help of a criminal intelligence analyst, if one is available, to support the investigation by evaluating and analysing all the evidence for any links or patterns. When evaluating evidence the ACFS should apply an investigative mindset to all source material, which initially involves assessing its provenance and characteristics. This will enable the ACFS to identify any characteristics that are particular to the source, which in turn will determine the way it is examined, thus ensuring that:

▪ The maximum amount of material is gathered.
▪ Its reliability is tested at the earliest opportunity.
▪ Immediate action is taken in relation to it.
▪ Relevant records are made.
▪ The material is appropriately stored.

(Stelfox, 2009: 168)

An additional component of the evidence gathering process is interviewing. Based on the original evaluation of the allegation, an ACFS should have identified any potential interviewees. These could be either witnesses, victims or both. Having done this, the officer in charge of the investigation should decide who is going to conduct the interviews, and if necessary task the relevant member of the investigation team accordingly, having fully briefed them on what information is required from the interview. The interview should take the form of a free recall interview which will be discussed in Chapter 6.

## Reporting

In order to comply with the CPIA Act 1996, all actions taken within the investigation will need to be fully documented by the ACFS (the relevant procedures are fully documented in Chapter 3). Not only does this ensure that the investigation is legally compliant, it also acts as a thorough record of all actions taken during the investigation and the thought process behind the decisions made should the investigation be assigned to another ACFS for operational reasons, or if the investigation is selected for a management check. The investigation report should be 'accurate, relevant and chronologically referenced' because this report may end up being used in court if it is decided that the case will be prosecuted (Fraud Advisory Panel, 2012: 2). Furthermore, if the case is referred to the police this will assist the ACFS in outlining the key stages of the investigation and the evidence obtained to facilitate an informed decision by the police on what further action is appropriate on the case.

## Taking Action

As the investigation progresses, should sufficient evidence have been gathered to cover the points to prove identified at the outset, at this point consideration will need to be given to interviewing the suspect(s). If enough evidence has been gathered to substantiate that a criminal offence has taken place, this interview should be conducted under caution. As discussed earlier in this chapter, if the ACFS is conducting a corporate fraud investigation, this should still have been carried out to the criminal standard, so an interview under caution is still a consideration at this stage. Finally, if the investigation relates to internal fraud the officer in charge will need to seek the views of the commissioning organisation as to what the next course of action should be. However, if criminal offences have been identified this should follow the criminal route. The next part of the process will be determined by the organisation employing the ACFS. If this is a public sector organisation such as the DWP, it is likely that the suspect will be invited to attend the office for an interview under caution, although in some cases, such as organised fraud, it is likely that the police will have to be consulted as the suspect will need to be arrested. In the case of corporate fraud investigations, if the police haven't already been consulted then it is at this point in the investigation that they should become involved. However the suspect is to be made available for interview, the ACFS will at this point need to formulate an interview plan for a conversation management interview, which will be discussed in detail in Chapter 6.

 ## INVESTIGATIVE DECISION MAKING

During the course of the fraud investigation an ACFS, either on their own or in consultation with senior management, will have to make some key decisions that influence the direction of the investigation. As previously discussed, each decision, including the thought process behind this judgement will need to be fully documented. In some serious and organised fraud investigations, these decisions may need to be recorded in a policy book which will then provide an additional transparent document open to independent scrutiny detailing all significant investigatory decisions made by the officer in charge and the investigation team when trying to progress the case. One way to think about decision making in the context of a counter fraud investigation is to consider the content of the decisions that need to be made. Using these criteria, five key decision types could be made during the investigation:

1. **Policy decisions:** Taken by the Senior Investigating Officer (SIO) and any management team. These set the broad parameters for an investigation.
2. **Knowledge decisions:** Are concerned with how particular units of information should be interpreted and treated by the enquiry team. That is, should they be understood as useful and contributing to the narrative of the case that is being developed, or should they be discarded as misinformation or disinformation?
3. **Action decisions:** Relate to what should be done, when and by whom. Action decisions look at the performance of key tasks and their order and timing.
4. **Logistic decisions:** Concern the support and infrastructure for an investigation. How many staff members should be available to the different components of the investigative system and for how long?
5. **Legal decisions:** Are essentially to do with how the investigation is related to the broader legal context in which it is located.

(Innes, 2007: 271)

Research also suggests that investigators rely on a set of rules that they develop from their own experiences of conducting an investigation (Adhami and Browne, 1996; Smith and Flanagan, 2000). Firstly, there is *personal bias*, whereby decisions made during an investigation can be unconsciously affected by personal perceptions of people, places and situations. An ACFS may also be influenced by *verification bias* (Tweney and Chitwood, 1995) which can result from developing a fixed view of what has occurred or who is responsible: there is a danger that they will focus on the material that supports that view. Finally, *availability error* (Stelfox, 2009: 163) may occur should decisions be based on material that is psychologically compelling because it appears familiar or is linked to a memory, but it may not necessarily reflect all the material at the ACFS's disposal. It is therefore imperative that the ACFS remain objective throughout the investigation, thus removing the risk of the decision-making process being influenced by the three aforementioned factors.

 ## ETHICAL INVESTIGATIONS

Historically there have been many issues relating to the way criminal investigations have been carried out. Although these criticisms have not been specifically directed at fraud investigations, they have resulted in a revised approach to criminal investigation that is underpinned by an ethical approach. To offer some background to this sea change, in the 1990s within the UK there was 'a growing call for independent oversight of the police, drawing upon the miscarriages of justice and other affairs in Britain, such as the Stephen Lawrence murder' (Punch, 2009: 149). As a result there was a stream of legislation and directives about police powers and police accountability (Reiner, 2000). The consequence was that the way in which investigations were conducted was fully reviewed, which resulted in the adoption of a more ethical approach to the process and the treatment of victims, suspects and witnesses.

The following principles are designed to ensure that investigations are conducted in ways which are ethical and encourage community support:

- When a crime is reported, or it is suspected that one has been committed, investigators should conduct an effective investigation.
- The exercise of legal powers should not be oppressive and should be proportionate to the crime under investigation.
- As far as operationally practical investigations should be carried out as transparently as possible (having regard) for individual confidentiality.
- Investigators should take all reasonable steps to understand the particular needs of individuals, including their culture, religious beliefs, ethnicity, sexuality, disability or lifestyle.
- Investigators should have particular regard for vulnerable adults and children.
- Investigators should respect the professional ethics of others.

(Association of Chief Police Officers, 2005a: 20)

The mnemonic PLAN is a useful aid to an ACFS when conducting an investigation, as it offers a reminder of the principles of 'proportionality, legality and necessity' (Wright, 2007: 592), that should always be a consideration when conducting any criminal or civil fraud investigation. This will result in a transparent investigation that can be subjected to any amount of scrutiny and should include keeping victims, witnesses and suspects regularly updated with developments in the investigation.

Returning to the subject of decision making, when conducting an investigation the ACFS should always have regard to ethics to ensure that the principles of proportionality, legality and necessity are observed. The process of ethical decision making should adhere to the following principles:

1. Identify the situation.
2. Decide what you need to achieve.

3. Examine what factors need to be considered.
4. Identify the various courses of action.
5. Identify which is the best and why.
6. Implement that course of action.

(Metropolitan Police, 2002: 6)

Another integral component is a suspect strategy because ethically it is important that all suspects are treated equally and without bias. Accordingly, it is imperative that an ACFS be fully conversant with the Equality Act 2010. Specifically, they must avoid actions that may be considered to be prohibited conduct or direct discrimination and they must also be aware of what the legislation defines as protected characteristics. These characteristics are what initiate the 'prohibition against discrimination' element of the statute and are defined within s. 4 of the Act as being; age, disability, gender reassignment, marriage and civil partnership, race, religion or belief, sex and sexual orientation. To ensure an ethical investigation and compliance with the statute, an ACFS should not treat any suspect 'less favourably' as a result of any of the aforementioned protected characteristics. Failure to comply with this requirement would be direct discrimination as defined within s. 13 of the Act. Other forms of prohibited conduct to be avoided during the investigation life cycle are defined within the Act as harassment (s. 26) and victimisation (s. 27).

However, if there is a legitimate reason for treating a particular suspect differently it is important that this is recorded on the case file, and if applicable, in the policy book (College of Policing, 2013a). This will then provide an explanation of why decisions were made, and may also contain a record of ethical considerations. Consequently, if there are any questions raised about the treatment of one individual in relation to another, possibly by the defence in court, then the case file notes and any policy book can be used to illustrate why certain courses of action were taken and that the investigation is ethically sound. Having identified a suspect, 'a strategy development approach can be adopted to gather material that will either implicate them in the offence or eliminate them' (College of Policing, 2013a).

 ## CORRUPTION

The antithesis of an ethical investigation is one that involves some element of corrupt practice, either within the decision-making process or in the treatment of victims, witnesses or suspects. Corruption may be defined as 'any type of proscribed behaviour engaged in by a law enforcement officer who receives or expects to receive, by virtue of his official position, an actual or potential unauthorised material reward or gain' (Barker and Roebuck, 1973). A similar definition is offered by Goldstein (1977) who suggests that it involves 'the misuse of authority by a police officer in a manner designed to produce personal gain for the officers or for others' (p. 188).

According to Punch (1985), corruption can be analysed in five dimensions:

1. The acts and actors involved
2. The norms they violate
3. The degree of support from their peer group
4. The extent to which the deviant practices are organised
5. The reaction of the police department.

It is imperative that an ACFS is aware of the issues of corruption, and should they suspect that this bad practice is occurring within any investigation they are leading, take the necessary action to alert senior management so that the relevant internal processes can be activated to investigate these suspicions. Corruption can be damaging to the reputation of any investigative agency, because if this is made public, the integrity of this organisation and any ACFS that is employed by them may be called into question. Furthermore, this may also cast doubt on the integrity of all previous investigations conducted by the organisation, specifically those that have resulted in the successful prosecution of a suspect.

Having covered the principles of investigation management and ethics, this chapter will now explore another key component of the investigative process referred to earlier – intelligence and its place within an investigation.

 ## INTELLIGENCE

Back in 1996 the Association of Chief Police Officers (ACPO) recommended that intelligence should play a greater role in policing (ACPO, 1996). However, while it had been used when dealing with serious and organised crime, it was not until around 2004 that it began to be fully embedded in more 'mainstream areas of policing' (John and Maguire, 2004: 7). The driver behind this development was to promote more efficient and effective deployment of resources (Maguire, 2000). The government strategy to increase joined up working between public sector organisations, in particular the sharing of data, also aided the development of intelligence-led investigation. As a consequence, non-policing organisations such as the Department for Work and Pensions began to develop an intelligence capability to support the concept of intelligence-led investigation. As time has passed, many other public bodies, including some local authorities, have also adopted the concept of intelligence-led investigation using a bespoke structure based upon the National Intelligence Model, which will be discussed later in this chapter. We will now explore the concept of intelligence and how this differs from information.

## Intelligence v Information

There is a distinct difference between information and intelligence, the former being raw data which may take many forms. Information can be passed on verbally, in writing or can be seen. It is the transfer of knowledge between one source and another. Information in its raw form can be useful because it is informative and can contain details of events, individuals or descriptions. In contrast, criminal intelligence is information that has been processed for a purpose, having been evaluated and subjected to some form of analysis. Intelligence is therefore:

- Information that is capable of being understood
- Information with added value
- Information that has been evaluated in the context of its source and reliability.

(United Nations Office on Drugs and Crime, 2010: 1)

In sum, intelligence is processed information designed for action that is used by law enforcement and investigative agencies to determine and support investigations. The analysis of information is intended to identify links, networks, associations, patterns and criminal business activity. Having been subjected to analysis intelligence products are developed which are used to identify priorities and inform the decision-making process when deploying resources (College of Policing, 2013b).

## The Intelligence Cycle

'Intelligence is also thought of as a process: a series of interactive steps, formally referred to as an "intelligence cycle"' (Johnson, 2007: 3). The process is outlined in Figure 4.1 and commences with *planning and direction* which is directed by operational needs and may be determined either by intelligence managers when harvesting strategic intelligence or by the ACFS in

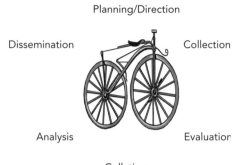

FIGURE 4.1   The Intelligence Cycle

(Adapted from Central Intelligence Agency, 1993: 14)

conjunction with the operational intelligence unit and the criminal intelligence analyst, if available, when this relates to intelligence required for a specific investigation. This discussion will focus on the latter which is most relevant to the operational ACFS.

Moving on, the next stage of the process is the formulation of a *collection plan* which should identify and describe the information needed and how and from what source it can be obtained. Having collected the information it then needs to be evaluated. *Evaluation* is an assessment of the reliability of the source and the quality of the information. This is normally conducted using a process of grading, referred to as 5 × 5 × 5, which will be discussed later in this chapter. Having evaluated the data collected, it then needs to be organised into a format from which it can be retrieved and analysed. Much of this *collation* process is now undertaken using computer based intelligence software, such as i2. The *analysis* phase is the most crucial because it examines the significance and importance of the information harvested and highlights both essential features and helps identify any information gaps that need to be addressed. Criminal Intelligence Analysts and the ACFS are then able to develop inferences from the data, drawing appropriate conclusions based on careful assessment of the information. At this stage it may be necessary to revisit and even revise the collection plan and obtain further information. The analysis phase will in turn lead towards completion of the intelligence cycle when the product of the analysis is presented to the ACFS leading the investigation and any other members of the investigation team who may have originally requested it. This is known as the *dissemination* phase. It may be necessary to move through the cycle again if as a result of subsequent investigations further intelligence requirements are identified.

The ACFS can use the intelligence gathered either tactically or operationally to inform the tasking and co-ordination process in terms of which suspects need to be investigated, the manner in which they should be investigated, and what investigative resources are required to progress the case. The use of intelligence also supports investigative direction as it allows:

- Control over events within the investigation
- Focused and directed planning
- Increased proactive activity
- Potential for more favourable investigative outcomes.

The use of the intelligence cycle can also help to inform future investigations through lessons learned from evaluation of the original planning and collection process, and whether the original objectives set were in fact appropriate.

## Intelligence Sources

Two of the main sources of intelligence are:

- **Open source:** examples of open source intelligence are newspapers and other types of publicly accessible media, the electoral roll, personal credit databases that the organisation subscribes to, the Land Registry and all publicly accessible internet sites.
- **Closed source (confidential data):** this can include intelligence harvested from a Covert Human Intelligence Source (CHIS), other law enforcement agencies such as the Police National Computer (PNC), databases accessible only by subscription such as Equifax, Experian and Callcredit, or from databases accessible via membership such as CIFAS, UK Payments Administration Limited or as a result of industry membership such as intelligence from the City of London Police Insurance Fraud Enforcement Department.

Any systematic collection and processing of intelligence from sources such as those described above would represent an intelligence system, or model, and accordingly would be subject to the governing legislation discussed in Chapter 3, including the Data Protection Act 1998, the Human Rights Act 1998 and if using a Covert Human Intelligence Source, the Regulation of Investigatory Powers Act 2000. The concepts of proportionality and necessity discussed earlier in the chapter should also be considered by the ACFS, including those employed by non-public bodies on the basis of best practice. Non-regulatory issues of commercial confidentiality might also be applicable in the private sector. In any case, any intelligence system should be operated in an ethical manner and in accordance with the law.

## The National Intelligence Model

Although there are bespoke intelligence structures at the organisational level, there is a national model, known as the National Intelligence Model (NIM), originally developed by the National Criminal Intelligence Service and given a statutory basis by the Police Reform Act 2002. It is a business model for law enforcement and takes an intelligence approach to policing. It takes the form of an 'information based deployment system' (ACPO, 2005b: 12) and facilitates the direction and deployment of resources 'to collect information to fill identified knowledge gaps' (p. 13).

The NIM provides, for the first time, a cohesive intelligence framework across the full range of levels of criminality and disorder (John and Maguire, 2004: 8). Accordingly, the model operates at three levels:

- **Level 1** represents local crime capable of being managed by local resources (which may include the most serious crime) and anti-social behaviour;
- **Level 2** represents force, inter-force and regional criminal activity usually requiring additional resources;
- **Level 3** represents the most serious and organised crime.

(ACPO, 2005b: 103)

The NIM facilitates the sharing of intelligence across all police forces and also with other law enforcement agencies and serves as a platform for standard working practices. The NIM is underpinned by the development and use of four specific products:

- **Analytical Products** are primarily brief reports drawn up by specialist intelligence units on the basis of analysis of information and intelligence from a variety of sources (within and outside the police)
- **Intelligence Products**, which may be broadly subdivided into Strategic Assessments; Tactical Assessments; Target Profiles; and Problem Profiles (hotspots or crime series), are used to inform

decisions on the prioritisation of problems and targets, to allo-
cate 'ownership' of problems to particular staff or units, and as
the basis for planning of operational responses
▪ **Knowledge Products** are products that will inform future development of the NIM itself and maintain quality within it. The model
already includes a wide-ranging list of examples, such as Data
Protection Act guidelines, intelligence training, and ECHR compliant codes of practice for policing activities
▪ **System Products** are designed to ensure that appropriate technical and computer equipment is available to the model for its effective operation and to minimise inefficient practices such as the use
of incompatible IT systems that act as a barrier to the sharing of
information. They are also used to ensure that access is secured
across the different levels, and to other agencies, and international
law enforcement bodies.

(John and Maguire, 2004: 9)

The tasking and co-ordination process is also an important facet of the
model which involves informed deployment of the tactical resource towards
priorities identified as a result of the intelligence analysis process. Accordingly,
another integral component of the NIM is the criminal intelligence analyst
which the ACFS should recognise as a useful resource to assist with the development and progression of complex fraud investigations involving multiple
suspects. The criminal intelligence analyst can support investigations by producing a range of reports, these being:

▪ **Network analysis:** not only describes the links between people who form
criminal networks, but also the significance of these links, the roles played
by individuals and the strengths and weaknesses of a criminal organisation.
▪ **Market profiles:** continually reviewed and updated assessments that sur-
vey the criminal market around a particular commodity, such as drugs or
stolen vehicles, or of a service, such as prostitution, in an area.
▪ **Criminal business profiles:** contain detailed analysis of how criminal
operations or techniques work, in the same way that a legitimate business
might be explained.
▪ **Target profile analysis:** embraces a range of analytical techniques to
describe the criminal, their criminal activity, lifestyle, associations, the
risk they pose and their strengths and weaknesses in order to give focus
to the investigation targeting them. Profiles may also focus on victims and
vulnerable persons.

- **Operational intelligence assessment:** involves evaluating incoming intelligence to maintain the focus of an operation on previously agreed objectives, particularly in the case of a sizeable intelligence collection plan or other large-scale operation.
- **Results analysis:** evaluates the effectiveness of law enforcement activities.

(ACPO, 2005b: 61)

More information on the National Intelligence Model and intelligence-led investigation can be found at:

http://www.acpo.police.uk/documents/crime/2007/200708-cba-intelligence-led-policing.pdf

http://www.app.college.police.uk/app-content/intelligence-management/

## Grading Intelligence (5 × 5 × 5)

The NIM also outlines procedures for handling and processing intelligence, specifically the grading of all intelligence using what is known as the 5 × 5 × 5 system, whereby each five represents one of three object categories, within which there are five grading choices available. The three object categories are:

- Source evaluation
- Intelligence evaluation
- Handling code (dissemination).

*Source evaluation* relates to the origins of the intelligence which could be from a human source, a document, information from a database or even something retrieved from CCTV footage. The individual receiving the intelligence must make a judgement as to whether the source is:

**A** Always reliable – (forensic and technical results)
**B** Mostly reliable (government agencies, police, etc.)
**C** Sometimes reliable
**D** Unreliable
**E** Untested source – (includes anonymous information).

*Intelligence evaluation* involves a judgement being made on the reliability of the intelligence itself, irrespective of the reliability of the source. The options available are:

1. Known to be true without reservation
2. Known personally to source but not to officer

3. Not personally known to source but corroborated
4. Cannot be judged
5. Suspected to be false.

The evaluation process should be carried out at the point the intelligence first enters the Intelligence System by the person who has gathered it. This evaluation should be objective and based upon professional judgement only.

Finally, the intelligence should be disseminated and therefore has to be allocated a *handling code* which informs the recipient of any restriction imposed on the intelligence received. Again, there are five options when disseminating the intelligence, these being:

■ **CODE 1:** Permits dissemination within the UK Police Service AND to other Law Enforcement Agencies as specified
■ **CODE 2:** May be disseminated to UK non-prosecuting parties
■ **CODE 3:** Permits dissemination to non-EEA foreign law enforcement agencies
■ **CODE 4:** Permits dissemination within originating agency/force. Specify internal recipients. (Must stay within originating agency)
■ **CODE 5:** Permits dissemination but receiving agency to observe conditions as specified:
  ▪ No further dissemination
  ▪ Recipients conditions specified
  ▪ To be discussed with originator and documented
  ▪ No further dissemination during life of the flag.

## REVIEW

This chapter has outlined the structure of a fraud investigation and the process of investigative decision making that an ACFS will need to undertake to ensure the investigation is efficient, legal and professional. The importance of recording all key decisions relating to the investigation, including the thought processes behind them, has also been explored. The question of ethics has also been discussed and how any decisions made by an ACFS during the course of the investigation should be underpinned by ethical considerations to prevent the risk of abuse of process or a miscarriage of justice. Finally, the chapter has outlined the importance of intelligence to the fraud investigation being conducted by an ACFS, including a review of the National Intelligence Model and guidance on the handling, grading and dissemination of intelligence.

**FURTHER READING**

Clark, D. (2007) Covert Surveillance and Informer Handling. In T. Newburn, T. Williamson and A. Wright (eds), *Handbook of Criminal Investigation*. Cullompton: Willan Publishing, pp. 426–449.

Fraud Advisory Panel (2012) *Fraud Facts: An Introduction to Fraud Investigations*. Issue 16, June 2012. Available from https://www.fraudadvisorypanel.org/ pdf_show_191.pdf [Accessed 13 April 2014].

Innes, M. (2007) Investigation Order and Major Crime Inquiries. In T. Newburn, T. Williamson and A. Wright (eds), *Handbook of Criminal Investigation*. Cullompton: Willan Publishing, pp. 255–276.

Neyroud, P. and Disley, E. (2007) The Management, Supervision and Oversight of Criminal Investigations. In T. Newburn, T. Williamson and A. Wright (eds), *Handbook of Criminal Investigation*. Cullompton: Willan Publishing, pp. 549–571.

Roberts, P. (2007) Law and Criminal Investigation. In T. Newburn, T. Williamson and A. Wright (eds), *Handbook of Criminal Investigation*. Cullompton: Willan Publishing, pp. 92–145.

Stelfox, P. (2009) *Criminal Investigation: An Introduction to Principles and Practice*. Cullompton: Willan Publishing, chapter 2: The development of investigative practice.

## CHAPTER FIVE

# Covert investigation

## CHAPTER **SUMMARY**

This chapter examines the regulatory position when covert investigative techniques are deployed as a means of gathering evidence during a fraud investigation and the protection that is afforded to public authorities from challenges to a breach of a subject's right to a private and family life when such methods are deployed. It examines the position of the ACFS operating in the commercial sector and the procedures that should be followed to ensure that actions for breaching a subject's Article 8 rights can be successfully defended. The two types of surveillance are defined, before moving on to discuss the role of the Covert Human Intelligence Source. Finally, the chapter considers how communications can be lawfully monitored and recorded.

 **INTRODUCTION**

The purpose of this chapter is not to describe the practical techniques and methods used to conduct surveillance – that would involve a book in its own right and is best left to your trainers to demonstrate and teach during ACFS training. However, the ACFS does need to understand the law relating to the use of such activity, so that their actions can remain lawful and stand up to legal challenge. In Chapter 3 we examined how the Regulation of Investigatory Powers Act 2000 (RIPA) regulated the use of covert investigative techniques by public authorities. If you recall, it is a piece of legislation that followed hot on the heels of the incorporation of the European Convention of Human Rights, by way of the Human Rights Act 1998, into UK law and it concerns itself with covert policing and investigations undertaken by public bodies as defined within the Act. As the term suggests, covert investigations involve activity of various kinds, such as surveillance, interception of communications, the use of informants and so on, carried out secretly. This is almost always likely to involve, in some way, interference with someone's privacy. Article 8 of the Human Rights Act guarantees the right to a private and family life. This obviously leads to conflict between the need to conduct covert investigations and people's human rights. The purpose of RIPA is to strike a balance between the two and provide a regulatory framework of accountability for public bodies to work within. It also provides public authorities with some protection from legal challenges asserting that the use of such investigative techniques has breached the subject's Article 8 rights. If the public authority (or indeed, any organisation that has used such methods) is able to demonstrate that their actions were proportionate, necessary and for one of the purposes specified in the legislation, then there will be an adequate defence to rebut such challenges.

Although the Act is aimed at public authorities (and not every public authority, only those specified in Schedule I of the Act) private organisations should pay regard to it and follow its principles. If a private organisation has gone to the lengths (and expense) of deploying such techniques then there is a likelihood that whatever is being investigated will result in a court or tribunal hearing. Although the organisation itself may not be a public authority the court or tribunal most certainly will be and if human rights issues are raised the court or tribunal will have to pay regard to them, which may result in the evidence being ruled inadmissible if RIPA principles have not been followed. As an example, consider *Campbell v Mirror Group Newspapers Ltd* [2004] UKHL 22. The model Naomi Campbell was covertly photographed coming out of a Narcotics Anonymous meeting and a story and photograph were published on the front page of the *Daily Mirror* on 1 February 2001. Campbell sued the newspaper for breaching her right to privacy and in their deliberations the House of Lords (which at the time was the most senior appellate court in the UK) gave consideration to Campbell's Article 8 rights. Neither Campbell nor the newspaper is a public authority but still the court was obliged to consider ECHR matters. In judgment, Lord Nicholls of Birkenhead stated:

> The values embodied in articles 8 and 10 are as much applicable in disputes between individuals or between an individual and a non-governmental body such as a newspaper as they are in disputes between individuals and a public authority.

The Financial Conduct Authority, for example, is deemed to be a public authority within Schedule 1 of RIPA, meaning that the Financial Services Ombudsman, who adjudicates on customer complaints against Banks, Insurance Companies and Building Societies etc., must be human rights compliant and, therefore, should comply with the requirements of RIPA.

Also, as will be seen, with the advent of Public Private Partnerships, Public Sector Private Finance Initiatives and the Government increasingly outsourcing functions to private sector companies, the lines are becoming increasingly blurred between the two sectors. This has led to a question mark arising over how far commercial companies should comply with human rights legislation. Where a public authority (or any organisation) contracts out investigative work this does not absolve it from having to ensure that the subject's rights are protected and that the techniques used are in accordance with RIPA. The contractor will be operating as the principal's agent, not as an investigative body in its own right. Therefore, rather than attempt to run parallel systems whereby different rules and procedures apply to different types of investigations, which can be very confusing, if not a complete distraction from the job in hand, it is suggested that attention should be paid to the overarching principles of RIPA which should be adapted to fit the purposes of non-public body investigators. This should ensure integrity of evidence, minimisation of risk, maximisation of duty of care and maintenance of an ethical investigative approach.

##  BACKGROUND TO RIPA

Prior to the introduction of the Act the law in relation to covert policing and investigations was fragmented. Indeed, what little legislation there was applied only to the police, the security services and Her Majesty's Customs and Excise.

Other public authorities and the private sector were completely unregulated and the use of surveillance was commonplace in many bodies, often being the first tool of resort when investigating social security fraud, for example.

As a result, disclosure became a minefield in covert cases and prosecutions collapsed or were withdrawn – the other side of the coin was that by insisting on full disclosure, the defence was given the opportunity to gain access to covert investigation methods, which often involved putting informants and innocent third parties at risk as well as exposing 'tricks of the trade' to criminals, which they could later circumvent.

The UK also suffered a number of adverse decisions at European Court of Human Rights in Strasbourg; prior to 2000, the UK, whilst a signatory to the Convention, did not have it enshrined in statute meaning that defendants were able to go to Strasbourg and have the decisions of domestic courts overturned, which was an embarrassment to the UK Government.

After 2000 the use of covert investigative techniques had to comply with the Human Rights Act and it clearly did not – which meant that something had to change to ensure that these valuable tools could continue to be used. Article 8 of the Human Rights Act had to be adhered to, which necessitated the enactment of RIPA prior to the entry into force of the Human Rights Act 1998 in October 2000, so enabling infringements of Article 8 rights to be 'in accordance with the law'. The Act applies to England, Wales, Scotland and Northern Ireland, with the exception of the regulation of surveillance and Covert Human Intelligence Sources in Scotland – these activities are covered by parallel Scottish legislation, the Regulation of Investigatory Powers (Scotland) Act 2000 (together with separately published Codes of Practice).

Like some of the other investigative compliance legislation, the Act is supplemented by a number of Codes of Practice to aid understanding from an operational perspective. The two that are relevant to the ACFS are the Code of Practice for Covert Surveillance and Property Interference and the Code of Practice for the Use of Human Intelligence Sources as they provide best practice guidance in these areas.

As described in Chapter 3 the part of RIPA that is applicable to the ACFS is Part II, which covers:

■ **Covert surveillance** – which is an expanding industry as companies, especially insurance companies, become bolder in the way they tackle suspected fraudulent activity. Perversely, there is evidence that the use of surveillance in the public sector has decreased (OSC, 2013). Probably this is because under RIPA surveillance is now the investigative tool of last resort and other options have to be considered first, which was not the case previously.

■ **Covert Human Intelligence Sources** – while 'informants' are widely used in law enforcement and are an integral part of policing, this is not the case in the commercial sector, though the issue does occasionally arise. There are various telephone reporting lines encouraging the public to come forward and inform on criminal activity, usually to do with fraud, an example being the Association of British Insurers' Cheat Line. However, there is a distinction to be drawn between an 'informer' (who would not fall within the scope of RIPA) and an 'informant' (who would fall within its scope), which will be discussed later. RIPA Part II also lays down guidelines on how to handle informants and has even coined a new term for such a person – a 'Covert Human Intelligence Source' (CHIS). There are good reasons why commercial organisations should take heed of the requirements of the Code – an example would be the duty of care owed to a CHIS. Imagine the reputational damage and probable litigation that would arise if a CHIS came to harm through the neglect of a commercial investigator. RIPA gives good guidance on issues such as this and it therefore makes sense to pay attention to it, whether acting for a public body or not.

 ## COVERT SURVEILLANCE

Before examining the law as it relates to covert surveillance, it may be prudent to take a step back and consider what surveillance, as a generic term, means. The Act defines it as:

> Watching or listening with a purpose, involving observation of an individual, group or venue in order to gather evidence . . .

In addition, it must be 'systematic' in nature in relation to the subject under surveillance and not just day-to-day general observation, for example watching a particular crime 'hot spot' such as a car park. It need not be covert and most surveillance is, in fact, overt, for example, CCTV.

Surveillance includes:

■ The monitoring, observing or listening to persons, their movements, their conversations or their other activities or communications – including post, correspondence and e-mails;

- The recording of anything monitored, observed or listened to in the course of surveillance – and recording can be as basic as pen and paper, such as surveillance logs;
- Surveillance by or with the assistance of a technical device – most commonly a camera of some sort, though transmitters and trackers would also be classed as surveillance devices. Even the live monitoring of someone moving about a secure building by following their use of a swipe card would be classed as surveillance.

RIPA does not cover 'ordinary' surveillance or surveillance per se. It deals exclusively with 'covert surveillance'. The questions therefore are, 'What is covert surveillance?' and 'How does it differ from non-covert surveillance?'

The answer to the first question is contained in s. 26 of the Act which gives covert surveillance a statutory definition:

Section 26 – Conduct to which Part II applies
(9)(a) [Any surveillance which] is carried out in a manner calculated to ensure that the persons subject to the surveillance are unaware that it is or may be taking place.

In other words: doing any of the activities previously described but undertaken without the subject's knowledge. This does not mean that the surveillance operatives are out of sight of the subject, indeed at times a good surveillance operative will be using a cover story in order to get really close to the subject so that evidence and/or intelligence can be gathered, which, at the end of the day, is what the surveillance will be aiming to achieve.

The following will not be classed as covert surveillance:

- Speed and traffic monitoring cameras;
- Public order filming – this is not aimed at a specific person but groups or crowds and is in full view of the people being filmed;
- Police vehicle cameras – whether marked or unmarked, but must be in connection with general observation and patrols;
- Photography in public places – obviously, if it is done overtly it cannot be considered covert surveillance. If, however, some cover story is being used to give a reason for the photography (for example, art students undertaking a project) then the photographing of the subject of an investigation will be covert.

But what about CCTV? The primary aim of CCTV is to be overt and so to act as a deterrent. Indeed, notices are required to be clearly displayed to indicate to people in the area that they may be subject to filming and the images recorded; the Information Commissioner has published a Code of Practice detailing how such notices should be displayed (ICO, 2008). Standard practice for a surveillance team following a subject into a town would be for a member of the team to find the CCTV control room for the area, locate the subject using the cameras and then to ask the controller to track the subject around the area, thus allowing other members of the team to draw back and limit their exposure to the subject, so extending their 'shelf life'. The CCTV system is now being used for a different purpose from the one it was set up for; there is systematic surveillance of an individual as part of a planned operation and the surveillance is being undertaken in a manner in which the subject is unaware of the fact that his movements are being tracked; the use of CCTV under these circumstances is therefore covert. But, you may say, CCTV is regularly used to track people who have just committed crimes or are known criminals, such as pickpockets for example. Under these circumstances the CCTV operator is responding to immediate events and so does not fall within the requirements of RIPA (this 'exemption' will be discussed further later on in this chapter).

## CATEGORIES OF SURVEILLANCE

RIPA defines two types of covert surveillance and it is important for the ACFS to be able to distinguish between the two as one of these types will most probably fall outside the remit of counter fraud work, meaning that if used the subject's Article 8 rights will probably be unlawfully breached.

**1. Intrusive surveillance:** This is defined as covert surveillance, carried out in relation to anything taking place on any residential premises or in any private vehicle and which involves the presence of an individual on the premises or in the vehicle or by way of a device placed therein (s. 26(3) RIPA 2000). Naturally, this leads to the question: 'What is the definition of a residential premises and private vehicle?' Fortunately these are defined by the Act.

*Residential Premises* – as well as a home this includes hotel rooms, bedrooms in barracks, hostels, caravans, etc. Common areas to which a person is allowed access such as reception areas, corridors, hotel bars, etc., are not classed as residential premises. The litmus test is what level of privacy is expected in a specific location? If you would expect a level similar to that which you would find in your own home then that will most probably be classed as 'residential premises'.

*Private Vehicle* – this includes any vehicle used primarily for the purposes of the person who owns it or otherwise has the right to use it – which can be implied or express. Therefore it will include company cars, leased vehicles or vehicles borrowed by the subject. It does not include hire cars or vehicles being used for paid journeys.

The important points to remember are that (a) the activity that is being monitored is taking place on residential premises or in a private vehicle *and* (b) the monitoring involves the presence of a surveillance operative or a surveillance device being on the premises as well.

There is a caveat to this – if the surveillance device is not on the premises or in the vehicle, but it *consistently* provides information which is of the same quality and detail as if the surveillance were conducted on the premises or in the vehicle, then the surveillance will be classed as being intrusive. The important word here is 'consistently' – if the subject is being watched in their own home from an observation post across the street and images are being recorded using a video camera with a 72x zoom lens, will the images consistently be of the same quality as if the camera were in the house? The answer is probably 'no' – the subject will be moving in and out of view as they move around the room.

As far as RIPA is concerned, intrusive surveillance is regarded as one of the most serious breaches of a person's Article 8 rights. It is therefore used very sparingly and only a limited number of public authorities are listed within Schedule 1 of the Act as being able to undertake such activity. The purposes for which intrusive surveillance may be lawfully authorised are:

▪ In the interests of national security – outside the scope of the ACFS;
▪ For preventing or detecting *serious crime*;
▪ In the interests of the economic well-being of the UK – some have argued that the prevention or detection of fraud is in the interests of the economic well-being of the UK. Although this is true when we consider the totality of fraud that is committed, RIPA authorisations are concerned with individual cases, not generalisations. The fraud would have to involve many millions of pounds and be likely to affect share prices (on the scale of the UBS fraud involving Kweku Adoboli, for example (British Broadcasting Corporation, 2010)) but then of course this would also be a 'serious crime'.

Note the highlighting of 'serious crime'. This means what it says and will involve offences where there is considerable harm or potential of harm and may involve organised crime. As can be seen, there will be very few situations where the ACFS will get involved in intrusive surveillance – if the fraud being investigated is of such magnitude as to be classed as 'serious crime', then the chances are that there will be police involvement and they will take the lead on the use of covert investigative techniques.

**2. Directed surveillance:** rather obviously, the Act describes this as 'surveillance which is covert but not intrusive'. However, it then further defines it as being undertaken:

- For the purposes of a specific investigation or operation, and
- In such a manner as is likely to result in the obtaining of private information about a person
- Otherwise than in response to immediate events or circumstances that would prevent an authorisation under the Act from being sought.

(s. 26(2) Regulation of Investigatory Powers Act 2000)

This is surveillance as very commonly carried out by Accredited Counter Fraud Specialists. While there still is an interference with an individual's right to privacy, it is less so than intrusive surveillance as it is generally undertaken in public places or other similar locations. Accordingly, there are less severe restrictions on this type of activity. To be more specific, directed surveillance is:

- Essentially any surveillance that isn't intrusive – as has previously been defined, but:
- Is connected to a particular investigation – no 'fishing' or 'mystery shopping' expeditions.
- Is likely to obtain '*private information*' about '*a person*'. The Act doesn't define what is meant by '*private information*' in detail, other than '*any information relating to his private or family life*' – it will certainly include things like details of bank accounts, relationships, home addresses and telephone numbers. As a rule of thumb think of information that you would be reluctant to disclose to a total stranger. It should also be noted that the Act says '*a person*', not 'the subject'. This means that if it is likely that private information about a third party will be discovered during the surveillance, then it will be 'directed surveillance', even if it is unlikely that private information about the subject will be learnt. This impact on the privacy of unconnected third parties is known as '*collateral intrusion*'.
- Is planned. The Act and Code recognise that there will be occasions where events unfold before an ACFS and it would be impractical to seek an authorisation. For example, you are travelling to a meeting when you see the subject of one of your investigations standing in the street, looking as if they are waiting for someone. You therefore take position in a telephone kiosk to covertly watch who they are meeting.

There must be a specific reason why the surveillance is necessary; the reasons are listed within the Act (and not all reasons are available for all of the public authorities that are listed in the Act's schedule – NHS Protect, for example, will be unable to use the reason that it is '*in the interests of National Security*' to justify surveillance activity). The reason most relevant to the work of an ACFS is for the '*prevention and detection of crime*'. It has been held that the investigation of crime is a crime prevention measure.

Before undertaking directed surveillance authorisation must be sought – for those organisations that are listed in Schedule 1 of the Act regulations will stipulate the rank or office of the person who can grant authority to conduct surveillance (the 'Authorising Officer'). Students should check within their own organisations to identify who their Authorising Officer is. For private organisations, the person who gives authority for the investigation should be a manager or supervisor, ideally one who is independent of the investigation so that they are able to take an unbiased and objective view as to whether the use of surveillance is justifiable. The Code of Practice recognises that in small organisations this may not always be possible.

A written application for authorisation to undertake surveillance must be made to the Authorising Officer; this must include:

▪ The reason why the surveillance is required. As stated previously, for ACFS work this will be for the purpose of preventing and detecting crime and there must be a genuine prospect of some criminal action being taken at the time of the application.
▪ An explanation as to why the surveillance is necessary, demonstrating how, for example, other lines of evidence gathering have been exhausted or rejected.
▪ An account demonstrating how the activity is proportional to what is being sought. Proportionality is one of the tenets of human rights legislation and the authorising officer must be satisfied that the directed surveillance is proportionate to what it seeks to achieve (the resulting evidence or intelligence is often referred to as the 'product' of the surveillance).
▪ The identity of the subject(s) of the surveillance.
▪ What evidence or intelligence is being sought.
▪ Details of any collateral intrusion that may occur (and how it will be minimised) together with reasons why such intrusion is necessary.
▪ Details of any confidential information that may be discovered. As with the term 'private information', neither RIPA nor the Code of Practice defines in detail what is meant by 'confidential information'; a good starting point

will be to consider material that falls within the definition of 'sensitive personal data' under the Data Protection Act 1998. Clearly, if confidential information is being sought then the grounds of necessity and proportionality need to be correspondingly higher.

The Authorising Officer's decision will be given in writing and good practice will dictate that they record why they consider the surveillance to be proportionate and necessary. If granted the authority to conduct directed surveillance will last for three months in the first instance. During this period the Authorising Officer will keep the authorisation under review and must cancel the authorisation if they become satisfied that the grounds for it are no longer present. The review will be recorded in writing and will be stored on the organisation's central record of authorisations. Reviews should be undertaken as frequently as is considered necessary. Before the end of the three-month period an application can be made for the authority to be renewed for a further three months, in a similar form to that made for the initial application but including a summary of activity so far and details of any product obtained. Authorities can be renewed more than once, although with the work that falls within the scope of the ACFS there will need to be exceptional reasons as to why the authority should be renewed beyond six months. If the ACFS hasn't met the objective within that time frame, it will be difficult to argue that the criterion of necessity is still valid.

Surveillance must cease on day of cessation of the authorisation – to do otherwise may render any subsequently obtained evidence inadmissible and leave the door open for action for breaching the subject's Article 8 rights.

To ensure proper oversight of the use of covert surveillance, Part IV of the Act provides for the Surveillance Commissioners who exercise their function across the whole of covert investigation activity as defined in the Act, although surveillance forms a substantial part of their oversight responsibilities. Nevertheless, the Surveillance Commissioners only have responsibility for examining the covert activities of those public bodies that are listed in the Act: 'To examine the systems, processes and administration of authorities granted under Part II RIPA 2000.' Their inspection regime does not extend outside this, but they do provide examples of best practice that is relevant to all organisations planning to utilise covert investigation techniques.

Commissioners examine and report on an organisation's compliance with RIPA and the Codes of Practice by inspecting:

▪ Policies and procedures – for instance, authorisation procedures and decision making.

- Availability of and adherence to the Codes of Practice.
- Record keeping: authorisations should be kept in a central record for the organisation.
- Security of evidence and material – so that it does not fall into the wrong hands.
- Training and education – in order that those involved with covert investigations, whether as a participant or Authorising Officer, understand their obligations and responsibilities.
- The content and relevance of associated risk assessments.

##  COVERT HUMAN INTELLIGENCE SOURCES

We turn now to the second aspect of Part II of RIPA that is relevant to the ACFS, Covert Human Intelligence Sources (CHIS). Prior to the introduction of RIPA these would commonly be referred to as 'informants', but the term CHIS is much wider than this. In the fight against crime in general, the use of informants cannot be underestimated:

> About one third of all crimes cleared up involve the use of informants.
>
> (Billingsworth, Nemitz and Bean, 2001)

Informants will typically, but not always, be criminals wishing to trade off information for immunity from prosecution or for financial reward. Occasionally, he or she might be a public spirited individual of good character wishing to ensure 'the right thing is done' in respect of any matter they perceive to be a serious transgression of the law. More controversially, they may be a protected person under the Public Interest Disclosure Act when their status can become confusing. However, this is the exception rather than the rule when the distinction is drawn between an informant and an informer.

The use of informants has a long history in criminal investigation, across the whole spectrum of crime. For example in Chitty, reporting a case heard in 1826 involving an informant, the following quote is to be found:

> The law confesses its weakness by calling in the assistance of those by whom it is broken. It offers premium to treachery and destroys the last virtue which clings to the degraded transgressor. Still, on the other hand, it tends to prevent any extensive agreement among atrocious criminals, making them perpetually suspicious of one another.
>
> (Chitty, 1826: 767)

The usefulness of a CHIS can be summarised thus:

■ They provide unrivalled access to criminals and criminal enterprises – as just seen, a third of all crimes are cleared up by the use of informants.
■ Their use frustrates criminals and creates a climate of mistrust and uncertainty – this was recognised as far back as 1826 in the case just mentioned. Indeed, the use and fear of informants also has a notorious history as a totalitarian political tool, for example, in the former Soviet Union and Eastern Bloc.
■ The information they provide gives investigative focus and leads to good evidence – having inside information allows the investigator to gain the initiative and plan his or her next moves with a degree of certainty. It also narrows down the lines of enquiry, thereby saving on investigative resource expenditure.
■ They are excellent for intelligence gathering: modern-day policing and investigation methods are now driven by intelligence (intelligence-led policing). The use of informants has become critical across the board, from local crime to international organised crime.

While being valuable in the fight against crime, informants have also caused a great number of difficulties over the years and their use is seldom without controversy. Because of the murky world in which informants move, the potential for corruption and unacceptable compromise is never far away and there have been many instances where handling of informants has gone wrong, such as the case of Delroy Denton who, while registered as an informant with the police, raped and murdered a woman called Marcia Lawes. An enquiry followed in which a number of police officers came close to prosecution and the informant handling system was laid bare as one riddled with mismanagement and illegality. There have also been instances of informants' identities being revealed by their handlers or colleagues, inadvertently or otherwise, to other criminals, resulting in serious risk to the well-being of the informant. In short, handling informants is a risky business.

RIPA regularises the use of informants and provides a legal framework in which they should be handled. It affords informants protection and establishes a duty of care towards them and others. It also identifies that there are other uses of human beings to covertly gather information and so confers a new title on such people – Covert Human Intelligence Source. But what exactly is a CHIS? What is the difference between a CHIS and an informer?

A CHIS is not:

■ An anonymous witness or tipster – who is essentially supplying information one way where there is no control at the receiving end.

- A Crimestoppers caller – even though Crimestoppers and TV programmes such as Crime Watch are formal routes to give information, people calling in will not be Covert Human Intelligence Sources so long as the flow of information is one way.
- A confidential contact (for example, whistleblowers or public spirited citizens) – according to the National Criminal Intelligence Service (which has now become the National Crime Agency) a confidential contact is 'an individual or member of an organisation who discloses information from which an individual can be identified and there exist personal, professional or other risks by doing so'. This could be considered a good description of a whistleblower or observant neighbour.

However, there is the potential for the ACFS to turn any one of these into a CHIS. Section 26 of the Act formally sets out what a CHIS is – someone who:

> [e]stablishes or maintains a personal or other relationship and uses such a relationship, covertly, to provide, obtain or disclose information to another person.

This is a very broad definition. 'Personal or other relationship' is not defined and could cover a multitude of relationship types. The Act defines covert in the context of a relationship:

> [A] purpose is covert, in relation to the establishment or maintenance of a personal or other relationship, if and only if, the relationship is conducted in a manner that is calculated to ensure that one of the parties to the relationship is unaware of the purpose.

What this means simply is that an element of secrecy and/or subterfuge will be involved – the two are obviously interlinked. It should be noted that there is no mention of 'private information' or 'confidential private information' – if a relationship is used secretly to find out *any* information then the person doing so will fall within the terms of being a CHIS.

As highlighted previously, there is the scope for an ACFS to inadvertently turn a whistleblower or other public spirited person providing information into a CHIS. This is known as 'tasking' – from a practical perspective, this is the crucial cross-over point between a person being an informer and becoming an informant (CHIS). Receiving information from 'informers' can be considered a passive process where the information is more or less one way. The point at which the handler starts 'tasking' the informer is when a CHIS situation arises.

Tasking involves the inducing, asking or assisting a person to engage in the use or creation of a relationship to obtain information covertly. Take, for an example, a neighbour telephoning the Housing Benefit fraud team to report that the benefit claimant next door has started work without notifying the Council or the DWP. The person taking the call, as a good investigator, starts asking lots of questions in order to glean as much information as possible. One question is asked, to which the neighbour doesn't know the answer. Their response is 'I'm going round there on Saturday, I'll see if I can find out for you.' If the neighbour pursues this course of action they will have become a CHIS as clearly they will not divulge to the claimant their reason for obtaining the information – they will be maintaining the relationship to covertly gather information, which they will then pass on to the investigator; they have become a CHIS. CHISs are not just restricted to third party sources. An ACFS can become a CHIS themselves, such as in an undercover operation. In the retail sector, for example, it is common practice for an investigator to pretend to be an agency worker who is then placed into a warehouse to identify who is stealing stock.

Like surveillance, the use of a CHIS is subject to authorisation and the same justifications for directed surveillance apply, that is to say, for the prevention and detection of crime, necessity and proportionality. Their use by public authorities is limited by RIPA – there are fewer organisations that can deploy a CHIS compared to those that can deploy directed surveillance. There is a separate Code of Practice and Chapter 5 of the Code details the process and information that must be supplied for an authorisation to use a CHIS. Much of this reflects what is required for an application to use directed surveillance but there are differences and the Code should be consulted before making an application. A key difference between an authority for directed surveillance and an authority to use a CHIS is that the latter will last for a period of 12 months.

As has been identified earlier in this section, the use of a CHIS can be a risky business and the following should be considered:

- **Who you are dealing with** – do not take it for granted that the name given is the correct one. CHISs are often criminals who are notorious for using false names and identities. Seek identification whenever possible. Undertake basic background checks as a minimum.
- **Identify their motivation** – is there a reward being offered or do they expect payment? What is their expectation? This brings with it problems when we later come to disclosure and the payment for information that is relied upon may undermine the prosecution case. However, there might be

other motivating factors such as revenge or thrill seeking. These are high risk indicators as such individuals can be extremely volatile.

▪ **Undertake a risk assessment (duty of care)** – is there risk of collateral intrusion into the privacy of persons other than those who are directly the subject of the covert operation? Is there a risk of 'vulnerable' people becoming involved (vulnerable people should only become involved in covert investigations in exceptional circumstances)? Is the risk of harm to the CHIS too great? The organisation has a vicarious responsibility to the CHIS: taking the example of the neighbour given earlier, if they were identified as the 'informant' what might the consequences be? A brick through the window? Verbal abuse? Violence? What are the risks to the ACFS, particularly if there is to be a meeting with the CHIS or if the ACFS is to become a CHIS?

 ## THE LAWFUL INTERCEPTION OF COMMUNICATIONS

Part I of RIPA covers the law relating to the interception of communications and the acquisition and disclosure of communications data. Currently in the UK, intercepted electronic communications are not admissible as evidence in a court of law and are considered a breach of Article 8 rights. Furthermore, intercepting communications without a person's consent can give rise to liability for an offence under s. 1 of RIPA, unless it has been undertaken in accordance with the provisions of the Act, which will involve the application for and the issuing of a warrant. RIPA provides that such applications can only be made on behalf of the Chiefs of the Intelligence Services, or Chief Constables or the Chief of Defence Intelligence, meaning that they will be outside the scope of an ACFS.

However, at the time that the legislation was being debated in Parliament, industry made representations to the department for Trade and Industry (DTI), to the effect that the clauses in Part I of the Bill would make routine business activity unlawful. It had been, and still is, common practice for calls received in call centres and other locations to be recorded. It had also been common practice for call centre supervisors to 'listen in' to calls, to ensure that members of staff were following procedures and that standards of service were being maintained. This was regularly done without the member of the public being aware. Industry also made the case that it would be almost impossible to monitor misuse of telecommunications in the workplace (such as making numerous personal calls, using the company's mail system for personal correspondence or accessing inappropriate internet content).

These representations led to the DTI laying Regulations before Parliament to enable these practices to be lawful after RIPA had been enacted. The legislation in question is the Telecommunications (Lawful Business Practice) (Interception of Communications) Regulations 2000, which came into force on 24 October 2000. Their purpose is to give businesses a lawful basis for the interception of business communications without the users' consent for a range of purposes. The Regulations cover all types of communications including those that are internet based, by fax, telephone, post and by e-mail.

The Regulations allow businesses, government departments, and any public authority to intercept, monitor or record communications for:

■ Establishing the existence of facts – such as for purposes of audit, verification of business transactions, dispute resolution etc.
■ Ascertaining compliance with practices or procedures – whether regulatory or self-regulatory.
■ Maintaining effective operating systems – especially from an information security perspective, for example, detecting viruses.
■ Prevention and detection of crime – most relevant to ACFS.
■ Safeguarding national security.
■ Detecting unauthorised use of electronic communications systems – such as the unauthorised use of a telecommunications system or misuse of the internet or e-mail.
■ Monitoring standards of training and service – which is something commonly heard as a standard recorded message when telephoning financial services companies.

This list covers practically all the reasons an employer might want to covertly monitor communications coming into and out of the business.

The Regulations allow monitoring of business systems in relation to:

■ Telephone calls/faxes
■ Post
■ E-mails
■ Internet and intranet use.

Telephone usage includes:

■ Fixed telephones on business premises – but not pay phones on business premises.

- Mobile phones for business use – interception is allowed to confirm that the phone is being used for business purposes.
- Fixed and mobile phones paid for by the organisation for business and private use anywhere – company mobiles, which are allowed to be used for private purposes, can be intercepted as can fixed line company phones installed at home.
- The references to mobile phones above will include voice, SMS and data services.

Post includes:

- Incoming addressed to the business.
- Incoming addressed to an individual at the business – even if it is marked confidential.
- Outgoing business and private if posted using business system and/or postage payment – which means that personal letters posted using the company despatch system can be intercepted as can personal letters posted with a stamp paid for by the company.

E-mail encompasses:

- Incoming addressed to the business.
- Incoming addressed to an individual.
- Any messages stored on the system.

This means that any e-mail travelling through the business's server can be intercepted, regardless of whether its content is private.

Internet and intranet use:

- All sites accessed with times and dates.
- Pages viewed and communications.
- Downloads.

In sum, organisations can intercept pretty much what they like if their communications network or system is being utilised. However, the reality is that the principles of fairness, proportionality and management accountability must be brought to bear when deciding on whether to employ interception techniques. It is also considered best practice for an organisation to explain the powers they have in this regard, for example, through their IT policy that should be brought to the attention of their workers.

The Information Commissioner has taken a view on the monitoring of staff at work and has issued guidance which is contained in the Employment Practices Data Protection Code (ICO, 2011). To be able to monitor and intercept communications at work, the organisation must make all reasonable efforts to notify users of the system that their communications may be monitored or intercepted. For staff members, this should not only be in the small print of an IT acceptable use policy but should be effectively communicated to them, for example by being displayed on the log-in screen. For members of the public, some organisations play a recorded message before a call is accepted by the system, while others ensure that messages are displayed on websites and advertisements.

Unlike RIPA, the Regulations do not impose a system of application and authorisation before monitoring can take place. However, good practice dictates that the ACFS will keep written documentation and obtain supervisory oversight before undertaking activity that is permitted by these Regulations.

 ## REVIEW

This chapter has examined the background to the regulation of covert investigative techniques following the introduction of the Human Rights Act 1998. It describes the reasons that must be present for an ACFS to be able to conduct such activity, whether by themselves or via an external party acting on their behalf. It has considered the position of the private sector and has explained how the courts are required to take into account breaches of Article 8 of the European Convention on Human Rights, even where none of the parties involved is a public body. The two types of surveillance have been defined, as has the Covert Human Intelligence Source, with some consideration as to how these may be encountered during the work of the ACFS. Finally, the law relating to the monitoring and interception of communications has been examined, identifying the requirements that must be present before this can be done in the workplace.

 ## FURTHER READING

Coleman, R. and McCahill, M. (2011) *Surveillance and Crime*. London: Sage.
Devon and Cornwall Constabulary (2010) *Compliance and Procedures for Covert Policing Activity*. Exeter: Devon and Cornwall Constabulary.
Stelfox, P. (2009) *Criminal Investigation: An Introduction to Principles and Practice*. Cullompton: Willan Publishing, chapter 5: The techniques of investigation.
Wakefield, A. and Brookman, F. (2009) Criminal Investigation. In A. Wakefield and J. Fleming (eds), *The Sage Dictionary of Policing*. London: Sage, pp. 65–70.

CHAPTER SIX

# Investigative interviewing

## CHAPTER **SUMMARY**

The background to the PEACE model of interviewing will be outlined, specifically the difference between interrogations and investigative interviews. The chapter will then define what is meant by a cognitive free call interview of a witness and how the model can be applied. The means by which the information obtained from a witness can be recorded in the form of a witness statement will then be discussed. Conversation management will be defined and the importance of constructing a detailed interview plan explained. The different methods of recording an interview and the types of records kept will be detailed. The chapter will conclude by outlining the difference between contemporaneous notes, records of a taped interview and short descriptive notes.

**INTRODUCTION**

A further critical component of the investigation process undertaken by an ACFS is that of interviewing. This may be the interviewing of a witness, or a victim as part of the evidence gathering process when progressing an investigation. Alternatively, it can be at the latter stage of the investigation when all evidence has been gathered and this confirms that a criminal offence has taken place necessitating an interview under caution with a suspect. Should the investigation have followed the civil route there is still a necessity for an ACFS working in the private sector to interview a suspect. Furthermore, as discussed in Chapter 4, any civil investigation should have been conducted to criminal standards, and therefore a corporate ACFS may also be required to conduct an interview under caution, albeit this being a joint interview with a police officer to whom the case has been referred.

Interviews with any suspects are also a crucial element of the investigation, and therefore require careful planning and delivery. This chapter will introduce the background to investigative interviewing, specifically the need to move away from interrogations. The chapter will explain how an ACFS can draw upon the PEACE model as a guide to the relevant stages of the interview process. The techniques of a free recall interview (witness) and a conversation management interview (suspect) will be discussed. The importance of interview planning will also be considered, and guidance offered on developing an interview plan.

 **BACKGROUND TO INTERVIEW TECHNIQUE TRAINING**

Historically, police interview training has concentrated on techniques for breaking down a suspect's resistance, suggesting that a certain amount of pressure, deception, persuasion and manipulation is essential if the truth is to be revealed (Gudjonsson, 2003: 7–8). Even interviewing manuals advocating a more psychological approach to interviewing still advocate an element of influence and persuasion (for example see Walkley, 1987). Research into police interview training manuals has identified that interviewers were instructed to look for signs that the suspect was lying and to identify guilt (Moston et al (1992) cited by McGurk, Carr and McGurk, 1993: 4). The conclusion was that the stressing of such abilities might appear to justify using them to manipulate suspects into confessing, either by playing on their vulnerabilities or by using trickery and deceit (McGurk, Carr and McGurk, 1993: 4). An explanation for the continued use of this style of interview is that most interviewing manuals are based on experience rather than objective and scientific data (Gudjonsson, 2003: 37).

Deceptive interrogation tactics identified as being used by US law enforcement interviewers include:

- Misrepresenting the nature or purpose of questioning.
- Misrepresenting the nature or seriousness of the offence.
- The use of promises.
- The use of fabricated evidence.

(Leo, 1992, cited by Milne and Bull, 1999: 83)

Research has also identified persuasive tactics being employed by interviewers in the UK including:

- Telling the interviewees that because of evidence against them they might as well admit the allegation.
- When a denial or refusal to answer was met officers often resorted to accusation and abuse.
- Trying to influence the suspect's assessment of the consequences of confessing.

(McConville and Hodgson, 1993: 127)

##  WHAT CAN GO WRONG DURING AN INTERROGATION?

Gudjonsson (2003: 34–36) identifies a number of ways in which interrogation may result in undesirable consequences for the criminal justice system:

- False confessions due to coercion
- Inadmissible confessions
- Coerced confessions resulting in resentment
- Coercion resulting in post-traumatic stress disorder
- Undermining public confidence.

In sum, the main persuasive ingredients in interrogation manuals involve exaggeration or misrepresentation of the evidence against a suspect. Many tactics encouraged include the employment of trickery, deceit and dishonesty. No interrogation will be completely free from coercion – the principal issue is the extent and nature of the manipulation and persuasion used (which varies between countries) (Gudjonsson, 2003: 36–37).

**INVESTIGATIVE INTERVIEWING**

The gathering of information from a well prepared and executed interview will contribute significantly to the quality of an investigation and increase the likelihood of a successful outcome. The key principles of investigative interviewing that an ACFS should consider are as follows:

i. The aim of investigative interviewing is to obtain accurate and reliable accounts from victims, witnesses or suspects about matters under police investigation.

ii. Investigators must act fairly when questioning victims, witnesses or suspects. Vulnerable people must be treated with particular consideration at all times.

iii. Investigative interviewing should be approached with an investigative mindset. Accounts obtained from the person who is being interviewed should always be tested against what the interviewer already knows or what can reasonably be established.

iv. When conducting an interview, investigators are free to ask a wide range of questions in order to obtain material which may assist an investigation.

v. Investigators should recognise the positive impact of an early admission in the context of the criminal justice system.

vi. Investigators are not bound to accept the first answer given. Questioning is not unfair merely because it is persistent.

vii. Even when the right of silence is exercised by a suspect, investigators have a responsibility to put questions to them.

(National Police Improvement Agency, 2009: 6)

 **THE PEACE MODEL OF INVESTIGATIVE INTERVIEWING**

The PEACE model of interviewing, developed from an enhanced cognitive interview procedure (Fisher and Geiselman, 1992), is an accepted method of conducting interviews with victims, witnesses and suspects employed by most UK law enforcement agencies. The acronym PEACE stands for:

**P** *Preparation and planning.* This includes knowledge of the case, what is required to be proved legally, arranging the interview and ensuring attendance and suitable facilities.

**E** *Engage and Explain*. This is the opening phase of the interview where introductions formally take place, legal requirements (e.g. reading the suspect his or her legal rights) are met and an explanation of the interview and its process take place.

**A** *Account*. Interviewees are asked to provide their account of events, which may require clarification and challenges.

**C** *Closure*. This involves the interviewer summarizing the main points from the interview and providing the suspect with the opportunity to correct or add anything.

**E** *Evaluation*. The account and evidence obtained during questioning need to be evaluated. The performance of the interviewers should also be evaluated.

(Gudjonsson, 2007: 470–471)

The core skills that an ACFS requires when using the PEACE model include:

- **Planning and preparation:** assembling the facts, knowledge of the location and circumstances of the offence, knowledge of the interviewee if practical, being methodical, legal knowledge and considering the timing, duration and location to conduct the interview. Selection of the interviewer and timing of breaks.
- **Establishing a rapport:** considering how to approach the interviewee, being aware of their needs, culture and background, language, displaying flexibility, approachability, not prejudging, avoiding being over officious and personal bias.
- **Listening skills:** developing the ability to listen actively, displaying empathy, consideration and tolerance. Using silence to obtain further information.
- **Questioning skills:** asking the right questions at the right time, use of appropriate language and perseverance.

(Association of Chief Police Officers, 2005a: 90)

A compatible, but slightly more detailed framework is outlined by the Home Office (2007) guidance for achieving best evidence, the stages being as follows:

- Planning and preparation
- Establishing rapport

- Initiating and supporting a free narrative account
- Questioning
- Closing the interview
- Evaluation.

 ## FREE RECALL INTERVIEWS WITH WITNESSES

In a free recall interview 'witnesses are simply asked an open ended question such as "Tell me what happened" and are allowed to give their own account of the event without interference or interruption' (Blackwell-Young, 2008: 211). Free recall tends to be very accurate, but can sometimes be incomplete, because people leave details out, particularly those they don't consider important. Research conducted by Lipton (1977) found that students only freely recalled 21% of the facts of a simulated robbery, but were 91% accurate.

### Memory

When interviewing a witness, it is important that an ACFS has an awareness of the process of memory and the impact this has on the ability of a witness to recall the events that are relevant to the investigation. Memory is where an individual retains their own personal life experiences of specific past events or episodes. There are three different types of memory:

- **Episodic memory:** is memory for specific events
- **Semantic memory:** relates to the retention of general knowledge which we accumulate through our lives. Also holds information about what to expect and how to act in certain situations
- **Procedural memory:** contains information that allows us to perform skills such as driving a car.

(Milne and Bull, 1999)

It is episodic memory that is relevant to free recall interviewing of witnesses. This is defined as 'the kind of memory that allows one to remember past happenings from one's life' (Tulving, 2001: 1505). The author further suggests that it is 'memory for personally experienced events or remembering what happened where and when' (p. 1506). Through the free recall interview process, by careful and well thought out questioning, the interviewer will attempt to take the witness on a journey back to the events that are relevant to the investigation via their episodic memory.

## Memory Processes

Memory is often described as a three part process (Melton, 1963), commencing with *encoding*, which is the process of entering information from experiences into the memory (Atkinson and Shiffrin, 1971). This information is then *stored* away in an individual's memory, the amount of which is determined by how much attention is paid to the events in question (Tulving, 1974). At a later date, for example when being interviewed as a witness, the interviewee will attempt to *retrieve* the information from their memory. Memory failure can occur at any one of these stages or a combination of them (Brainerd, Reyna, Howe, and Kingma, 1990). When an interviewee is unable to remember something, it could be that the information was not sensed, and consequently the interviewee did not encode the information into memory for later use. Alternatively, it may be that encoded information may be inadequately stored, or just cannot be retrieved (Milne, 2004). When interviewing a witness who is unable to retrieve some potentially relevant information, an ACFS would need to consider whether that information has been lost from memory or whether the interviewee, for some reason, finds it difficult to retrieve this information. Milne and Bull (1999) suggest that this is often 'a problem of retrieval rather than loss' (p. 12). Evidential support that retrieval is frequently the issue is offered by what Brown and McNeill (1966) cited by Milne and Bull (1999: 12) refer to as 'the tip of the tongue phenomenon' which occurs when it is known that the information has been stored but for some inexplicable reason, at that moment in time, it cannot be retrieved. To overcome this issue with a witness, an ACFS may need to resort to employing various retrieval cues such as directive prompts within their questioning style to help the witness recollect information and events (Gilbert and Fisher, 2006).

## Environmental Factors

Some elements of memory can be determined by the environmental factors at the time of the incident being recalled. Following the *R v Turnbull* (1976) *63 Cr App R 132* ruling, when the issue of personal identification arises in court, judges in England and Wales are required to inform the jury about such factors as the quality of lighting when the incident occurred, the length of time during which the observation took place and the distance between the witness and the person being observed. All of these factors can have a significant effect on the quality of the witness's recall of the events. The guidelines issued in this ruling are intended to assist in evaluating the quality of the identification. The court advised:

> *In our judgement when the quality is good as for example when the identification is made after a long period of observation, or in satisfactory conditions by a relative, a neighbour, a close friend, a workmate and the like, the Jury can safely be left to assess the value of the identifying evidence even though there is no other evidence to support it.*

If the quality of identification is considered poor, the following guidance was issued:

> When in the judgement of the Trial Judge, the quality of the identifying evidence is poor as for example when it depends solely on a fleeting glance, or on a longer observation made in difficult conditions, the situation is very different. The Judge should then withdraw the case from the Jury and direct an acquittal unless there is other evidence which goes to support the correctness of the identification.

When interviewing a witness, to ensure that all the necessary information is obtained by asking the right questions, an ACFS should refer to the eight-point mnemonic ADVOKATE:

**A** – Amount or length of time the witness had the suspect under observation;

**D** – Distance between the witness and the suspect during the observation;

**V** – Visibility conditions during the observation;

**O** – Obstructions to the observations, whether they temporarily or partially inhibited the observation;

**K** – Whether the suspect is known to the witness in any way;

**A** – Any particular reason the witness has for remembering the suspect or event;

**T** – Time the witness had the suspect under observation and the amount of time elapsed since the event;

**E** – Errors in the description provided by the witness compared with the actual appearance.

Descriptions should be obtained as soon as possible while the recollection is fresh in the mind of the witness. In some cases the suspect may still be in the locality and may not yet have had the opportunity to alter their appearance or to conceal/dispose of evidence.

(College of Policing, 2013a)

## The Importance of Witness Statements

Information from a witness aids an investigation in the following ways. It:

- Governs the direction of the investigation.
- Helps in the choice of the offence to be charged.
- Helps in the selection of possible defendants.
- Outlines the points to prove.
- Helps in the planning and preparation prior to the interview with the suspect.

(Milne and Bull, 1999)

The ACFS should also take account of additional factors relating to the witness, for example the ability to recall can be significantly impaired if the witness has ingested alcohol prior to the incident observed. Similarly, if the witness is suffering from stress, they may also find it difficult to recall in sufficient detail what they have observed.

## Question Types

There are eight question types that may be used in interviews, as outlined in the Griffiths Question Map (Griffiths and Milne, 2006: 182–183):

1. Open questions
2. Probing questions
3. Appropriate closed yes/no questions
4. Inappropriate closed yes/no questions
5. Leading questions
6. Multiple questions
7. Forced choice questions
8. Opinion or statement.

These eight question types are defined as either appropriate or unproductive. For the purpose of this Handbook, the chapter will focus on what are determined to be appropriate questions.

An *open question* is the best kind of question from the point of view of gaining good quality information. Therefore, this type of question should be used predominantly during the interview (Powell and Snow, 2007). Questions commencing with the words 'explain' and 'describe' are ones that an ACFS should consider when attempting to get the witness to talk in detail about what they saw. The questioning style should commence with very general open questions before moving on to more specific open questions that seek some additional clarification of the events from the witness to set the scene.

Having evaluated the suspect's response to an open question, an ACFS may decide to follow this up because it is incomplete and they believe there may be more information that the witness can offer. A *probing question* is therefore designed to 'clarify, elaborate and motivate the interviewee to give additional information' (Lord and Cowan, 2011: 107). These are more intrusive questions in order to obtain 'a more specific answer' (Griffiths and Milne, 2006: 182). Probes often use the opening words 'who',' what', 'where', 'when' and 'why'. However, while these 'W' questions can be framed as open questions, they are much more commonly used as probing questions (Milne and Bull, 1999).

Finally, *appropriate closed yes/no questions* 'are used at the conclusion of a topic where open and probing questions have been exhausted' (Griffiths and Milne, 2006: 182). While these types of questions are sometimes considered to be counterproductive, they do have a place within the witness interview, and can also be used when dealing with 'reluctant interviewees who will not give detailed responses' (Black, 2013: 130).

 ## CONVERSATION MANAGEMENT

Conversation management was developed by Eric Shepherd in 1983 as an innovative approach to investigative interviewing. In 1986 the conversation management interview was further developed into a formal investigative interview model (Shepherd, 1986) and has subsequently been incorporated into the PEACE interviewing package.

When an ACFS is required to interview a suspect, they will need to draw upon conversation management skills and use the PEACE interviewing model to guide them through the interview. This way the maximum potential should be gained from the interviewing process, and by referring to this model, all the necessary topics will be covered, all relevant evidence introduced, and by managing the interview, an adequate account of events obtained from the suspect. Remember, this is what the whole investigation has invariably been leading up to, this is the opportunity for the ACFS to conduct a thorough, fair and balanced investigative interview to seek explanations and obtain further details relating to the points to prove that were identified when formulating the investigation plan at the onset of the investigation.

## Interview Planning

All stages of the PEACE model are important, but to get the interview off to a good start and ensure that all the relevant aspects of the investigation are covered during the interview, careful planning is paramount. Accordingly, it is essential that the ACFS develops a thorough and well thought out interview plan, prior to engaging with the suspect. This will aid the conversation management process, and support the objective of conducting a successful investigative interview.

A well-constructed interview plan should cover the following points relating to the investigation:

- Potential offences
- Points to prove
- Possible defences that might be offered
- Purpose of interview
- Facts already established during the investigation
- Facts to be determined
- Evidence to support allegation/suspicion(s) of fraud
- Information to be disclosed to suspect's legal representative.

The ACFS should also refer to the seven principles of investigative interviewing referred to earlier in this chapter, and also consider the following points to prove:

- The intent (*mens rea*) – what was in the mind of the suspect at the time the act took place? Why did they commit the crime?
- The action that occurred (*actus reus*) – what did the suspect actually do?
- The method used to commit the alleged offence (*modus operandi*) – how did the suspect commit the crime?

Another consideration for the ACFS is that of pre-interview disclosure to the suspect's legal representative. The following are factors worthy of consideration;

- What information/evidence to disclose
- When to disclose

- How disclosure will take place – verbally or in a written format
- What not to disclose to the legal representative
- Why this information will be held back
- How to handle non-disclosure if challenged by the legal representative.

The last criterion warrants careful consideration because while there is no legal obligation to disclose any information or evidence to the suspect's legal representative prior to the interview, if material is held back and then introduced during the interview it is likely that the legal representative will ask for the interview to be suspended so they may consult with the suspect. Additionally, the ACFS may be asked to justify this non-disclosure. There may be legitimate reasons why certain aspects of the case have been held back, and these should be outlined when challenged, however if there are not, then in the interests of a free flowing interview it may be advisable to consider disclosure of all materials. For example, the interview may be progressing well, and the suspect fully engaged and responding to the questions posed. That engagement and rapport may prove difficult to retrieve following the suspension of an interview as a result of the sudden introduction of undisclosed evidence.

## Managing an Interview

Managing an interview in an investigative context is an intricate and difficult task which requires an interviewer to be aware of, and manage, both their verbal and non-verbal behaviour, the interviewee and any third parties such as the second interviewer, legal advisor, appropriate adult or an interpreter (Milne and Bull, 1999: 56). Five key elements have been identified as being essential to managing an interview, these being:

- **Contact:** which includes establishing rapport and setting out the aims and objectives of the interview.
- **Content:** eliciting facts using appropriate questioning strategies.
- **Conduct:** the way in which the content is covered.
- **Credibility:** the way in which the interviewer is perceived.
- **Control:** directing the overall flow of the interview.

(Walkley, 1987)

## Ethical Pressures when Interviewing

Another challenge facing the ACFS during the interview is achieving a balance between the rights of the suspect and victim as a result of the ethical pressures that may be placed upon an interviewer. These may partially result from 'the political, economical and sociological nature of contemporary democratic societies' and as a consequence, these factors create ethical pressures on interviewers because they generate two contradictory social trends, one of them seeking to increase, and the other to decrease the safeguarding of suspects (Roy, 2006: 298). Accordingly, there are certain values an ACFS needs to balance when interviewing a suspect, the issue in question being 'how can we legitimately balance the victim's right to justice and security with the suspect's right to dignity and to the presumption of innocence?' (p. 304).

An important consideration for the ACFS therefore is the extent to which this pressure should be transferred to the suspect. An interesting view is offered by Landry and St-Yves (2004), who argue that in the UK, the PEACE approach avoids putting psychological pressures on suspects because pressure was already applied through the legal warning issued at the time of the arrest. However, this does suggest that some pressure is required, either before or during an interview, to obtain a confession (p. 25). There will of course be instances, particularly with an uncooperative suspect, that some pressure will be required, particularly at the challenge stage of the PEACE model. What an ACFS needs to determine is how much pressure may be placed on a suspect before the interview may become oppressive and interrogatory. In summary, to ensure that an interview remains just that – a mechanism for establishing facts – an ACFS should always remember that whilst a confession is a desirable outcome, this should never be the primary objective of a suspect interview. The purpose of the investigative interview with a suspect is to establish the facts of the case and to test the evidence that has been obtained during the investigation. Simply looking for a confession may result in an unethical interview that puts unreasonable psychological pressure on a suspect that not only breaches the governing legislation of the Police and Criminal Evidence Act 1984, but also violates the suspect's human rights. Furthermore, applying unreasonable pressure may also result in false confessions being obtained which is of no value to the investigation whatsoever.

## Developing Rapport

An important aspect of any investigative interview is the development of rapport between the interviewer and the suspect. Rapport may be defined as 'relationship building; two people connect. The interviewee needs to feel comfortable with and trust the person who is asking the questions. Rapport building does not require emotional involvement, but rather psychological closeness' (Lord and Cowan, 2011: 70). Accordingly, an interview in which rapport has been developed equates to a natural environment which carries the participants along with it in a relaxed manner (McKenzie and Milne, 1997). To achieve this, the ACFS will need to project openness and transparency, trustworthiness and professionalism by interacting 'meaningfully with the interviewee, contributing as an interested party' (Bull, 1992), and not simply asking a list of predetermined short answer questions (Milne and Bull, 1999).

The rapport phase should also be used to allow the interviewer to become more familiar with the victim's communicative strengths and limitations (Milne and Bull, 2001). Furthermore, one of the core principles of cognitive interviewing is developing rapport (Fisher, Brennan and McCauley, 2002). In fact, research has found that interviewees who are approached initially with rapport building are more likely to provide complete answers to questions posed (Collins, Lincoln and Frank, 2002; Holmberg, 2004). To emphasise the impact that rapport building can have to the interview, it is interesting to note that some investigators in the US are trained to establish rapport with and flatter the suspect (Davis and Leo, 2006: 130; Holmberg and Christianson, 2002). Rapport as a conversational skill can be achieved through two mechanisms; attention to the processes of social skills and through the use of active listening strategies (Milne and Bull, 1999: 66). To clarify, a social skill can be defined as: 'the extent to which [a person] can communicate with others in a manner that fulfils one's rights, requirements and satisfactions or obligations to a reasonable degree, without damaging the other person's similar rights' (Phillips, 1978: 13), the skills required being:

- **Proxemics:** This term refers to the distance and the effects of differing distances between individuals (that is, the interviewer and interviewee in an interview situation). The interviewer should recognise that their behaviour can affect the interviewee's behaviour in negative ways (Milne and Bull, 1999: 66). For example, their behaviour following what they perceive to be an invasion of personal space may result in the interviewer perceiving them to be lying.
- **Posture and orientation:** The angle or orientation at which people stand or sit in relation to one another can convey information about attitude, status and affiliation within an interview situation (Sommer and Becker, 1969; Cook, 1970).
- **Non-verbal signals:** Strategic use of non-verbal behaviour can help in the development of rapport at the start and across the whole interview. A speaker will look up at the possible end of an utterance, seeking some

form of response (Kendon, 1967). A response such as a nod of the head is an indication that it is appropriate to continue.

■ **Active listening:** From the rapport phase of the interview through to closure the interviewer and interviewee should 'reinforce' each other's statements through a number of non-biasing behaviours which include 'summarising, echo probing and querying' (Milne and Bull, 1999: 66).

It is therefore essential that the ACFS takes these factors into account during the interview to aid the conversation management process.

## Within-interview Behaviour

Having established a need to interview, care and attention also need to be given to within-interview behaviour. According to Shepherd (1984; 1986), it is necessary to use both psychological and social aspects of communication within four interview phases known by the acronym GEMAC:

■ Greeting
■ Explanation
■ Mutual activity
■ Close.

Bennett (1992), cited by Milne and Bull (1999) describes these four phases as, engage, explain, execute and exit. Shepherd (1986) considers there to be six micro skills which enable an interviewer to conduct an effective interview:

1. Observation and memory
2. Listening and assertion
3. Initiating and regulating through the processes of control and social reinforcement
4. Appropriate questioning
5. Active listening
6. Confronting feelings.

Establishing and maintaining a relationship is also critical during the conversation management interview. 'Here the interviewer needs to demonstrate the understanding of the situation from the interviewee's perspective' by letting the suspect discuss their concerns about the incident under investigation (Milne and Bull, 1999: 41). An empathetic approach may in turn assist the ACFS to lay the building blocks for establishing a relationship with the suspect and thus begin to direct the interview towards meeting the desired aims and objectives. To develop and sustain the desired relationship there are five basic rules considered to be essential to conducting a successful investigative interview, these being: keeping an open mind and remaining objective, building a rapport, paying attention, keeping a professional attitude and knowing how to conclude (St-Yves, 2006: 88). When concluding the interview, the ACFS should always ensure that all the legal arguments have been covered, that the suspect has nothing to add, that the suspect has been informed of what is going to happen next and, finally, that they remain professional even if a confession has not been obtained (p. 93).

 ## INTERVIEW UNDER CAUTION PROCEDURE AND RECORDS

All interviews under caution where the investigation has followed the criminal route and the interviewee is suspected of committing an indictable or triable-either-way offence should be tape recorded. As previously discussed, civil investigations should be conducted to the criminal standard so again, wherever possible, these should be tape recorded and conducted under caution. If a suspect is charged following a tape recorded interview, a record of the interview may be required. The interview record:

- Enables the prosecutor to make a decision informed by what was said at interview.
- Is an exhibit to the officer's statement.
- Will be used for the conduct of the case by all parties where it is accepted by the defence.

(Crown Prosecution Service, ndb)

### Interview under Caution Procedures

Code of Practice E of the Police and Criminal Evidence Act 1984 offers the following instructions:

4.3 When the suspect is brought into the interview room the interviewer shall, without delay but in the suspect's sight, load the recorder with new recording media and set it to record. The recording media must be unwrapped or opened in the suspect's presence.

4.4 The interviewer should tell the suspect about the recording process and point out the sign or indicator which shows that the recording equipment is activated and recording.

The interviewer shall:

(a) say the interview is being audibly recorded
(b) subject to paragraph 2.3, give their name and rank and that of any other interviewer present
(c) ask the suspect and any other party present, e.g. a solicitor, to identify themselves
(d) state the date, time of commencement and place of the interview
(e) state the suspect will be given a notice about what will happen to the copies of the recording.

4.5 The interviewer shall:

- caution the suspect
- remind the suspect of their entitlement to free legal advice.

4.6 The interviewer shall put to the suspect any significant statement or silence.

The ACFS will also have to deal with objections or complaints by the suspect. For example, interviewees can object to the interview being audio recorded. In such cases the interviewee's objections should be audio recorded before the recording equipment is switched off (PACE Code of Practice E 4.8). If this occurs, the ACFS will need to make a written record of the interview. If, however, the ACFS reasonably considers they may proceed to question the suspect with the audio recording still on, they may do so.

At the conclusion of the interview, the suspect shall be offered the opportunity to clarify anything he or she has said and asked if there is anything they want to add (PACE Code of Practice E 4.17). The ACFS should also record the time that the recording stopped, seal the master recording with a master recording label and treat it as an exhibit, sign the label and ask the suspect and any third party present during the interview to sign it. If the suspect or third party refuse to sign the label an officer of at least inspector rank, or if not available the custody officer, shall be called into the interview room and asked to sign it (PACE Code of Practice E 4.18). If the interview is taking place at a location other than a police station, the interviewer should get a senior manager to sign the tape seal. Finally, the suspect should be given a notice that explains how the recording will be used, how they can obtain access to it and if they have been charged or advised that they will be prosecuted that a copy of the audio recording will be supplied as soon as practicable, at an agreed time or by order of the court (PACE Code of Practice E 4.18).

All sealed master tapes should be kept securely and a record of tape movements documented. If it is necessary to gain access to the master recording, the seal must be broken in the presence of a representative of the Crown Prosecution Service. The defendant or their legal adviser should be informed and given a reasonable opportunity to be present. If no criminal proceedings result or the criminal trial and, if applicable, appeal proceedings to which the interview relates have been concluded, the chief officer of police, or senior manager if a non-police organisation, is responsible for establishing arrangements for breaking the seal on the master recording, if necessary. When the master recording seal is broken, a record must be made of the procedure followed, including the date, time, place and persons present (PACE Code of Practice E 6.1–6.4).

Guidance on written records of an interview may be found in the Police and Criminal Evidence Act 1984 Code C which provides guidelines on detention treatment and questioning. The following is of relevance to an ACFS should they have to complete a written record of an interview under caution:

11.7  (a)  An accurate record must be made of each interview, whether or not the interview takes place at a police station.
      (b)  The record must state the place of interview, the time it begins and ends, any interview breaks and, subject to paragraph 2.6A,[1] the names of all those present; and must be made on the forms provided for this purpose or in the interviewer's pocket book or in accordance with the Codes of Practice E or F.
      (c)  Any written record must be made and completed during the interview, unless this would not be practicable or would interfere with the conduct of the interview, and must constitute either a verbatim record of what has been said or, failing this, an account of the interview which adequately and accurately summarises it.
11.8  If a written record is not made during the interview it must be made as soon as practicable after its completion.
11.9  Written interview records must be timed and signed by the maker.
11.10  If a written record is not completed during the interview the reason must be recorded in the interview record.

---

[1] Nothing in this Code requires the identity of officers or other police staff to be recorded or disclosed: Unless either (a) the name of the officer is not used, or (b) if the officer or police staff reasonably believe recording or disclosing their name might put them in danger. In these cases, they shall use their warrant or other identification numbers and the name of their police station.

11.11 Unless it is impracticable, the person interviewed shall be given the opportunity to read the interview record and to sign it as correct or to indicate how they consider it inaccurate. If the person interviewed cannot read or refuses to read the record or sign it, the senior interviewer present shall read it to them and ask whether they would like to sign it as correct or make their mark or to indicate how they consider it inaccurate. The interviewer shall certify on the interview record itself what has occurred.

## Records of Interviews

There are four types of written interview record that an ACFS needs to know about:

- Contemporaneous notes
- Short descriptive note (SDN)
- Record of taped interview (ROTI)
- Transcript.

Full details regarding the provision of a record of an interview can be found in the National Prosecution Team (2011) *The Prosecution Team Manual of Guidance: For the Preparation, Processing and Submission of Prosecution Files*. Detailed guidance on providing a written record of an interview and general requirements for interviews not audio or visually recorded can be found in PACE (2012) Code C, Revised, *Code of Practice for the Detention, Treatment and Questioning of Persons by Police Officers* Section 11.1a–11.6. Therefore a brief synopsis of each record is offered, commencing with contemporaneous notes.

*Contemporaneous notes* are a verbatim and contemporaneous account that records in full the following details from the interview; the caution, all questions and responses and any explanations offered by the suspect. The record should be timed and signed, gaps ruled through and any errors deleted with a single line and initialled. At the conclusion the interviewee may read, add to, clarify or correct these notes and then sign the document, which is form MG15. An example of wording used at the end of the contemporaneous note is 'I have read the above record, and I have been able to correct, alter or add anything I wish to do so. I agree that it is a true record of what was said.' This record then becomes an exhibit.

*Short descriptive notes* are also recorded on form MG15 and are the shortest form of interview notes (National Prosecution Team, 2011: 1.13.1). They are frequently used in what may be considered straightforward cases, that is to say, where a guilty plea is anticipated and an abridged rather than a standard prosecution file is likely to be required. If after the first court hearing a guilty plea is not offered by the defendant, then either a ROTI or full transcript may be required. Short descriptive notes are written in the third person, although any admissions which prove the rudiments of the offence are written in direct speech, and are not offered as an exhibit. These notes should also include denials, explanations for committing the offence and any mitigation (National Prosecution Team, 2011: 1.13.2). In serious and complex fraud cases, even if a guilty plea is anticipated, a full interview record is likely to be required.

A *record of taped interview (ROTI)*, also recorded on form MG15, is a more comprehensive record, but only contains the salient points of the interview and is therefore shorter than a full transcript. This record is produced after the interview has been conducted and is exhibited along with the tapes of the interview. In all cases the record must include:

(i) the admin section at the top of the form fully completed;
(ii) the fact that the caution was given (this need not be written out in full as the wording is prescribed);
(iii) that the suspect was reminded of their entitlement to free legal advice (if they changed their mind and either subsequently requested legal advice or declined it, this too must be noted);
(iv) any significant statement or silence before the interview was put to the suspect;
(v) use of any special warnings and responses given;
(vi) details of any offences to be taken into consideration (TIC).

It should also include:

▪ All admissions made to the offence(s) under investigation and questions and answers leading to the admission – write these out in the words used by the suspect.
▪ Statements or questions about possible defences, alibis, assertions that others were involved, ambiguous/qualified admissions, any questions asked by the suspect and answers dealing with the issues of bail and/or alternative pleas/charges.
▪ Responses regarding aggravating factors and/or mitigating circumstances (can be summarised in the third person).

(National Prosecution Team, 2011, 1.13.6–1.13.7)

A *transcript* is a 'full verbatim record of what was said' (National Prosecution Team, 2011: 1.13). It is completed after the interview and therefore does not require any endorsement by the interviewee. The need for a full transcript will be determined by the seriousness of the case and role and importance of the interview in relation to the facts to be proved or inferences to be drawn (National Prosecution Team, 2011: 1.6.7).

 ## REVIEW

This chapter has explored the concept of investigative interviewing of both suspects and witnesses. The PEACE model of interviewing has been explained, and how an ACFS should differentiate between investigative interviews and interrogations and not consider a confession to be the primary goal of the interview. The chapter has explored the cognitive free recall interview with a witness and how an ACFS can use prompts to aid the memory retrieval process. The importance of interview planning has been emphasised and how establishing rapport with the interviewee can assist in the conversation management process. Finally, the chapter has examined ways in which an interview with a suspect can be recorded and the circumstances in which a full transcript is required.

 ## FURTHER READING

Black, I. S. (2013) *The Art of Investigative Interviewing*. Waltham, MA: Butterworth–Heinemann.

Blackwell–Young, J. (2008) *Witness Evidence*. In G. Davies, C. Hollin and R. Bull (eds), *Forensic Psychology*. Chichester: John Wiley & Sons, pp. 209–233.

Davis, D. and Leo, R. (2006) Strategies for Preventing False Confessions and Their Consequences. In M. R. Kebbell and G. M. Davies (eds), *Practical Psychology for Forensic Investigations and Prosecutions*. Chichester: John Wiley & Sons, pp. 121–149.

Milne, R. and Bull, R. (1999) *Investigative Interviewing: Psychology and Practice*. Chichester: John Wiley & Sons.

Roy, R. (2006) Investigative Interviewing: Suspects' and Victims' Rights in Balance. In T. Williamson (ed.) *Investigative Interviewing: Rights, Research, Regulation*. Cullompton: Willan Publishing, pp. 292–317.

## CHAPTER SEVEN

# Rules of disclosure and evidence

## CHAPTER **SUMMARY**

This chapter examines the material that the ACFS will gather during the course of an investigation and how it is introduced into a legal process to determine the facts. The manner in which material is gathered, stored and presented will be described, considering best practice techniques to ensure that evidence remains admissible in proceedings and to prevent claims of unfairness. The more common and relevant rules relating to evidence are described so that the ACFS can gather evidence that will be admissible in proceedings. Finally, the chapter looks at how a prosecution file should be compiled.

##  INTRODUCTION

During the course of an investigation an ACFS will gather material – in some investigations there may only be a handful of documents, in others there may be mountains of material (well, filing cabinets full). Some of it will be used as evidence and as such will have to comply with legal rules if it is to be admissible in proceedings. Some of it will not be used but it can't simply be discarded; it must still be recorded and some of it will have to be disclosed to the prosecutor who will determine whether it should be revealed to the defence. Such 'unused' material may be mundane and will cause no concern if it is disclosed; some of it, however, may be 'sensitive' and could cause lots of problems if it falls into the wrong hands.

This material, both sensitive and non-sensitive, is governed by the Criminal Procedure and Investigations Act 1996 (CPIA), which was explained in Chapter 3. CPIA introduces to the ACFS the four 'Rs' – Record, Retain, Review, Reveal, and, as if in a stick of rock, these words should run through all stages of the investigation. You will recall from the earlier chapter that these words refer to 'Relevant Investigation Material' and you should now be able to identify what this is. Such material must be **R**ecorded (notes of telephone calls, e-mails, witness statements, interview notes, etc.) and then **R**etained securely. (In years gone by when bad practice wasn't treated as seriously as it is now an important piece of equipment for the investigator was the shredder!) This material must be kept under continuous **R**eview by the Disclosure Officer (who may also be the Investigator) and items that might undermine the prosecution case or which might assist the defence must be **R**evealed to the prosecutor.

One aspect of CPIA that wasn't mentioned in Chapter 3 is that it places a duty on the investigator to '. . . pursue all reasonable lines of inquiry, whether these point towards or away from the suspect' (CPIA Code of Practice 2005). As well as ensuring fairness (which is the under-riding tenet of the Act) this imposes an ethical responsibility on the ACFS and underpins the principles of good practice promulgated by the Counter Fraud Professional Accreditation Board. The Crown Prosecution Service recognises that in the early stages of an investigation 'Following reasonable lines of enquiry and recording and retaining relevant material involve the exercise of considerable professional expertise' (CPS, 2014).

The CPS (in its Disclosure Manual) recognises the close link between CPIA and the preparation, processing and submission of prosecution files – rather than repeat what was said in Chapter 3, this section will concentrate on what is required of the ACFS in producing documentation that will lead to the successful submission of a file to the prosecutor, demonstrating that the requirements of CPIA have been complied with.

We discovered in Chapter 3 that CPIA defines what a criminal investigation is. To determine whether someone should be charged with an offence or whether someone charged with an offence is guilty of it, evidence will be required. We can therefore develop the CPIA definition to the following:

> An investigation is the process undertaken to establish whether an act, intention to act or omission may have given rise to a civil or criminal liability and, if it has, the collection of evidence to determine those responsible and how they will be dealt with in terms of redress and/or sanction.

This identifies the collection of evidence as being a central part of a fraud investigation, whether criminal or civil. This chapter will therefore examine the rules that relate to evidence, so that the ACFS can gather the best possible evidence to determine liability, responsibility, redress and sanction.

 **EVIDENCE**

The term 'evidence' is used to indicate the means by which any fact or point in issue, or question, may be proved or disproved in a manner complying with the legal rules governing the subject. It is information that may be presented to a court so that it may decide on the probability of some facts asserted before it, in other words, information by which facts in issue tend to be proved or disproved. Facts in issue are those facts which must be proved in order to establish guilt or liability, such as the defendant's conduct *(actus reus)* and their state of mind *(mens rea)*.

## Standard of Proof

The probability of facts is considered by the jury and the prosecution has to pass the test required by the standard of proof which, in criminal trials, is that the evidence must prove the case 'beyond a reasonable doubt'. This was an issue in the well-reported first trial of Vicky Pryce, the former wife of ex-Minister Chris Huhne, in relation her taking his penalty points for speeding. The jury asked the judge to explain what was meant by the term 'beyond a reasonable doubt'.

Mr Justice Sweeney's response was 'A reasonable doubt is a doubt which is reasonable. These are ordinary English words that the law doesn't allow me to help you with . . .' (British Broadcasting Corporation, 2013).

In the civil arena the standard of proof is determined on the 'balance of probabilities', meaning that the most likely version of events is true. This can be as fine as 49% in one direction and 51% in the other. However, as a result of the decision in *S and M Carpets Ltd v Cornhill* [1981] 1 Lloyd's Rep 667, in civil fraud trials the balance needs to be tipped further than this:

> If a defendant or plaintiff is to allege fraud, then the standard of proof is somewhat higher than that ordinarily applicable to civil matters, but not as high as that relating to criminal matters.

It is worth considering at this point the 'burden of proof', which has a distinct meaning and is sometimes erroneously confused with 'standard of proof'. In criminal trials, the burden of proof lies with the prosecution, who must prove the case 'beyond a reasonable doubt'. There is no burden on the defendant to prove anything although, in reality, the defence will normally present evidence to rebut the prosecution case. In civil cases the principle is that 'he who asserts must prove' – in other words, the claimant.

## Admissibility and Weight of Evidence

When considering evidence there are three questions that must be asked about it:

1. **Relevance:** this is the connection between the item of evidence and the fact that the party tendering it is trying to prove. In the majority of cases relevance is not determined by the law but by common sense. As a result of *R v Turner* [1975] QB 834, irrelevant evidence is inadmissible. The aim of only admitting relevant evidence is to avoid matters that may confuse a jury or give rise to speculation.
2. **Admissibility:** is to be decided by the judge and will be based on whether the evidence is of a type that is admissible in law (by either statute or case law).
3. **Weight:** how much effect does it have on proving or disproving the case? Questions of weight are normally determined by the jury, however there are occasions where a judge will exclude a piece of evidence because its prejudicial effect outweighs its probative value.

## Types of Evidence

Evidence can fall into one (or more) of the following categories:

- **Original evidence:** this is where a witness is giving direct testimony about a fact of which he or she has personal or first-hand knowledge (for example, 'I did this . . .', 'I saw that . . .'). It is presented as evidence of truth and is capable of direct cross-examination.
- **Real evidence:** usually takes the form of a material object (known as an 'exhibit' in court) and its production proves that material object exists, or enables inferences to be drawn from the jury's own observation as to an object's value or physical condition. It will usually be accompanied by written testimony to connect the object with the case.
- **Secondary evidence:** this is evidence of an inferior kind, such as a copy of a document which may be admissible if the original has been lost or destroyed. Copies of documents may also be admitted as secondary evidence where there has been a failure of a party to produce the original by order of a court or where production of the original would be overly inconvenient (for example, the Register of Births). It will also include evidence of items where production of the original is impossible (such as a photograph of graffiti on a wall).
- **Documentary evidence:** is a document produced for inspection by a court either as real, hearsay or original evidence and includes maps, plans, graphs, drawings, photographs, CCTV etc. As with real evidence it should be accompanied by testimony from a witness identifying its relevance to the case.
- **Prima facie evidence:** is evidence that would, if uncontested, establish a fact or raise a presumption of a fact and will form the basis of the prosecution or claimant's case. In certain proceedings such evidence is untested but is used as a benchmark to determine whether there appears to be a case to answer before the next stage of the proceedings can follow.
- **Circumstantial evidence:** is evidence of relevant facts from which the facts in issue may be presumed with more or less certainty. A good explanation of circumstantial evidence was given by Pollock CB in *R v Exall* (1866) 4 F and F 922, comparing it to a rope comprised of several strands:

  One strand of the cord might be insufficient to sustain the weight, but three stranded together may be quite of sufficient strength. Thus it may be in circumstantial evidence – there may be a combination of circumstances, no one of which would raise a reasonable conviction, or more than a mere suspicion: but the whole taken together, may create a strong conclusion of guilt, that is, with as much certainty as human affairs can require or admit of.

Examples of circumstantial evidence will include:

- Evidence of fact supplying a motive
- Evidence that suggests planning and preparation
- Evidence of mental or physical capacity to do a particular act
- Evidence of opportunity
- Evidence of identity (such as fingerprints or DNA).

## Rules of Evidence

- **Best Evidence Rule:** dates back to 1745 and requires that 'the best evidence must be given of which the nature of the thing will allow'. In other words, for example, an object should be produced for the court to examine, rather than a witness describing it. It requires that only people having immediate personal knowledge of a fact in issue could give evidence as to that fact. Although the rule is now antiquated and is not referred to, in practice its principle remains good and the ACFS should strive to produce evidence from the best practicable source.
- **Hearsay evidence:** this is defined by s. 114(1) Criminal Justice Act 2003 as '[a] statement not made in oral evidence in the proceedings, which is admissible as evidence of any matter stated'. In general terms it will be evidence based on what someone has told the witness and not of their direct knowledge. The rule applies to both parties to the proceedings during examination-in-chief and in cross-examination. It was originally a common law rule intended to prevent rumour, gossip and unreliable information from being tendered as evidence. However, over the years it became ambiguous in definition due to numerous exceptions and application of the rule was inconsistent, so much so that it began to negatively impact upon the administration of justice.

## Hearsay Evidence Reform

The Civil Evidence Hearsay Act 1995 paved the way for reform of the rule and hearsay is now allowed in civil proceedings subject to discretion of the court. The Criminal Justice Act 2003 (implemented in April 2005) reformed the hearsay rule in criminal trials and provides a statutory framework for it. It allows hearsay evidence to be admitted if:

1. It meets one of the statutory provisions (for example for business documents).
2. It is information contained in public records.
3. All parties to proceedings agree to its admission.
4. The court is satisfied that it is in the interests of justice for it to be admissible.

## Hearsay Evidence – An Investigator's Perspective

Despite the reforms, the law relating to hearsay evidence continues to be a minefield, with documents particularly being susceptible to hearsay arguments. If you are in any doubt as to whether something is hearsay it is best to include it in a statement. It is ultimately for the lawyers and then a court to determine what is and what is not admissible but, if they are unaware of its existence, it will never be an issue. The job of the ACFS is to gather and present the best possible evidence.

- **Opinion evidence:** the general rule is that opinion evidence is not admissible. A witness should not be able to give an opinion as to what the defendant was thinking, for example. There are, however, some exceptions:
  - *Lay opinion evidence*: this is often evidence relating to the identification of a person (for example, 'he was six feet tall' – unless the witness took out a tape measure he doesn't know this to be a fact), or to the speed of a moving vehicle ('The car that hit me was travelling about 50 mph.' Did the witness have a speed measuring device with them?). It can also relate to a witness's evidence of time, temperature, or the value of an item (unless specialist knowledge is required).
  - *Expert evidence*: under the common law, expert opinion is admissible where issues are beyond a court's competency, that is to say, outside their experience or knowledge. The expert is there only to assist the court (not the side that is paying their fee) in deciding facts of the case and not to apportion blame or guilt. Obviously high standards of knowledge, accuracy and objectivity are required.
- **Evidence of bad character:** such evidence has been allowed in civil proceedings (subject to the provisions of the Rehabilitation of Offenders Act) but was generally forbidden in criminal trials under common law, subject to two exceptions. Since December 2004, however, it has been allowed by provisions contained in the Criminal Justice Act 2003 (ss 98–111), if it is

deemed relevant to the matter being tried. It still remains a controversial subject, however, for the law is complex and there is a growing body of case law. Section 98 of the 2003 Act defines bad character evidence as '. . . evidence of, or a disposition towards, misconduct on his part . . .' and which is not evidence to do with the alleged facts of the case for which the defendant is being tried. An example would be adducing evidence about a member of staff who has made false entries in a time-sheet (for which they received a verbal warning) during their trial for falsifying an expense claim.

## Other Evidential Considerations

▪ **Competence and compellability:** *competence* relates to those persons who are permitted by law to give evidence; *compellability* relates to those persons who may be compelled by law to give evidence. The general rule is that all persons who are competent to give evidence are compellable (Youth Justice and Criminal Evidence Act 1999). As you might expect, there are some exceptions to this rule:
  1. Persons who are unable to understand questions and give answers that can be understood.
  2. Defendants, liable to conviction, are not competent to give evidence for the prosecution.
  3. Defendants, liable to conviction, are not compellable to give evidence on their own behalf. However, where a defendant decides not to give evidence in his own defence (or, if having decided to do so, refuses to answer one of the questions) the court or jury may draw inferences from this when determining guilt. If a defendant refuses to answer questions and instead reads out a pre-prepared, entirely exculpatory statement then this can be deemed inadmissible on the basis that it is self-serving (*R v Pearce* (1979) 69 Cr App R 365).

▪ **Interview and confession evidence:** from a criminal perspective, this subject is governed by the rules of PACE and HRA. Evidence obtained through oppressive or coercive interviewing may be excluded under s. 76 PACE and will also be a breach of Articles 3 and 6 HRA.

▪ **Unfair evidence:** this is dealt with by s. 78 PACE, which gives a discretionary power to judges and magistrates to exclude evidence on which the prosecution seeks to rely if it appears that 'having regard to all the circumstances, including the circumstances in which the evidence was obtained, the admission of the evidence would have such an adverse effect on the fairness of the proceedings that the court ought not to admit it'.

▪ **Entrapment and 'agent provocateur':** the use of such investigative techniques will lead to evidence being compromised when an investigator steps beyond 'essentially passive' investigation of a suspect's criminal activities, and will most likely lead to the defence making an application for the evidence to be excluded under s. 78 PACE. The ACFS must not exercise influence so as to incite commission of an offence, nor create crime artificially. The subject is fully explored in *R v Loosely (Re Attorney General's Reference No 3 of 2000)*[2001] UKHL 53.

▪ **Legal privilege:** The scope of legal professional privilege is reflected in s. 10 PACE, which defines three categories:

1. Communications between a professional legal adviser and his client (or any person representing his client), made in connection with the giving of legal advice to the client. This advice can be of any kind and does not have to be in connection with litigation or the prospect of it. It includes communications between an 'in-house' lawyer and employees of the organisation.

2. Communications between a lawyer, client and third parties for the purpose of pending or contemplated litigation. The communication between the parties must have the litigation as its dominant purpose in order to attract protection.

3. Includes all items enclosed or referred to by communications described at 1. and 2. above.

Legal professional privilege will not protect communications where the purpose is to facilitate a crime or fraud, nor will it protect criminal or fraudulent activities carried out by investigative agents employed by law firms in connection with litigation or otherwise.

 ## GATHERING EVIDENCE

Evidence will be gathered from a range of sources:

▪ From witnesses, their original evidence will be gathered during an interview and will be put into their statement; they may produce 'real' or 'documentary' evidence as well, which will need to be referred to in their statement.

▪ From suspects, again this will be obtained during an interview but will be put into the form of a transcript or Record of Taped Interview.

▪ Forensic evidence will be obtained by expert analysis of the item.

▪ Physical or 'real' evidence may be obtained by search and seizure.

**SEARCH AND SEIZURE**

The ACFS has no criminal law powers of search but can accompany the police, if required, whilst they conduct a search of premises (PACE Code B – Note 3C). There are occasions, however, when the ACFS may be able to undertake a search without the police. The Civil Procedure Act 1997 allows the High Court to grant search orders (in effect civil search warrants) which are sometimes referred to as Anton Pillar Orders (*Anton Pillar KEG v Manufacturing Process Ltd* (1976)). This enables the claimant to secure evidence in civil fraud cases where there is a likelihood of it being destroyed if the defendant becomes aware of proceedings (an *ex parte* application is made to the court).

In the corporate world, most common search and seizure cases involve employee fraud or serious professional misconduct. Warrants or orders are not required if the search is conducted on the client's premises with management consent (which should be in writing). Issues may arise when the suspect's personal space becomes involved – such as a locker or cupboard that has been provided by the organisation for the purpose of storing 'personal effects' whilst at work. Searching this type of space would probably lead to a breach of Article 8 rights, unless the subject's contract of employment or other policy specifically allows for this.

## Search and Seizure Stepping Stones

In deciding whether to undertake a search of the workplace, the following should be taken into consideration:

- Review standing disciplinary procedures, fraud policy or contract of employment (any mention of a right to search?).
- Consider the reasonableness of action to search (is material likely to be found?) and whether it is a proportionate response (ECHR).
- Consider having suspect present. There are advantages and disadvantages to this – it will prevent allegations of 'planting' evidence but will also reveal to them what has been found (and missed!) allowing them the opportunity to create an explanation prior to being interviewed.
- Appoint search leader and an administrator (Exhibits Officer).
- Plan and prepare the search, undertaking a risk assessment and deciding what action should be taken to protect the scene.
- Carry out a briefing of those participating.
- Photograph or video the scene before searching and consider drawing a sketch plan, labelling the key items (which makes life much easier later on

when trying to describe exactly where an item was found – 'Filing Cabinet 3, Drawer 2' is much easier than 'The second filing cabinet to the left of the desk, third drawer down').

- How will the searching be conducted? For example, devise a methodical method so that nothing gets missed.
- What equipment will be required? Exhibit bags, labels, gloves, overalls, tools, keys, etc.
- Record everything (time, day, date, place, team composition, chronology, etc.).
- Ensure that there is communication between the team whilst the search is underway. When things are found, let the others know.
- Seize property/material/exhibit; precisely describe; who recovered and where; consider safe storage. **N.B. Remember chain of custody (continuity).**
- Conclude, leaving the premises as you found them.
- Debrief, with team members completing statements producing the items seized.

 ## DEALING WITH EXHIBITS

When dealing with an exhibit there are four aspects to consider in order to preserve its integrity: contamination, security, continuity and accuracy.

- **Contamination:** will reduce the effectiveness of forensic examination or even prevent the examination. If contaminated, there may be accusations of interference or tampering with the exhibit, which may lead to the evidence being ruled inadmissible.
- **Security:** the ACFS has a duty of care to prevent theft or loss of the exhibit. If the exhibit is not stored securely it again may lead to accusations of interference or tampering, which again will put the exhibit at risk of being excluded. Exhibits are often kept in a sealed plastic bag, which has a serial number unique to that investigation. If, for any reason, the bag has to be opened, the reason for doing so should be recorded. Once that reason is past, the exhibit should be placed in a new sealed bag, with the old bag being placed inside with the exhibit.
- **Continuity:** records should be kept that demonstrate the passage of an exhibit through the investigative process, showing an audit trail between witnesses and locations. Continuity is maintained by all witnesses who

handle or have custody of the exhibit signing the exhibit label. They should also provide a witness statement describing why they had the exhibit and what they did with it whilst it was in their custody.

◼ **Accuracy:** in relation to the description of the exhibit, in relation to its handling, and in relation to what has happened to it. Accuracy leads to less confusion at court (and to less embarrassment of the ACFS!). Once a description has been given to the exhibit (which will be written on the exhibit label), exactly the same description should be used every time the exhibit is described.

Each exhibit will be given a reference number that is unique to that investigation. The reference number is made up of the initials of the person finding or producing the exhibit, plus a consecutive number. So, if I was to find a receipt book in the suspect's desk drawer, and this was the first exhibit that I had dealt with in this investigation, I would give it the reference AW1. Similarly, if my colleague Sarah Mills found a blank invoice, she would give it the reference SM1. The next item I found would have the reference number AW2, and so on. If I was taking a statement from a witness and they produced an exhibit to me (perhaps something that they had created, such as a spread sheet), it would have their reference number, not mine. If there are two people working on an investigation with the same initials, then the second letter of the family name should be used, for example, Andrew Whittaker – AWh1, Anne West – AWe1.

Finally, where an exhibit has been seized and it contains other items which might later be identified as exhibits, it will still be given a reference number as described above but then items that are found inside will be given the same number plus a suffix. For example, if I seized a box file full of documents I would give it the reference number AW1. If I later sifted through it and found a number of documents that I wanted to use as evidence, these would be given the reference numbers AW1/1, AW1/2, AW1/3, and so on, indicating that they all came from AW1.

When dealing with digital evidence the above aspects will be enhanced by following these principles that have been produced by the Association of Chief Police Officers:

Principle 1: No action taken by law enforcement agencies or their agents should change data held on a computer or storage media which may subsequently be relied upon in court.

Principle 2: In exceptional circumstances, where a person finds it necessary to access original data held on a computer or on storage media, that person must be competent to do so and be able to give evidence explaining the relevance and the implications of their actions.

Principle 3: An audit trail or other record of all processes applied to computer based electronic evidence should be created and preserved. An independent third party should be able to examine those processes and achieve the same result.

Principle 4: The person in charge of the investigation (the case officer) has overall responsibility for ensuring that the law and these principles are adhered to (ACPO, 2008).

 ## EVIDENCE GATHERING TECHNIQUES

The ACFS should have an awareness of the various expert methods that are available to gather evidence from documents – all of these have been used during fraud investigations:

**The 'super glue' fuming method:** Latent fingerprints must first be made visible before they can be used for identification. When you touch an object, your fingers leave material behind. Although the material is mostly water (which evaporates) there are also amino acids, glucose and other proteins. The fuming method employs the concept of introducing a chemical that will react with some of the material that your fingers leave behind. This will change the chemical composition and make the latent prints visible. The surface to be checked is placed in an airtight container with a small heater. Cyanoacrylate (super glue) is introduced to the 150°F environment where it evaporates and creates an environment of gaseous cyanoacrylate. As the gas contacts the print, the fingerprint is 'developed'. The process is accelerated by fans in the container which circulate the gas ensuring even distribution and contact time. Finally, the sticky chemical formed that details the fingerprint is dusted with a coloured powder that allows the fingerprint to be photographed.

**Fingerprints (or, more correctly, finger marks) – Latent print evidence collection guidance:** Latent finger mark evidence can typically be divided into two categories: porous and non-porous. Porous evidence such as paper, unfinished wood, cardboard, etc., is normally conducive to the preservation of prints because latent print residue can soak into the surface. Non-porous evidence such as plastic, glass, metal, foil, etc., is much more fragile because the latent print residue may just be lying on the surface. Even the slightest handling can 'wipe away' a latent print on non-porous surfaces.

**Borderline or questionable surfaces?** If you aren't sure whether a drop of water would soak into a surface, treat it as non-porous. You may otherwise 'wipe off' valuable latent prints during shipment to the lab. Many latent prints are destroyed on shiny magazines and shiny cardboard cigarette cartons by failing to treat them as non-porous. All porous evidence must be submitted to the laboratory for latent print processing and should be packaged as conveniently as possible. Wear gloves when handling the evidence and allow wet or damp evidence to dry before sealing and taking to the fingerprint expert. Do wear gloves and assume that any area your gloves touch will destroy identifiable latent prints on non-porous or semi-porous surfaces. Keep all gloves clean: touching a contaminated surface (such as scratching your oily nose) will result in fabric impressions from the gloves (or your own fingerprints when thin surgical gloves conform to your underlying friction skin ridges) later developing on the evidence . . . possibly obscuring an otherwise identifiable latent print from the offender. Clean gloves will not harm latent prints on papers or other porous surfaces. If you keep cloth gloves just for handling evidence, keep several pairs so you can rotate and launder them routinely. When you see investigators in the movies pick up a firearm or drinking glass with their hand covered by a handkerchief, you are seeing an example of how to almost certainly destroy the offender's latent prints on those smooth, non-porous surfaces.

Avoid unnecessary writing or marking on surfaces to be processed for latent prints (not only might you be damaging hidden evidence, you are 'changing' the exhibit). Avoid taping or sticking labels on the surfaces to be processed for latent prints.

## Electrostatic Detection Apparatus (ESDA)

This technique detects indented handwriting impressions on paper. The document in question is covered with a piece of thin clear plastic film called Mylar. A strong electric field is passed over the document and a static charge collects in the indentations. The Mylar is then coated with an electrically charged black powder that collects in the indented areas, producing a copy of the indented writings on the Mylar without harming the document. The ESDA process can:

- Produce a permanent trace of any impressions present.
- Produce good results with very faint impressions.
- Produce results with old impressions.
- In some circumstances enable the sequence of ink writings and impressions on a sheet to be established.

The ESDA process will not:

- Produce good results with very deep impressions.
- Produce results from documents which have been treated with a liquid, for example, documents that have been treated to develop fingerprints.
- Produce good results from documents that have been in contact with certain plastics, particularly file sleeves (commonly known as 'poly-pockets').
- Produce good results from very poor-quality papers or smooth surfaces such as magazine covers.

Documents intended for examination should be:

- Handled as little as possible – ESDA is affected by fresh fingerprints.
- Packaged in paper envelopes (in a sandwich between two sheets of cardboard) or in cardboard boxes.
- Protected from solvents and liquids.
- Protected from the addition of extra impressions (for example, they should be placed in envelopes after the address or identifying mark has already been written).

 ## HANDWRITING ANALYSIS

Examinations involve the comparison of a known handwriting specimen against the questioned document. The characters in the specimen and the questioned handwriting are examined to determine the range of variation and allowing an assessment of the similarities and differences to be made. If the writings are similar then this constitutes evidence of common authorship. The strength of this evidence will depend on the distinctiveness of letter formations, the amount of handwriting in dispute and the suitability of the handwriting of known authorship.

When obtaining samples the offender may try to disguise their handwriting. Always assume the specimens are disguised and try to get some non-request known writing examples.

Some points to consider:

- Source – Where do you get them from? (it must be lawful).
- Proof – You must be able to use them in court (there will need to be witness testimony to describe where they have originated).

▪ Date – They should be contemporary with that in question as our hand-writing changes with time.

The best specimens include both request and non-request samples. If obtaining request samples you should ask the suspect to write a series of specimens containing the same words as on the questioned document.

## COMPUTER BASED ELECTRONIC EVIDENCE

> Electronic evidence is valuable evidence and it should be treated in the same manner as traditional forensic evidence – with respect and care. The methods of recovering electronic evidence, whilst maintaining evidential continuity and integrity may seem complex and costly, but experience has shown that, if dealt with correctly, it will produce evidence that is both compelling and cost-effective.
>
> (ACPO, 2008)

Data is stored in bits on a disk. A bit is a zero or a 1, which equates to a 'cell' on the disk being magnetised or un-magnetised. A character requires one byte of storage space on the disk and there are 8 bits in a byte. Many computers today are being built with hard disks that have a capacity of 1 terabyte (1 Tb); 1Tb = 1024 Gigabytes (Gb); 1Gb = 1024 Megabytes (Mb). An average CD-ROM holds 600 Mb, therefore 1Tb holds the equivalent of 1,747 CD-ROMs (1024/600×1024). If you were to print 1Tb of data onto A4 paper it would result in a pile 134.582 kilometres or 84.11 miles high! An external hard drive, 1Tb in size, can now be purchased for a little over £50.00, meaning that huge amounts of data can be cheaply stored in a very portable format. Given also our increased reliance on digital media to conduct business, this means that computer based electronic evidence is not only a vital source of evidence; it is also an increasingly common source of evidence, particularly in fraud investigations. Think also of the disclosure challenges when dealing with a pile of paper 84 miles high! Dealing with this latter point, a court will not expect an ACFS to have examined every sheet of paper in that pile to look for material. The Attorney General's Guidance on Disclosure sets out what should be the approach:

> ... it might be reasonable to examine digital material by using software search tools, or to establish the contents of large volumes of material by dip sampling. If such material is not examined in detail, it must nonetheless be described on the disclosure schedules accurately and

as clearly as possible. The extent and manner of its examination must also be described together with justification for such action.

(Attorney General, 2013)

Evidence that is based on a computer or on computer media is subject to the same rules and laws that apply to documentary evidence, that is to say:

> The onus is on the prosecution to show to the Court that the evidence produced is no more and no less now than when it was first taken into their possession.
>
> (ACPO, 2008)

The statement means it is the responsibility of the prosecution to prove that the evidence has not been tampered with in any way, and remains in exactly the same state as when it was seized.

It is essential to demonstrate to a court both integrity and continuity of evidence. It is also necessary to show how evidence has been recovered and the process that was followed. Evidence should be preserved and contemporaneous notes made. The notes should be complete enough to allow an appropriately qualified third party to be able to repeat the same process and arrive at the same result as that presented to a court.

## Analysis of Mobile Telephones and Personal Digital Assistants (PDA)

This is a specialist area within Forensic Computing. Mobile phones are now one of the most widely available personal accessories and are used in all corners of the world. Most modern phones manufactured in the last few years have cameras built in; they also have the ability to record video, and to record voice and sound. Smart phones are able to access the internet and can control other devices remotely. More memory is being added to mobile phones, which makes their storage capacity greater than ever. Forensic mobile phone examinations go far beyond normal data recovery techniques and go into areas and files on the media not normally accessed by the ordinary user.

## E-mails

Web based e-mail (such as Hotmail, Yahoo, Gmail, etc.) comes under internet analysis as the data is stored on a web server and each page is downloaded by your browser in order to be viewed. Client based e-mail (such as Outlook, Thunderbird, Eudora, Lotus Notes) store files on an e-mail server, the local machine, or both. Investigators should consider obtaining relevant areas of e-mail servers to capture this data.

E-mails may also be setup to synchronise with mobile devices such as a Blackberry, Smartphone or Personal Digital Assistant (PDA). E-mail clients not only provide access to e-mails, but also contacts/address books, diaries/calendars and to do lists/tasks.

## Deleted Files/Folders

Allocated areas of disk space are those which contain live files, that is to say, files that are stored. The operating system remembers where the file is stored, and provides access to users and programs that need them. The remainder of the disk (the part not taken up by live files) is known as unallocated space. In order to provide access to a file, the operating system needs to know where on the disk the file is stored. To do this, it maintains a pointer to the file. When a file is 'deleted' by the user, the operating system removes the entry, or pointer, which links the file to its location on the disk. This means that the file can no longer be viewed through the operating system. The operating system, and therefore the user, has no way to recover the pointer information, and so the file is lost somewhere on the disk. The file itself however, remains on the disk until it is overwritten. Because the operating system no longer identifies the area as being used, it can be overwritten with any other data. Whether or not this happens depends on the length of time since the pointer was destroyed, the remaining available space on the hard disk, and other factors. In general, once a file has been *overwritten* it cannot be recovered by software tools. It is however possible that even if part of a file has been overwritten, the remainder of the file may be present. For example, consider a video tape, which you use to record a football match. Having watched the footage, you put it on the pile for re-recording. All the time that the tape is on this pile, it is possible to recover the footage on the tape. Then you record 'Coronation Street' over the top. Some of the football match will undoubtedly be overwritten, but depending on the position of the tape when you started recording, a portion of the football match will remain on the tape.

## Graphic and Video Files

Forensic software can be used to review images and graphics from across the whole operating system in one view (known as a Gallery Review). This allows the examiner to quickly scroll through all the images. There may be many thousands, and they will include system files as well as user files. Examples are icons, logos, diagrams, clip art, photographs, images viewed in web pages, images in documents, frames, indicators and more. Deleted graphics can also be recovered from unallocated space. This will include all of the above types of images, and is likely to result in many tens of thousands of images to review on a standard 40GB hard drive. Live video files can also be searched for according to file extension and/or signature. There are methods available to recover deleted videos, and partially overwritten or corrupted videos can sometimes be spliced back together or modified so that they play.

## Internet History

In order to view a web page, the component parts must be stored locally on the user's machine. Therefore, when a user browses a web page, the individual parts (for example, images) are downloaded to a collection of folders called 'Temporary Internet Files'. This area is also often referred to as a 'cache'. Once the web page has been viewed, the items can be deleted, however if disk space permits it, it can be useful to keep these files, in case you revisit the web page again. This is because the web page will load quicker if it doesn't have to download the component parts again. This means that all information that the user has browsed must have been on the PC at some point. Whether it has been deleted and overwritten will depend on the length of time since that item was viewed, and the size of the hard drive. It is often possible to recover web pages from the cache, or from unallocated clusters, which depict web mail (such as Hotmail, Yahoo, e-mail etc.), internet banking, internet search engine searches, and other browsing. Furthermore, most browsers maintain an 'Internet History'. This allows the user to revisit pages they have previously visited if they cannot remember how they found it, or its address. It works by maintaining a list of previously visited addresses, including the dates and times that the page was visited. History files are also deleted after a set period of time (can be defined by the user), but it is often possible to recover history files from unallocated space.

## Seizing and Packaging Electronic Evidence

Always consider consulting a computer forensic expert prior to undertaking a search. Even if the expert doesn't take part in the search, knowing that one is at the end of a telephone to offer guidance and support may mean that their help can make the difference between evidence being admissible and being excluded.

- **Continuity:** ensure that a record of custody for the items is continuously maintained (that is to say, items are logged in and out of an examiner's possession).

- **Accuracy:** ensure that no changes are made to any of the data on any areas of the evidence. To avoid data being changed, machines must not be accessed, booted, or shut down after they have been seized. Data is captured in a forensic manner using devices which prevent any modification of original data. If the machine is running at the time of seizure, call the expert for advice.
- **Security:** any seized items must be sealed with individual seal numbers to ensure integrity and continuity.
- **Contamination:** packaging should protect the device from damage or interference. Mobile devices including phones, PDAs, Blackberries, or any devices which use a wireless signal, should be sealed in a Faraday bag to prevent the signal being received and making data changes (that is to say, if more data is received, new e-mails, text messages, phone calls etc.). Power should be maintained to mobile devices, to prevent data loss.

 ## COMPLETING A PROSECUTION FILE

Having gathered investigation material and identified what is going to be used as evidence and what is going to be unused material, the ACFS must now marshal all of that material into a format that can be passed to the prosecutor. This will be the prosecution file and there is an agreed format for its creation, so that there is consistency in preparation and adherence to standards. The format is fully described in the Prosecution Team Manual of Guidance for the preparation, processing and submission of prosecution files. It has been compiled by representatives of the Crown Prosecution Service (CPS), the Association of Chief Police Officers and the National Policing Improvement Agency (the latter's responsibility for this work has now passed to the College of Policing). This section of the book is not designed to replace the Manual, nor is it intended to reproduce it. However it is worth bringing certain aspects of the Manual to the attention of the ACFS.

The Manual consists of three sections:

1. A concise outline of the case file building process, required file contents and the process for obtaining CPS charging advice where necessary.
2. Guidance to managers regarding the supervision of case files. It outlines the responsibilities that managers have in respect of the endorsement of particular forms, and in supervising the content in terms of quality assurance.
3. Examples of the forms that are to be used within the file – these are referred to with the suffix 'MG' (Manual of Guidance). This section of the Manual gives an example of each form, annotated where necessary to assist completion.

Each of the MG forms carries a Header and a Footer that indicate how the form should be treated under the Government Protective Marking Scheme (GPMS). GPMS categorises material into four classes, namely 'Restricted', 'Confidential', 'Secret' and 'Top Secret'. The MG forms will fall in either the 'Restricted' or 'Confidential' categories and those that are completed by the ACFS will most probably be classified as 'Restricted'. There may be some circumstances however, such as the use of covert investigative techniques, where a 'Confidential' classification will be appropriate. A full description of the 'Restricted' and 'Confidential' classifications can be found in the Manual.

Responsibility for deciding whether to prosecute an individual is split between the police and the CPS. The ACFS's employing organisation may have agreements with the CPS or the police for the direct referral of cases for prosecution (for example, NHS Protect) or, alternatively, the ACFS may have to approach the police in the first instance (particularly if the case requires police powers to be used). If the case is referred to the police they will take forward completion of the prosecution file but may well ask the ACFS to provide certain completed MG forms. In deciding whether to prosecute, the CPS will apply two tests:

1. Is the evidence sufficient to provide a realistic prospect of conviction? and, if it is,
2. Is a prosecution in the public interest?

Only if both tests are passed will a prosecution be launched.

The form of the file will be dependent on whether a 'guilty' or 'not guilty' plea is anticipated at court and is based on the National File Standard, details of which are given in the Manual. In order to meet Disability Discrimination Act requirements, typed copies of case file documents should be in either Arial or Verdana font 12.

The ACFS should be aware of the following MG forms:

## MG5 Police Report

Formerly known as the 'Case Summary', this document is now more streamlined and sets out the key aspects of the case. The section entitled 'Summary of the key evidence' should describe in chronological order the facts of the case, in other words, 'telling the story'. All key witnesses and exhibits should be referred to, so that the prosecutor can understand the part that they play. The summary should demonstrate how each of the points to prove has been met. There is also a section on the form that indicates that there will be an application for compensation (by means of completing form MG19) – redress is a key aspect of the Comprehensive Approach to countering fraud and so this should not be forgotten.

## MG6 Disclosure Series

There are six forms in the MG6 series of forms, each of which deals with a separate aspect of the disclosure process. The MG6 form should be used by the ACFS as a means of passing additional confidential information to the prosecutor (such as the demeanour of a witness when interviewed). The MG6C form is the schedule of unused non-sensitive material, the MG6D is the schedule of unused sensitive material and the MG6E is the disclosure officer's report.

## MG9 Witness List

The purpose of this form is to provide the prosecutor and the Witness Service with witness information and contact details; it also indicates to the prosecutor the number of statements and whether or not the statement has been attached to the case file (some witnesses may provide more than one statement in a case).

## MG10 Witness Non-availability

This provides the prosecution team with an easily accessible overview of witness availability, so that court dates can be selected when all witnesses are available to attend. This information will be drawn from the rear of the MG11, where details of a witness's prior commitments should be recorded.

## MG11 Witness Statement

You will become familiar with this document during the investigative interviewing stage of ACFS training. There is no set format (each case is different) but there are some key principles that should be followed. The statement should start by 'setting the scene' – who is the witness and what is their relevance to the case? It should then describe in chronological order what happened, producing exhibits where appropriate. The witness should sign after the last word of their statement as well as at the bottom of each page; they should also read the declaration and sign this. The statement should be written in black ink, with alterations being made by a single strikethrough, which the witness should initial to indicate that they have seen it. Remember to include ADVOKATE where the witness is giving evidence of identity. It is also important to ensure that the reverse of the form is fully completed prior to the end of the interview as it contains important information that will need to be referred to during the case management stages.

## MG12 Exhibit List

This summarises all the exhibits in the case and will provide the prosecutor with details of where the exhibits are located if a copy hasn't been included in the case papers.

## MG15 Record of Interview

The purpose of this form is to present the 'highlights' of the interview with the suspect and should include all the salient points of the interview as well as any admissions, aggravating factors, mitigating circumstances, significant silences, etc. Where a recording device is unavailable or faulty, the MG15 should be used to make a handwritten contemporaneous record of the interview.

 **REVIEW**

This chapter examined the material that the ACFS will gather during the course of an investigation and how it is introduced into the investigative process to determine the facts. The manner in which this material is gathered, stored and presented has also been discussed, offering guidance on best practice techniques to ensure that evidence remains admissible in proceedings and to prevent claims of unfairness. The more common and relevant rules relating to evidence have been described, specifically admissibility and weight, so that the ACFS can gather relevant material that will be admissible in proceedings. The rules relating to search and seizure have been explored including how an ACFS should deal with exhibits. Finally, the chapter explored the key components of a prosecution file.

 **FURTHER READING**

Johnston, D. and Hutton, G. (2013) *Blackstone's Police Manual Volume 2: Evidence and Procedure 2014.* Oxford: Oxford University Press.

CHAPTER EIGHT

# The courtroom process

## CHAPTER **SUMMARY**

This chapter will commence by explaining the workings of Her Majesty's Court Service and the different types of courts, including describing the typical layout of a magistrates' court and a Crown Court. The roles of the judiciary, court officials and lay persons will be discussed. The actions a Counter Fraud Specialist is required to take before attending court to ensure that they are fully prepared when required to give evidence will be identified. The principles of advocacy will be outlined and the experience of being cross-examined by a solicitor or counsel will be described. The chapter will conclude by explaining the process for obtaining warrants within the magistrates' court.

 **INTRODUCTION**

English law is the legal system of England and Wales and is the basis of the common law legal systems used in most Commonwealth countries and the United

States (as opposed to codified or multiple systems in other countries, such as Scots Law). It was exported to Commonwealth countries during the period of the British Empire, and it forms the basis of the jurisprudence (legal theory) of most of those countries. English law that existed prior to the American Revolution still forms part of the law of the United States, and provides the basis for many American legal traditions and policies, though it has no superseding jurisdiction.

Our current legal system dates back to the Norman Conquest. Following the 1066 invasion there developed, alongside the existing Saxon shire courts, the feudal courts of the barons and the ecclesiastical courts of the church. From the King's Council there also developed the Royal Courts, presided over by professional judges, which over time gradually absorbed the jurisdictions (legal powers) of the baronial and ecclesiastical courts. By 1250 the royal judges had amalgamated the various local customs into the system of common law – that is, law common to the whole country.

1362 saw the introduction of the Pleading in English Act (during the reign of Edward III), which complained that because the French language was still relatively unknown in England the people had no knowledge of what was being said for them or against them in the courts, which used French. The Act therefore stipulated that:

> All Pleas which shall be pleaded in Courts whatsoever, before any of his Justices whatsoever, or in his other Places, or before any of His other Ministers whatsoever, or in the Courts and Places of any other Lords whatsoever within the Realm, shall be pleaded, shewed, defended, answered, debated, and judged in the English Tongue, and that they be entered and inrolled in Latin. (sic)

The oldest court still in existence is the Coroner's Court which dates back to 1194 when the office of Coroner was formally established as an independent judicial officer charged with the investigation of sudden, violent or unnatural deaths. Over the subsequent years the courts system developed into what we have today.

All criminal cases will commence in the magistrates' court, whether they be minor matters such as dropping litter or the most serious, such as murder. Magistrates' courts are a key part of the criminal justice system and more than 90% of cases are completed there. In addition, the magistrates' courts deal with a number of civil matters, for example, Council Tax Liability Orders, but many civil matters that they used to deal with have now passed to Local Authorities, such as liquor licensing.

##  CLASSIFICATION OF OFFENCES

Each crime is classified according to the way in which it can be dealt with by a court. The Act that creates the offence will detail the penalties that are available and the penalty will determine how the offence can be dealt with. For some offences there will only be a penalty on summary conviction, for some there will be two penalties, one on summary conviction and one for conviction on indictment and finally for some offences (the most serious) there will only be a penalty for conviction on indictment.

**Summary-only offences** – these are offences which can *only* be heard in the magistrates' court. This restriction is imposed by the statute which creates the offence and applies to minor offences where it is right that the case should be heard at this level. Examples of summary-only offences include speeding, being drunk and disorderly and committing criminal damage (to a value below £5000).

**Either-way offences** – the majority of criminal offences fall within this category, including offences under the Fraud Act 2006. An offence will fall within this category if the statute that created it gives penalties for both summary trial and trial on indictment. An Indictment is the document on which the charges against an accused appear, for trial in the Crown Court. The defendant has the right to have his case heard in the Crown Court if it is an either-way offence, even if the value is low. For example the theft of a bottle of milk and the theft of a diamond ring worth £500,000 are both contrary to s. 1 of the Theft Act 1968, which is an either-way offence and so both can be tried in the Crown Court. If the defendant who stole the ring applies to have his case heard in the magistrates' court then the case will be committed by the magistrates to the Crown Court on the basis that if the defendant were to be found guilty then their sentencing powers would be insufficient to deal with the seriousness of the offence.

**Indictable-only offences** – these are the most serious offences and include murder, robbery and arson. The only penalty available is one on indictment, i.e. a penalty imposed by the Crown Court. If the defendant pleads not guilty or declines to indicate a plea at the magistrates' court, a mode of trial hearing will take place. If the magistrates decline jurisdiction (normally because they feel that their sentencing powers are insufficient for the circumstances of the offence) or the defendant elects to be tried at the Crown Court, the case will be adjourned for committal proceedings. In committal proceedings the magistrates will consider the prosecution evidence and decide whether there is a case to answer. If there is, they will commit the case to the Crown Court which will then take ownership of the case. If the offence charged is indictable only, then the magistrates will formally send the case to the Crown Court for proceedings to continue.

 ## THE COURTS

### Magistrates' Court

Cases in the magistrates' courts are usually heard by a panel of three magistrates (otherwise known as Justices of the Peace or lay magistrates) supported by a legally qualified Court Clerk. The magistrates are collectively called a Bench and are assigned to a Local Justice Area but have a national jurisdiction pursuant to the Courts Act 2003. Magistrates are appointed by the Crown (retiring at the age of 70). They are not paid but may claim expenses and an allowance for loss of earnings. They come from all walks of life and do not usually have any legal qualifications. Qualified clerks advise them on the law. They are unpaid but receive travel and a subsistence allowance. There are around 30,000 in England and Wales. They undergo a substantial amount of training supervised by the Judicial Studies Board. In addition, there are also about 130 District Judges. District Judges in magistrates' courts are required to have at least seven years' experience as a barrister or solicitor advocate and two years' experience as a Deputy District Judge. They sit alone and deal with more complex or sensitive cases, for example, serious fraud, and until August 2000, were known as stipendiary magistrates, but were renamed to identify them as members of the professional judiciary.

Magistrates cannot normally order sentences of imprisonment that exceed six months (or 12 months for consecutive sentences), or fines exceeding £5000. In cases triable either way the offender may be committed by the magistrates to the Crown Court for sentencing if a more severe sentence is thought necessary. Normally cases are prosecuted by the Crown Prosecution Service, however some matters can be prosecuted by other agencies, such as the RSPCA. The layout of a typical magistrates' court can be found at Figure 8.1.

Key:  A Witness   B Magistrates   C Clerk of the court
D Lawyers for the prosecution and defence
E Court usher   F Defendant   G Others

**FIGURE 8.1**   Inside a magistrates' court

(Cheshire Constabulary, nd)

## County Court

The County Court is the first tier court in the civil process; often referred to as the Small Claims Court, it deals with civil matters, such as:

- Claims for debt repayment including enforcing court orders and return of goods bought on credit
- Personal Injury
- Breach of contract concerning goods or property
- Family issues such as divorce or adoption
- Housing disputes, including mortgage and council rent arrears and re-possession.

Unlike the magistrates' court, some cases will by-pass the County Court and make their first appearance at the next tier, the High Court. For further details on the civil justice system please see Chapter 9.

## Crown Court

The Crown Court deals with more serious criminal cases as explained earlier. Before the Crown Court came into existence in 1972 cases were heard at what were known as 'Assizes'. The Crown Court is a single entity but is based at 77 centres across England and Wales – most have resident judges who are based at one particular court. The most serious cases (indictable only) will be heard by a circuit judge, who will visit a number of courts within a Courts Service region (formerly known as circuits).

The Crown Court sitting at the Central Criminal Court deals with major criminal cases from Greater London and, in exceptional cases, from other parts of England and Wales. It is the Crown Court for the City of London and so hears many fraud cases. The name Old Bailey is drawn from the street in which it is sited – Bailey meaning fortified wall.

The Crown Prosecution Service is the government department responsible for determining the charge and prosecuting criminal cases investigated by the police in England and Wales. Created by the Prosecution of Offences Act 1985, it is an independent body that works closely with the police. The head of the Crown Prosecution Service is the Director of Public Prosecutions (DPP), currently Alison Saunders CB, who is the first DPP to be drawn from the CPS. The DPP is superintended by the Attorney General, who is responsible to Parliament for the Service. The CPS employs around 6800 staff, including around 2500 lawyers and every year they deal with more than 1.3 million cases in the magistrates' court and about 115,000 in the Crown Court. In the Crown Court, their role is to prepare the case and to instruct a barrister who will present the case to the court.

The role of the judge within a Crown Court is to manage the proceedings and to interpret and make decisions about the law. Throughout a trial, the judge makes sure that the jury is aware of its legal role and what it should and shouldn't do so that the court case stays within the law. Following the jury's decision, if the defendant is found guilty of the offence(s) charged then the judge's role is to impose a sentence that is appropriate for the circumstances of the case and which is within the parameters set by the statute which created the offence.

The presence of a jury in a Crown Court trial is a cornerstone of our judicial system, in that the finding of guilt (or not) is determined by the defendant's peers, i.e. ordinary people drawn from the community. A jury is comprised of twelve people who are drawn at random from a pool of jurors – technically known as a panel, who have been summoned for jury service from the electoral roll. Twelve names will be called at random from the panel and those persons will enter the jury box and take the juror's oath.

Historically, only barristers had a right of audience as an advocate in the Crown Court. However, in recent years this has changed and now suitably qualified solicitors have the right to present their client's case to the Crown Court; these solicitors are known as solicitor advocates.

The Crown Court deals with cases transferred from the magistrates' courts and it also deals with cases sent for sentence from magistrates' courts and hears appeals against decisions of magistrates' courts.

The Court of Appeal Criminal Division will hear appeals against decisions made by the Crown Court. These can be appeals against conviction or sentence. The only automatic right of appeal is where a question of law only is involved. On all other matters the appellant requires leave to appeal to be given by the Court of Appeal. The layout of a typical Crown Court can be found in Figure 8.2.

## The Court of Appeal

The Court of Appeal, which sits in London at the Royal Courts of Justice, consists of two divisions:

1. The *Civil Division*, which hears appeals:
   ■ from the three divisions of the High Court (Chancery, Queen's Bench and Family Division)
   ■ from the County Courts across England and Wales
   ■ from certain tribunals, such as the Employment Appeal Tribunal.
2. The *Criminal Division*, which hears appeals from the Crown Court.

The Court of Appeal is the highest court within the Senior Courts, which also include the High Court and Crown Court. It normally sits in up to twelve courts in the Royal Courts of Justice in the Strand in London. The Right Honourable Lord Dyson, the Master of the Rolls, is the President of the Court of Appeal, Civil Division and is Head of Civil Justice.

## The Supreme Court

As well as being the final court of appeal, the Supreme Court plays an important role in the development of UK law. It is the highest court in the UK and its decisions are binding on all lower courts. In August 2009 the judges moved out of the House of Lords (where they sat as the Appellate Committee of the House of Lords) into their own building, the Middlesex Guildhall. They sat for the first time as a Supreme Court in October 2009.

Key: **A** Witness  **B** Judge  **C** Clerk of the court
**D** Lawyers for the prosecution and the defence
**E** Members of the jury  **F** Defendant

**FIGURE 8.2**  Inside a Crown Court

(Cheshire Constabulary, nd)

 ## CRIMINAL PROCEEDINGS

Just as the civil courts have rules governing the process to be followed, so the criminal courts have their own rules – Criminal Procedure Rules. The Criminal Procedure Rules are published on the Ministry of Justice's website and determine the way a criminal case is managed as it progresses through the criminal courts in England and Wales. They are made by the Criminal Procedure Rule Committee, and apply in all magistrates' courts, the Crown Court and the Court of Appeal (Criminal Division). The Criminal Procedure Rules are augmented by the Criminal Practice Directions, which are published by the Lord Chief Justice.

Proceedings start with either a person being charged with an offence or by being served with a summons to appear at the magistrates' court. A person is charged with an offence by the police after being arrested and then detained at a police station whilst the matter is investigated. The defendant will then remain in custody to appear at the next available court or may be released on bail to appear at a certain court on a given day at a certain time. If a person hasn't been arrested, or a prosecution is being brought by an agency other than the police, then a summons can be issued by a magistrates' court, directing the defendant to appear at that court on a given day at a certain time.

Where a person has been arrested by the police the CPS now has a role in determining whether that person should be charged with an offence and, if so, what offence they should be charged with. The aim of this is to ensure that the evidence has been reviewed by a lawyer and that there is a more realistic chance of a conviction. The CPS will then take over management of the case from the police; when proceedings have commenced the prosecutor will undertake the requirements of CPIA and the defence will respond accordingly.

##  GIVING EVIDENCE

As a witness you will give evidence as a matter of truth and will do so after having taken the oath or solemn affirmation. You will then be bound to tell the truth as described by the oath or affirmation – not to do so would expose you to the risk of prosecution for perjury, for which the penalty is a maximum of seven years' imprisonment. The oath is taken by those who hold religious beliefs and the witness will hold their holy book in their right hand whilst reading the words of the oath from a card. The affirmation is taken by the witness holding up their right hand and reading the words from a card.

**The Oath:** 'I swear by almighty God that the evidence I give shall be the truth, the whole truth and nothing but the truth.'

**The Solemn Affirmation:** 'I do solemnly, sincerely and truly declare and affirm that the evidence I shall give shall be the truth, the whole truth and nothing but the truth.'

## Examination-in-chief

After taking the oath or affirmation the witness will be asked to identify themselves, normally by stating their name and occupation. The advocate representing the side that has called the witness will then take the witness through their evidence as contained within their statement. In doing so, the advocate seeks to adduce testimony which supports the facts that the prosecution wish to establish to prove the case beyond a reasonable doubt. The witness will have had the opportunity to read their statement before going into the court in order to refresh their memory and the prosecutor will have a copy in front of them and will be familiar with its contents. The questions will be simple and open and will be designed to elicit from the witness the relevant evidence, for example, 'What happened next?' Some leading questions are allowed on matters which are not disputed by the defence, for example, the place and time of the incident. The prosecutor can only ask questions about the content of the witness's statement and is not entitled to draw new evidence from the witness. During the course of giving evidence exhibits may be referred to and these should be in court and available to be produced. The court will then issue its own exhibit number which will thereafter be used when referring to the exhibit. Occasionally the magistrate or judge may ask questions to clarify specific points.

## Cross-examination

For the witness, this is often seen as the most stressful part of the trial process. The cross-examination will be undertaken in such a way as to test the witness's knowledge or recollection, to test their credibility or to reveal the existence of any bias or prejudice. Leading questions can be used to do this, as well as questions that highlight evidence of earlier statements which are inconsistent with their evidence in chief.

## Re-examination

Following cross-examination the advocate who called the witness may wish to re-examine them, with the aim of mitigating any damage that was done during cross-examination. New evidence cannot be adduced during re-examination, nor can leading questions be used, but the advocate will try to maximise the positive aspects of the witness's evidence.

## Release

Following examination the prosecutor may ask the court if the witness can be released, that is to say, leave the proceedings. The witness should discuss this with the prosecutor before being called into the witness box.

The manner of giving evidence remains basically the same whatever the court, although there are some minor differences. In the County Court the judge and lawyers will be wearing suits as opposed to being robed and the courtroom is more business-like than a criminal court. There will not be examination-in-chief as such, instead you will be asked to confirm that you have provided a statement for the proceedings and that the content is true. The other side will then ask questions about those matters that are contested; re-examination may then follow.

In the magistrates' court the lawyers will normally be wearing suits but the courtroom will be more official in appearance, with a dock for the defendant and a box or stand for the witness. In the Crown Court the judge and barristers will all be robed and there is a more formal 'air' to the proceedings. Again there will be a dock for the defendant and a witness box for the witness. The prosecution barrister will be seated nearest the witness box and the defence barrister nearest the jury.

Although it is unlikely that your fraud work will require you attend a Youth Court it is worth mentioning it here, as there are some noticeable differences. The proceedings are more informal and the defendant will be addressed by their first name. The bench must comprise both male and female magistrates and members of the public are not admitted (although the press may be present).

Normally you should expect to give your evidence on only one occasion; however there are times where it will be necessary to give your evidence again:

- Retrial – where the jury is unable to reach a verdict and a completely new trial has to take place.
- Appeal – in most appeals the Court of Appeal will normally review the case by using documents and court records. However, where a witness's evidence forms grounds for the appeal that witness may be called to give their evidence to the Court of Appeal.
- Concurrent cases – you may have to give evidence in both the criminal and civil trials. If the criminal trial has taken place before the civil trial, then the outcome of that case will be binding on the civil proceedings.
- Trial within a trial – otherwise known as a voir dire – this often occurs when there is an issue about the way in which evidence has been obtained.

The jury will be asked to leave and the witness will be called into court. They will be asked to take a different oath 'I swear by Almighty God that I will answer truthfully any questions the court may ask of me' and will then give their evidence and be cross-examined. The judge will then make a ruling as to whether the evidence is admissible or not. If it is to be allowed then the jury will be recalled, the witness will take the normal oath and will give their evidence again and will be cross-examined a second time.

## Witness Safeguards and Support

The Criminal Justice and Public Order Act 1994 and the Criminal Justice and Police Act 2001 create offences of witness interference and intimidation. If an allegation of either is made then the burden of proof rests with the defendant to show that such intimidation or interference did not take place.

If there is any suspicion of such behaviour then the police should be advised as soon as possible.

Many non-professional witnesses can be daunted by the prospect of giving evidence in court. Although times have changed it is still easy for those whose day-to-day work is spent in the courtroom to forget how a witness may be feeling – after all, courts are not designed to be friendly places!

The Witness Service is established to support witnesses before, during and after a trial. They will offer support on the day of the trial but can do more to help if the witness gets in touch with them earlier – for example, organising a visit to the courtroom before the trial so that the witness knows what to expect. Make use of the Witness Service yourself if you've never been to court, or a particular court building, before.

As an ACFS you will be viewed by the court as being a 'professional witness' – you should therefore do everything you can to prepare yourself for appearing in court as a witness – remember, you can only create one first impression. If you've never been to court before try to find an opportunity to visit a court and to view a trial in progress. Find one of the ushers and explain your reason for being there – they will happily identify the best case for you to watch. It is a key principle of our criminal justice system that proceedings are open to the public.

You must remember that your primary duty is to the court – as an ACFS your responsibility is to gather and present the best possible evidence; it is for the magistrates or jury to decide on guilt. Whilst giving evidence you must therefore remain objective, honest, clear and helpful. It is not always easy to stay in control of your nerves or to avoid inadvertently using jargon. You may be unsure who to talk to or look at – the advocate asking the question, the defendant, the judge or the jury? The following points should help you to present yourself as a professional witness, who is in control and knows what they are doing.

### What to take into the witness box

The only things that you need to take into the witness box are original notes that were made at the time of the incident or as soon as reasonably practicable thereafter. You should also have the original exhibits that you produced during your statement. Taking other documents with you may lead to problems in the witness box – having your papers falling over the courtroom floor doesn't look very professional. A copy of the trial bundle will be available if you need to refer to anything in it.

### What to aim for in the witness box

Your objectives are to be professional, calm and reliable.

## Examination-in-chief

The party who calls a witness asks that witness questions. As described above, the witness will first take the oath or affirmation and will then be asked to state their name and address. You will then find the advocate that has called you already on their feet and looking at you, ready to take you through your evidence. In civil proceedings the witness may not be asked many, if any, questions during examination-in-chief.

## Cross-examination

The lawyer for the other party will ask questions of you, the professional witness. Their aim is twofold:

1. To advance their own case by eliciting testimony from you that is favourable to them and developing their own case theory by getting you to agree with certain propositions.
2. To undermine your case by limiting the effect of your testimony; this can be done by questioning your area of expertise, qualifications and length of experience; by challenging the admissibility of evidence by discrediting your testimony, questioning your methodology, the terms of reference of the investigation or your interpretation of facts; or by discrediting you as a witness (being biased or inconsistent).

## Prepare Yourself

There are lots of things that can be done to prepare yourself prior to giving evidence. You should have a detailed knowledge of the investigation and should be familiar with possible defences that may be put forward. You should re-read your statement and/or report but don't try to memorise these – you will be sure to forget something. Be familiar with other evidence such as the exhibits.

## The Procedure

Most witnesses give their evidence whilst standing but there are no rules to prevent you from sitting if this will be more comfortable. When the advocate is asking you questions, look at them as this is not only polite but will aid your understanding of what is being asked. Direct your answers to the jury or judge, not to the person who asked the question. The judge will be taking notes and will appreciate you speaking in a clear, steady voice; keep an eye on their note taking and try to keep pace with it. Court is a formal occasion and you should dress appropriately – the jury will be making subconscious assessments of you and a shabbily dressed ACFS will lead them to think that you are a shabby ACFS in your work.

If you think that you will be nervous whilst in the witness box consider researching some stress-relieving techniques beforehand. Do not be tempted to have an alcoholic drink for 'Dutch courage' or to take any drugs (prescription or otherwise) that may impair your ability. You should remain impartial throughout, keeping your evidence factual and avoiding assumptions. If interrupted or contradicted you should remain calm and not allow yourself to be drawn into an argument. On arrival at the court make yourself known to one of the ushers, so that they know that you're there.

Finally, it is worth summarising some things that you should and shouldn't do in the witness box:

1. Speak clearly, slowly, pause, breathe.
2. Speak to the decision makers.
3. Listen carefully to the questions. Ask if you need the question repeated.
4. Do use your notes/documents/photographs etc. to assist in answering questions.
5. Answer what is asked (but only what is asked).
6. Don't be biased.
7. Avoid jargon/technical terms.
8. Don't avoid answering questions.

9. Correct incorrect assertions.
10. Correct mistakes – apologise and move on. If you don't correct a mistake it will probably lead to you say something later on in your evidence that will expose the earlier mistake, which may then be viewed as you having deliberately misled the court.
11. Don't argue and don't raise your voice, even if the advocate does so.
12. Don't ask the lawyer questions
13. Don't make up things you don't know the answer to. If you don't know something, say you don't know.
14. Do stay within your knowledge/expertise, don't speculate.
15. Acknowledge professional limitations.
16. Ignore rudeness, stares, silence.
17. Do help the decision maker.

 ## REVIEW

This chapter has examined some of the history and the structure of the judicial system in England and Wales. It has identified the courts that the ACFS may be called to in order to give evidence and has described the process of bringing the defendant before those courts. The classification of offences has been explained. Finally, the chapter has reviewed the process of giving evidence and has identified some useful points to equip the ACFS so that they can present themselves as a professional witness.

 ## FURTHER INFORMATION

For further information about the court you are due to attend, visit the court and tribunal finder website: https://courttribunalfinder.service.gov.uk/courts

CHAPTER NINE

# Civil law

## CHAPTER **SUMMARY**

Knowledge of how the law is formed and developed is one of a number of foundation stones for the ACFS. This chapter will describe how the law has developed within England and Wales and examine some of the advantages and disadvantages of both the civil and criminal law systems. It will outline some of the civil law tools that are available to the ACFS when investigating fraud and when considering the recovery of money or other assets that have been obtained by the fraudster. As more public services are being contracted out, such as with the commissioning of primary healthcare services and welfare to work schemes, the ACFS can find themselves dealing with companies, both private and public limited, when investigating fraudulent activities. This chapter therefore also examines some of the more common trading entities that may be encountered and the main offences that they may commit.

**INTRODUCTION**

In simple terms the law consists of rules that generally reflect the accepted norms of society and they regulate the conduct of citizens. Laws are laid down by those in authority and are enforced by the courts and officials. If a criminal law is broken, the offender is liable to punishment. If there has been a breach of civil law there will be remedy or restitution.

The present legal system in England and Wales dates back to the twelfth century and the rapid expansion of institutions that followed the Norman Conquest in 1066. Unlike the rest of Europe where countries based themselves on Roman law, the system of English common law has developed uniquely.

The law in England and Wales may be divided into two, namely:

- Common law
- Statute law.

Civil justice in England and Wales is administered mainly by the County Courts and the High Court, with the High Court handling the more substantial and complex cases. In Scotland, the bulk of civil business is dealt with in the Sheriff Court. County Courts also handle family proceedings, such as divorce, domestic violence and matters affecting children. Proceedings are controlled by the Civil Procedure Rules, which are binding on all parties to a case and are published by the Ministry of Justice; failure by a party to comply with the rules will have an adverse effect on their case.

Most civil disputes do not go to court at all and, of those that do, most do not reach a trial having been settled before that stage is reached. This is a key feature of civil justice and is not replicated in the criminal system, although elements of 'plea bargaining' are starting to appear. One of the principles of the Civil Procedure Rules is to encourage parties to settle as much as they can before the case appears before a court. Many civil matters are dealt with through statutory or voluntary complaints procedures, or through mediation and negotiation. Arbitration is also common in commercial and building disputes. Ombudsmen have the power to determine complaints in the public sector and, on a voluntary basis, in some private sector activities – for example, banking, insurance and pensions.

A large number of tribunals exist, most dealing with cases that involve the rights of private citizens against decisions of the state in areas such as social security, income tax, mental health and also in relation to breaches of employment law. Tribunals in England and Wales deal with over one million cases a year. Successful actions taken in the civil courts can result in damages being awarded to the person pursuing the claim and the amount being awarded varies according to the circumstances of each case.

Her Majesty's Courts Service (an executive agency of the Ministry of Justice) is responsible for the administration of the civil justice system: the High Court, County Courts, the Probate Service and a number of tribunals.

 ## THE CIVIL COURTS

There are 228 County Courts in England and Wales, handling claims in contract and in tort (179 of these also deal with family issues). The majority of claims dealt with by County Courts concern the recovery and collection of debt. The next most common types of claim relate to recovery of land and personal injury. Although a primary component of the criminal justice system, magistrates' courts also have limited civil jurisdiction, such as in family matters (when they sit as a Family Proceedings Court), licensing and in relation to various miscellaneous civil orders, such as Anti-Social Behaviour Orders (although breach of an Anti-Social Behaviour Order is a criminal offence). Most County Courts are assigned at least one circuit judge and one district judge. Circuit judges generally hear cases worth over £15,000 or involving greater importance or complexity. They also hear many of the cases worth over £5000 but not over £15,000.

The next tier in the civil justice system is the High Court, which has three divisions:

- the *Queen's Bench Division*, which deals with disputes relating to contracts, general commercial matters (in a specialist Commercial Court) and breaches of duty – known as 'liability in tort' – covering claims of negligence, nuisance or defamation;
- the *Chancery Division*, which deals with disputes relating to land, wills, companies and insolvency;
- the *Family Division*, which deals with matrimonial matters, including divorce and the welfare of children.

All three divisions have an appellate jurisdiction, which means that they hear appeals from other courts, as well as hearing 'first instance' cases. Proceedings (whether for damages or for a specified sum) may not be started in the High Court unless the value of the claim is more than £100,000 unless they include a claim for damages in respect of personal injuries, and the value of the claim is £50,000

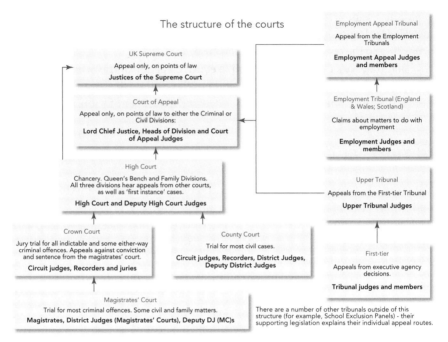

The structure of the courts

**Employment Appeal Tribunal**
Appeal from the Employment Tribunals
**Employment Appeal Judges and members**

**UK Supreme Court**
Appeal only, on points of law
**Justices of the Supreme Court**

**Employment Tribunal (England & Wales; Scotland)**
Claims about matters to do with employment
**Employment Judges and members**

**Court of Appeal**
Appeal only, on points of law to either the Criminal or Civil Divisions:
**Lord Chief Justice, Heads of Division and Court of Appeal Judges**

**High Court**
Chancery. Queen's Bench and Family Divisions. All three divisions hear appeals from other courts, as well as 'first instance' cases.
**High Court and Deputy High Court Judges**

**Upper Tribunal**
Appeals from the First-tier Tribunal
**Upper Tribunal Judges**

**Crown Court**
Jury trial for all indictable and some either-way criminal offences. Appeals against conviction and sentence from the magistrates' court.
**Circuit judges, Recorders and juries**

**County Court**
Trial for most civil cases.
**Circuit judges, Recorders, District Judges, Deputy District Judges**

**First-tier**
Appeals from executive agency decisions.
**Tribunal judges and members**

**Magistrates' Court**
Trial for most criminal offences. Some civil and family matters.
**Magistrates, District Judges (Magistrates' Courts), Deputy DJ (MC)s**

There are a number of other tribunals outside of this structure (for example, School Exclusion Panels) - their supporting legislation explains their individual appeal routes.

**FIGURE 9.1**　The structure of the courts (Civil and Criminal Justice systems)

(Courts and Tribunals Judiciary, nd)

or more (Civil Procedure Rules, Practice Direction 7A). The High Court also deals with applications for Search Orders and Freezing Injunctions (see later). Figure 9.1 outlines the hierarchy of the courts for both criminal and civil justice route.

## THE OBJECTIVES OF CIVIL LAW

The objectives of civil law are different from other types of law – in civil law there is the attempt to right a wrong, honour an agreement, or settle a dispute. If there is a victim, they get compensation, and the person who is the cause of the wrong pays, this being a civilised form of, or a legal alternative to, revenge. If it is an equity matter, there is often a pie for division and it gets allocated by a process of civil law, possibly invoking the doctrines of equity. In criminal law the objective is usually deterrence and punishment (with a view to rehabilitation). An action in criminal law does not necessarily preclude an action in civil law which may provide a mechanism for compensation to the victims of crime.

A tort is the French word for a 'wrong'. A tort is a civil wrong and involves a breach of a duty owed to someone else, as opposed to criminal wrongdoing which involves a breach of a duty owed to society. Torts are civil wrongs other than breaches of contract and certain equitable wrongs.

Civil law courts provide a forum for deciding disputes involving torts (such as accidents, negligence, and libel), contract disputes, the probate of wills, trusts, property disputes, administrative law, commercial law, and any other private matters that involve private parties and organisations, which may also include central and local government. An action by an individual (or legal equivalent) against the Attorney General is a civil matter, but when the state, being represented by the prosecutor for the Attorney General, or some other agent for the state, takes action against an individual (or legal equivalent including a government department), this is public law, not civil law. Public law includes the criminal law, as well as procedural law, constitutional law, administrative law and tax law. Civil law is based on common law and cases are decided with reference to precedents set by superior courts.

 ## ADVANTAGES AND DISADVANTAGES OF USING THE CIVIL LAW

When considering how to deal with a suspected fraud, Counter Fraud Specialists should consider using both the civil and criminal law. The civil law option should also include staff disciplinary action and referral to a regulatory body in relevant cases. Research shows that a criminal sanction is achieved in only about 0.4% of frauds (Button et al, 2012), yet the civil law is rarely used by Counter Fraud Specialists, primarily due to a lack of knowledge and understanding. It is therefore worth considering the pros and cons of the civil justice system, so that the relative benefits can be identified:

- **Lower standard of proof:** normally the standard of proof in civil matters is 'on the balance of probabilities', that is, the scales of justice have to tip slightly in one direction for the case to be proved. However, as a result of a ruling in *S and M Carpets v Cornhill Insurance* [1981] 1 Lloyd's Rep 667, 'If a defendant or plaintiff is to allege fraud, then the standard of proof is somewhat higher than that ordinarily applicable to civil matters, but not as high as that relating to criminal matters.'
- **Better chance of recovery:** civil procedure is designed to achieve redress so the courts are more familiar with this objective.

- **Can keep control of the case:** civil action allows the Counter Fraud Specialist (and his employing organisation) to have control over the direction of the case and decisions that need to be made. If the case is referred to the police for criminal action then control is also passed to them. The aim of the police will be to prosecute the offender, rather than seek recovery of the money defrauded or compensation. The final decision to prosecute will be taken by the Crown Prosecution Service, which, as well as considering the strength of the evidence, will decide whether it is in the public interest to instigate criminal proceedings.

- **More options:** the civil law provides the Counter Fraud Specialist with a range of options for dealing with the fraudster, rather than just prosecution.

- **Admissibility of evidence:** the rules relating to the admissibility of evidence in civil proceedings are more flexible than those that apply in criminal trials.

- **Speed:** Civil Procedure Rules impose time limits, meaning that things have to happen within set periods of time

- **Can settle before trial:** in recent years the civil system has moved to the trial being a tool of last resort, with procedures encouraging dispute resolution by means of mediation or arbitration. Settlement can be reached right up to the last minute, with negotiations often achieving recovery of at least a proportion of the assets stolen.

- **Costs can be recovered:** just as the civil courts are geared for recovery of losses, so they are also geared for the recovery of costs – the aim being, as far as possible, that the claimant is put back into their original position with no loss having been suffered. Increasingly, there is a move in criminal cases to recover investigation costs as compensation, although these rarely reflect the true cost of the investigation and, just as in civil cases, are subject to the defendant's ability to pay.

- **Costs!** as you will no doubt be aware, legal costs can be very high, often amounting to sums greater than the original loss. A risk when facing civil litigation is that the case will not be won and the claimant will have to bear their own costs and possibly those of the other side.

- **No rehabilitation:** in civil cases there is no opportunity for the probation service to become involved or for community penalties to be imposed.

- **No punitive element:** unless the defendant lies in court or in documents provided to the court terms of imprisonment cannot be imposed. However, the civil courts can impose exemplary damages, which are intended to punish the defendant for the wrongful act and consequently an award will 'overcompensate' the victim. An example can be seen in *AXA v Jensen*

(Birmingham County Court) 10 November 2008, where exemplary damages of £4000 were awarded.

▪ **We have to do the work:** the investigation and subsequent case management will have to be undertaken by the Counter Fraud Specialist where civil action is undertaken. However, often when a case is referred to the police much investigative work is still carried out by the organisation that has referred the case.

▪ **Not as good a deterrent as a criminal prosecution:** a criminal conviction is seen by many as the ultimate penalty for fraud. If a criminal conviction does not follow, this can often be viewed as 'he got away with it', despite the fraudster losing his job, pension, house or other assets. A civil judgment is not a conviction and does not lead to a criminal record. It can, however, pose problems for the individual concerned as the obtaining of credit or insurance may become difficult and expensive.

 ## CIVIL LAW TOOLS

### Injunctions

An injunction is an equitable remedy in the form of a court order, whereby a party is required to do, or to refrain from doing, certain acts. The party that fails to adhere to the injunction faces penalties and may have to pay damages or accept sanctions for failing to follow the court's order. In some cases, breaches of injunctions are considered serious and may result in imprisonment.

### Freezing Orders

These are usually applied for before proceedings are issued and when the applicant fears that the respondent will dispose of or dissipate its assets before judgment can be obtained and enforced. It is only possible to freeze those assets over which a judgment can be attached – money held in bank accounts, land, vehicles, shares, bonds and other financial instruments. They can apply to assets held within England and Wales or to assets held overseas. Onerous duties are imposed on the claimant regarding the strength of evidence and there has to be a cross-undertaking in damages (that is, an agreement to pay any damages that the respondent sustains by reason of the freezing order if it later turns out that the order should not have been granted). As a result they can be costly to obtain and are potentially high risk, so are appropriate for 'high value' cases only and should be considered in the early stages of an investigation when the risk of dissipation is greatest.

## Search Orders

These are effectively civil search warrants and are obtained *ex parte* from the High Court (that is, the other side will be unaware of the application). They allow for the securing of evidence when there is reason to believe that material will be destroyed if the respondent becomes aware of the investigation; this must be a genuine belief, preferably supported by some evidence. They are comparable in seriousness to freezing orders in that onerous duties are imposed on the claimant; the same considerations also apply as far as timing is concerned. Items to be sought must be clearly listed in the application and on the order – if not listed they cannot be seized. Search orders are served and supervised by an independent solicitor; the respondent is allowed to obtain legal advice but cannot deny entry whilst waiting to receive such advice. Those undertaking the search must provide a written record of everything seized to the respondent.

## Non-compliance

In the case of non-compliance with any of the above the circumstances can be brought before the court that issued the order, which might decide on one of the following sanctions:

- Imprisonment and/or fine
- Seizure of assets
- Subjecting the respondent to oral examination
- Obtaining a security to ensure future good behaviour
- Imposing a remedy at the respondent's own expense.

## Insolvency and Bankruptcy

Insolvency is the inability of a business to meet its liabilities and pay debts when they are due (a civil court judgment constitutes a debt), whereas bankruptcy is the state of one who is declared unable to pay current debts by a court. Therefore insolvency applies to companies, bankruptcy to individuals. Both processes are governed by Insolvency Act 1986 as amended by the Enterprise Act 2002.

Insolvency involves Liquidators and Receivers appointed by creditors or the debtor company and can result in the winding up of company (it will cease to exist as a legal entity) and the liquidation of its assets among creditors. Insolvency can be used unscrupulously by some companies, where the defaulting company is 'wound up' and then starts trading the following day under the guise of a completely new company, trading from the same premises and being run by the same directors. These are often known as 'phoenix companies' ('risen from the ashes') and the process is perfectly lawful.

Bankruptcy can be voluntary or alternatively applied for by a creditor. If this is the case there must be an undisputed, unsecured debt owed in excess of £750 (a judgment is classed as 'undisputed'). They are administered by the Official Receiver as Trustee in Bankruptcy, being appointed after an order is granted by a court. The bankrupt must submit to interview by the Official Receiver to identify their assets and financial affairs. The disclosure of assets is subject to perjury law, so lying about assets can result in criminal proceedings. Being made bankrupt imposes restrictions on the debtor regarding the obtaining of credit, having bank accounts and other commercial activities. For some generations great stigma is attached to being made bankrupt but for other people they are seen as an easy way out of significant debt. Since 2004 a bankruptcy order is considered discharged after one year (down from three) though they can be extended up to 15 years by means of a Bankruptcy Restriction Order for 'bad bankrupts', for example, fraudsters.

## Individual Voluntary Arrangement (IVA)

These are also governed by the Insolvency Act 1986 and are an alternative to bankruptcy, avoiding the more severe consequences; they have been described as 'Bankruptcy Lite'. Essentially they are a compromise agreement to repay debt, usually a proportion thereof, over an agreed period of time. Arrangements are enforceable by the courts but once implemented a debtor is protected from the imposition of other methods unless the arrangement is breached. They are supervised by an Insolvency Practitioner.

## Judgment and Enforcements

Judgment is the most common method of civil recovery and leads to several methods of enforcement. Proceedings are commenced by submitting a 'claim form' (formerly a writ) to the court providing the particulars of claim, the amount (loss) and the allegation (the circumstances that led to the debt). Any prior defendant admissions, confessions or findings of guilt (dismissal, formal caution or conviction) are important evidence. Once the claim is served the defendant has 14 days to formally acknowledge and a further 14 days to serve their defence (a 'bare denial' defence is no longer allowed under the Civil Procedure Rules). The defence must be verified by way of a statement containing a 'Statement of Truth':

Civil Procedure Rule 32.14
Proceedings for contempt of court may be brought against a person if he makes, or causes to be made, a false statement in a document verified by a statement of truth without an honest belief in its truth.

The sanction for contempt of court is up to two years' imprisonment or an unlimited fine. There is also the potential for perjury where the debtor lies during cross-examination in court.

## Judgment

Default judgment can be obtained if there is no acknowledgement of the claim or there is no defence served within the prescribed time limit. Summary judgment can be obtained after the time limit if the claimant can persuade the court that the defendant has no realistic prospect of successfully defending the claim or there is no compelling reason why the matter should be disposed of by trial ('slam dunk evidence'). Otherwise the case will go to trial.

Once judgment has been obtained it can be enforced against the defendant's assets – there is a six-year time limit. If there is an immediate risk of asset dissipation a post-judgment freezing order can be applied for (unlike pre-judgment freezing orders there is no requirement for a claimant's cross-undertaking in damages). A 'writ of fi fa' or Warrant of Execution entitles the Sheriff (High Court) or Bailiff (County Court) to seize a debtor's property in lieu of the judgment debt. Some property is excluded for the purposes of trade and basic domestic needs.

Other options available for recovery post-judgment are:

- Third party debt order – enables a creditor to freeze money owed by a third party to the judgment debtor;
- Charging order, stop order and stop notice – obtained against a debtor's property, for example, investments, shares, bonds and real estate;
- Attachment of earnings order – compels a debtor's employer to pay a specified sum to the judgment debtor;
- Insolvency/bankruptcy.

 **REGULATORY SANCTIONS**

A further option worth consideration by an ACFS is that of a regulatory sanction, which would be applicable if the perpetrator of the fraud is a professional. This is a sanction that is frequently available to regulators through their relevant legislation (Macrory, 2006: 19). The policy of parallel sanctions, which involves the pursuit of criminal or civil proceedings, disciplinary action and seeking to have the fraudster removed from a professional register where a licence to practice has been issued is one that has been adopted by the NHS for a number of years. Guidance issued to counter fraud practitioners recommends that 'working in tandem' with the relevant professional regulatory body can 'prevent a practitioner from practising on either an interim basis pending serious complaints being investigated or a permanent basis where the facts are very clear' (NHS Counter Fraud Service, 2007: 30). In the context of healthcare provision, these professional bodies would include the General Medical Council, General Dental Council, General Optical Council, Nursing and Midwifery Council, General Pharmaceutical Council and the Health Professions Council (NHS Protect, 2013: 4).

## Dentist struck off for dishonesty, false accounting and fraud

A dentist has been struck off by the General Dental Council (GDC) following a public hearing.

The allegations against Mr X were heard by the GDC's Professional Conduct Committee. The charges he faced were that on or about 19 July 2012 he was convicted of the following criminal offences:

> 20 counts of False Accounting, contrary to Section 17(1)(a) and (2) of the Theft Act 1968;
> 1 count of Evasion of a Liability by Deception, contrary to Section 2(1)(c) of the Theft Act 1968;
> 1 count of Fraud, contrary to Section 1 of the Fraud Act 2006.

In making its decision the Committee noted that: 'Mr X's actions amount to a course of serious dishonest conduct which took place over a period of about 18 months and occurred in the context of his professional practice. He has not engaged with these proceedings and so the Committee has not been able to establish whether he has any insight, has done anything to remediate his actions or is now contrite. The Committee is in no doubt that criminal convictions for false accounting, deception and fraud would not in any event be easily remedied in the light of the effect such conduct will have had on the public's confidence in the profession.'

(General Dental Council, 2013)

The imposition of regulatory sanctions can also be applied to a variety of professionals outside the healthcare system including barristers, solicitors, accountants and even veterinary surgeons, as the following case study illustrates.

When considering the importance of regulatory sanctions it is worth considering the criminological debate relating to what punishment sets out to achieve. For example, Croall (2003) observes that crime control gives emphasis to punishment for the purposes of deterrence and incapacitation as well as to 'underline society's disapproval' (p. 46). Similarly, the use of a regulatory

## Vet convicted of fraud struck off

A vet has been removed from the register of the Royal College of Veterinary Surgeons (RCVS) following a Crown Court conviction for fraud.

The college's disciplinary committee ruled on 24 July that Mr X was unfit to practise veterinary surgery following his conviction. During a one-day hearing, the Committee heard that while working as a veterinary surgeon, Mr X abused his position by defrauding insurance companies of around £10,000 with fictitious claims for veterinary treatment on non-existent pets.

Following an investigation by the City of London Police's Insurance Fraud Enforcement Department (IFED), Mr X was convicted on five counts of fraud by false representation on 21 February 2013 at the Old Bailey in London, and later sentenced to eight months' imprisonment, suspended for two years, and 200 hours of unpaid community work. He was also ordered to pay just over £10,000 in compensation and costs.

Mr X left the UK shortly after his sentencing and the committee hearing proceeded in his absence, on the basis that he was deliberately avoiding the disciplinary proceedings.

It found that the five counts of fraud were deliberate crimes of dishonesty, committed over a significant period of time and for significant financial gain, which abused the trust that the insurers placed in him as a professional. Committee chair said: 'The committee has no real confidence that there is no significant risk of repeat behaviour from the Respondent. His conduct subsequent to the criminal proceedings gives it no confidence that he has reformed himself to the extent that he will in the foreseeable future be fit to return to practice. So far from satisfactorily completing his criminal sentence, it appears that the Respondent has deliberately gone abroad to avoid doing so.'

(Haslers, 2013)

sanction will also achieve these objectives. The withdrawal of a licence to practice may act as a deterrent to some potential fraudsters, thus forming a component of an organisation's counter fraud strategy. Moreover, by ensuring that a fraudster has their licence to practice revoked, or at least suspended until the full facts of the case are established, it will result in incapacitation, thus removing the opportunity to commit further fraudulent transactions.

## INNOVATIVE SANCTIONS

A further consideration for an ACFS working within a relevant industry is to ensure that a fraudster's details are recorded on any industry based fraud register. For example, the Insurance Fraud Register which is funded by the Association of British Insurers and operated by Insurance Fraud Bureau. The register will include information on persons found to have made a fraudulent insurance claim or acted in some other way to facilitate insurance fraud. The criteria for placement on the register have not, at the time of writing, been published, but will include many who have not been convicted in the criminal courts. Access to the register will only be for members, and arguably is the equivalent of the Violent and Sexual Offender Register for insurance fraudsters. There will be significant implications for those placed upon it, as they will find it difficult to take out new insurance, or to renew existing policies. They may also experience difficulties when trying to secure other financial products such as loans or mortgages.

Another example is the CIFAS (Credit Industry Fraud Avoidance System) staff fraud database which seeks to prevent individuals dismissed for committing fraud and theft from moving unchallenged to a new and unsuspecting employer. Three hundred public and private sector organisations share fraud information through CIFAS to prevent and detect fraud and financial crime. They include those from the banking, grant giving, credit card, asset finance, retail credit, mail order and online retail, insurance, savings, telecommunications, factoring, share dealing, vetting agencies, contact centre and insurance sectors (CIFAS, nd).

## EXAMPLES OF CIVIL CASE LAW

The following cases show how fraud is dealt with by the civil courts and demonstrate how the courts' attitude to fraud has developed over the years.

## Derry v Peek [1889] LR 14 App Cas 337

This is the benchmark case for defining fraud in the civil courts. It established the three elements that must be present for the tort of deceit. Civil fraud can be shown to have happened when:

1. A false representation has been made.
2. The person making the representation did so knowingly without belief in its truth; or recklessly or careless as to whether it was true or false.
3. As a result a party suffered a loss.

## Orakpo v Barclays Insurance Services CA [1995] LRLR 443, CA

Mr Orakpo was owner of a bed-sit that suffered damage following ingress of water during a severe storm; as a result the tenants had to move out. He claimed the following from his insurance company – storm damage of £39,093, dry rot repairs (as a result of the damp) of £22,805 and loss of rent of £77,233. Investigation by the insurers found that only 3 of 13 bedsits were occupied prior to the storm and that the dry rot was known to Orakpo before the policy was taken out. As a result his claim was rejected by the court with the following comment: '. . . if the insured knows that if he is fraudulent, at least to a substantial extent, he will recover nothing even if his claim in part is good . . .'

## Galloway v Guardian Royal Exchange (UK) [1999] Lloyd's Rep IR 209

Galloway submitted a claim to his insurers, following a burglary at his home, for £18,133.94. The loss included a computer allegedly worth £2000. It transpired that the computer receipt submitted by Galloway as proof of existence and ownership was false (Galloway was convicted of attempting to obtain money by deception) but he still pursued the full loss in his claim. The judge stated '. . . size is irrelevant . . .' (referring to the part of the claim that is fraudulent) '. . . the making of dishonest claims has become all too common. There seems to be a widespread belief that insurance companies are fair game and that defrauding them is not morally reprehensible. The rule may appear to be somewhat harsh, but is in my opinion a necessary and salutary rule, which deserves to be better known to the public . . .'

## Direct Line v Khan and Another [2001] EWCA Civ 1794

This is another insurance fraud where Mr and Mrs Khan were joint policy holders on a domestic insurance policy. The property caught fire and they made a claim for repairs to the fire damage of £61,000; they also claimed for alternative accommodation (to the value of £8000) whilst their home was repaired. It was discovered that this accommodation was actually owned by Mr Khan and, as a result, there was no liability to pay to use it; he furnished false rental agreement and receipts for rent. The whole claim was declined by the insurers and recovery sought for interim payments that had already been made. The judge upheld the recovery claim saying '. . . the fraud of the first defendant (Mr Khan) would taint the whole policy. If policyholders seek to top up their honest claims by adding bogus claims they are at peril of losing everything . . .'

 **COMPANY LAW**

The word 'company' can be misused when referring to trading entities – the dictionary defines it as 'a trading enterprise' – so it is worth examining the different types of business entity that might be encountered when investigating fraud.

### Sole Trader

Often a 'one man band', a sole trader is the most simple and also the most unregulated form of trading entity. Anyone can set up a business and start trading by themselves, perhaps using a name for the business (trading as . . .), or even employ people to work for them. The person retains 100% control of their business but conversely also carries 100% liability for the debts and actions of the business. There is no requirement to keep documents (other than for tax purposes) or to produce documents.

### Partnership

'Partnership is the relation which subsists between persons carrying on a business in common with a view of profit' (Partnership Act 1890, s. 1(1)). A minimum of two people is required for a partnership but there is no maximum (take John Lewis Partnership, for example). This form of entity is required in some professions before they can start trading (for example, solicitors and accountants). There is no difference between the assets of the partnership and those of individual partners so, as with sole traders, any of the partners can be pursued for the debts of the partnership. Partners are accountable to each other and so must agree on decisions affecting the way in which the business operates. They are also liable for decisions made by each other and must bear the consequences of those decisions, that is, if partner A makes an error and the partnership is sued, then partner B is equally liable. As with the case of sole traders, there is little regulation attached to a partnership with no requirement to file accounts or documents. The agreement to operate in partnership does not even have to be made in writing, although it is best practice to do so.

The Limited Liability Partnerships Act 2000 allows professions who have to trade by means of a partnership to create a 'limited liability partnership' (LLP), which allows them to restrict their liability for general trading debts but not their individual liability for negligence, so that the interests of their clients are protected.

## Private Limited Company (Ltd)

This is the most common trading entity and is subject to most company law. The company is created by a process of incorporation and must be registered with the Registrar of Companies at Companies House. Incorporation of a company creates it as a separate legal identity, apart from its owners. As a general rule, therefore, the owners are not liable for debts of the company, and are said to enjoy 'limited liability', restricted to the amount of shares owned, for example, if S owns 25 50p shares his liability will be limited to £12.50. Most limited companies are owned by the 'members' who are usually referred to as shareholders; control of the company sits with the members and one share carries one vote on decisions that affect the company. Day-to-day management of the company sits with the directors, all of whom must be registered as such with Companies House; it is quite common for directors to also be shareholders. Shares in a Private Limited Company cannot be publicly traded (on the stock exchange) and the primary legislation that governs limited companies is contained within the Companies Act 2006. This imposes considerable accountability and regulation, requiring companies to hold regular meetings, to keep a series of registers (such as registers of members and directors) and to file certain documents with the Registrar, such as accounts (which will outline the financial position of a company) and an Annual Return (which provides a snapshot of the company's shareholders, directors and finances). Documents filed at Companies House are generally held to be public documents and copies may be obtained on application (for which a nominal fee will be charged).

## Public Limited Company (PLC)

A Public Limited Company is the largest and most complex trading structure. It is also registered with the Registrar of Companies and many Public Limited Companies start as Private Limited Companies, changing their status later on as the business grows. The key difference between the two is that the shares of a Public Limited Company are traded publicly, which means that the company can raise large sums of money by selling shares to members of the public. Another difference is that a Public Limited Company must have a minimum of £50,000 in capital, whereas a Private Limited Company has no minimum capital requirement. The Companies Act 2006 places a higher burden of accountability and regulation on Public Limited Companies, restricting the freedom of the directors and requiring greater disclosure of information. As with Private Limited Companies, the shareholders of a Public Limited Company are limited in their liability for the debts of the company and debtors cannot pursue their personal assets beyond this liability. Public Limited Companies that wish to trade their shares are listed on the London Stock Exchange and are often known as 'listed companies'. Listing attracts additional regulation and scrutiny from the Exchange, so affording investors some reassurance that the company is bona fide.

 **CORPORATE PERSONALITY**

As has been identified above, the assets of limited companies, both private and public, are separate from the assets of the owners. This is because a limited company is a separate legal entity (see *Salomon v Salomon and Co.* (1897)) which separates assets of the company and shareholders. It also means that a limited company can sue and be sued and enter into contracts (such as a contract of insurance, for example); it will continue to function after the death of a shareholder and can own other companies (group and parent) or be owned by another company (subsidiary).

This separation of liabilities between the company and its members is recognised in law and is known as the 'veil of incorporation'. Very occasionally, the courts are prepared to ignore the barrier between the two and will hold members personally liable for the debts of the company – this is known as 'lifting the veil' – and provisions to do this are contained in statute and common law. The aim of these provisions is to prevent the protection of limited liability offered by incorporation being used to perpetrate fraud or other wrongdoing. When the veil is lifted it will only be partially lifted, so that only those who caused the wrongdoing will become liable (for example, directors).

Two of the statutory occasions where the veil can be lifted are when 'fraudulent trading' or 'wrongful trading' has taken place.

## Fraudulent Trading

Section 993 Companies Act 2006 creates the offence of Fraudulent Trading:

Section 993 – Fraudulent trading
1. If any business of a company is carried on with intent to defraud creditors of the company or creditors of any other person, or for any fraudulent purpose, every person who is knowingly a party to the carrying on of the business in that manner commits an offence.
2. This applies whether or not the company has been, or is in the course of being, wound up.
3. A person guilty of an offence under this section is liable—
   (a) on conviction on indictment, to imprisonment for a term not exceeding ten years or a fine (or both);
   (b) on summary conviction—
      (i) in England and Wales, to imprisonment for a term not exceeding twelve months or a fine not exceeding the statutory maximum (or both);
      (ii) in Scotland or Northern Ireland, to imprisonment for a term not exceeding six months or a fine not exceeding the statutory maximum (or both).

As can be seen, the offence (and penalty) is reflected by s. 9 Fraud Act 2006 – Participating in fraudulent business carried on by sole trader etc., which captures fraudulent trading committed by trading entities that aren't limited companies. The Insolvency Act 1986 (s. 213) allows the veil to be lifted if, during the course of winding up the company, it appears that fraudulent trading had taken place.

## Wrongful Trading

Section 214 Insolvency Act 1986 creates a sanction where wrongful trading has taken place:

Section 214 – Wrongful trading
1.  Subject to subsection (3) below, if in the course of the winding up of a company it appears that subsection (2) of this section applies in relation to a person who is or has been a director of the company, the court, on the application of the liquidator, may declare that that person is to be liable to make such contribution (if any) to the company's assets as the court thinks proper.
2.  This subsection applies in relation to a person if —
    (a)  the company has gone into insolvent liquidation,
    (b)  at some time before the commencement of the winding up of the company, that person knew or ought to have concluded that there was no reasonable prospect that the company would avoid going into insolvent liquidation, and
    (c)  that person was a director of the company at that time;

A key feature of this is not just what the director actually knew, but what he should have known had he been a reasonable director. So, the court can consider what a reasonable company director in that situation should have done.

**Common law** – the courts will lift the veil where it is held that the company has been used as a 'sham' or 'façade' to hide some dishonest purpose. This would be the case where there has been a 'long firm' fraud. Similarly, should a company decide to enter into a risky venture it may decide to create a subsidiary company, with the aim that should the subsidiary fail then the assets of the parent company would be safe. The courts have been prepared to treat the parent and subsidiary as one and the same, although their approach has not been consistent.

 **REVIEW**

This chapter has examined the civil law and some of the tools that it offers the Accredited Counter Fraud Specialist when investigating fraud. These are often overlooked during the course of an investigation, with focus being solely on a criminal sanction. For the ACFS working within the corporate world, however, often the primary objective of the employer or client is one of recovery, which is where knowledge of the civil law is essential. The content of this chapter has therefore been designed to give the ACFS an overview of the civil system and the tools that it offers when dealing with fraud. It has also provided a brief explanation of the more common trading entities that might be encountered and how these are regulated.

 **FURTHER READING**

Button, M., Lewis, C., Shepherd, D., et al (2012) *Fraud and Punishment: Enhancing Deterrence through More Effective Sanctions.* Portsmouth: Centre for Counter Fraud Studies, University of Portsmouth.

CHAPTER TEN

# Resource compendium

 **INTRODUCTION**

This chapter provides links to the most important bodies, websites and operational guidance for the Counter Fraud Specialist. Copies of the relevant templates, forms and aide memoires that an ACFS will require during the course of the investigation are also included.

 **REGULATORY BODIES**

Where a fraudster holds a professional status, there might also be opportunities to sanction them through their regulatory bodies. Some of the most significant are listed below.

### Accountants and Actuaries

Accountants and Actuaries: **Accountancy and Actuarial Discipline Board**
https://www.frc.org.uk/About-the-FRC/FRC-structure/Former-FRC-structure/
Accountancy-and-Actuarial-Discipline-Board.aspx

## Aviation

Aviation related occupations: **Civil Aviation Authority** http://www.caa.co.uk/

## Financial

Various financial services related occupations **Financial Conduct Authority** http://www.fca.org.uk/firms/being-regulated/enforcement

## Gambling

Gambling occupations: **Gambling Commission** http://www.gamblingcommission.gov.uk/

## Lawyers

Solicitors: **Solicitors Regulation Authority** http://www.sra.org.uk/home/home.page and **Legal Ombudsman** http://www.legalombudsman.org.uk/consumer/index.html

Barristers: **Bar Standards Board** https://www.barstandardsboard.org.uk/complaints-and-professional-conduct/concerns-about-a-barrister/

## Medical and Care Related

Chiropractors: **General Chiropractors Council** http://www.gcc-uk.org/

Dentists: **General Dental Council** http://www.gdcuk.org/Pages/default.aspx

Doctors: **General Medical Council** http://www.gmc-uk.org/

Nurses and Midwifes: **Nursing and Midwifery Council** http://www.nmc-uk.org/

Optometrists and Dispensing Opticians: **General Optical Council** http://www.optical.org/

Osteopaths: **General Osteopath Council** http://www.osteopathy.org.uk/

Pharmacists and Pharmacy technicians: General Pharmaceutical Council http://www.pharmacyregulation.org/

Arts therapists, biomedical scientists, chiropodists/podiatrists, clinical scientists, dieticians, hearing aid dispensers, occupational therapists, operating department practitioners, orthoptists, paramedics, physiotherapists, practitioner psychologists, prosthetists/orthotists, radiographers, social workers in England and speech and language therapists: **Health and Care Professions Council** http://www.hcpc-uk.org/

Social care workers, qualified social workers, and social work students on approved degree courses in Wales: **Care Council for Wales** http://www.ccwales.org.uk/

Social care workers, qualified social workers, and social work students on approved degree courses in Northern Ireland: **Northern Ireland Social Care Council** http://www.niscc.info/

### Surveyors

Surveyors: **Royal Institute of Chartered Surveyors** http://www.rics.org/uk/regulation/complaints/

### Teaching

Teachers (England): **National College for Teaching and Leadership:** https://www.education.gov.uk/help/contactus/nctl

Teachers (Scotland): **General Teaching Council for Scotland** http://www.gtcs.org.uk/home/home.aspx

Teachers (Wales): **General Teaching Council for Wales** http://www.gtcw.org.uk/gtcw/index.php?lang=en

### Vets

Vets: **Royal College of Veterinary Surgeons** http://www.rcvs.org.uk/home/

### Other

For a list of government regulators and related bodies go to https://www.gov.uk/government/organisations and professional bodies http://www.totalprofessions.com/profession-finder

 ## INVESTIGATIVE AND ENFORCEMENT BODIES

The City of London Police is the most important body in the criminal investigation of fraud as the national lead police force and hosting a number of specialist units related to fraud and economic crime: http://www.cityoflondon.police.uk/Pages/default.aspx

For the most serious frauds and related crimes the relevant body is the Serious Fraud Office: www.sfo.gov.uk

Frauds perpetrated by organised criminals are the responsibility of the National Crime Agency: http://www.nationalcrimeagency.gov.uk/

The NHS has its own service which co-ordinates fraud and security called NHS Protect: http://www.nhsbsa.nhs.uk/Protect.aspx

Some frauds related to companies are the responsibility of Companies Investigation: http://www.bis.gov.uk/insolvency/Companies/company–investigation

Frauds and other financial related deviance are often the responsibility of the Financial Conduct Authority Enforcement: http://www.fca.org.uk/firms/being-regulated/enforcement

For insurance fraud there is an industry funded unit within the City of London Police called the Insurance Fraud Enforcement Directorate and there is also another important industry funded body, The Insurance Fraud Bureau: http://www.insurancefraudbureau.org/

## MAJOR FRAUD REPORT RECEIVING BODIES

All Fraud Via Action Fraud: www.actionfraud.police.uk/report_fraud

Anonymous General Reporting: https://crimestoppers-uk.org/

Benefits Fraud: https://www.gov.uk/report-benefit-fraud

Tax Fraud: http://www.hmrc.gov.uk/reportingfraud/

Insurance Fraud: https://www.insurancefraudbureau.org/report/

NHS Fraud and Corruption: https://www.reportnhsfraud.nhs.uk/

Share/Boiler Room Fraud: http://www.fca.org.uk/consumers/scams/investment-scams/share-fraud-and-boiler-room-scams/reporting-form

EU Related Fraud: http://ec.europa.eu/anti_fraud/investigations/report-fraud/index_en.htm

## LEGAL PROSECUTING BODIES

The main prosecution body in England and Wales is the Crown Prosecution Service and they have a specialist fraud division: http://www.cps.gov.uk/your_cps/our_organisation/cfg/ The Serious Fraud Office also has this role for the most serious economic crime.

In Scotland the responsibility is with the Crown Office and Procurator Fiscal Service: http://www.copfs.gov.uk/

In Northern Ireland it is the Public Prosecution Service: http://www.ppsni .gov.uk/About-the-PPS-5014.html

In England and Wales private prosecutions are also possible, and there are some firms of solicitors which specialise in this, for example EdmondsMarshallMcMahon: http://www.emmlegal.com/

 ## IMPORTANT COUNTER FRAUD/CORRUPTION BODIES

CIFAS provides a range of services which can be used to help prevent fraud based upon databases of known fraudsters: http://www.cifas.org.uk/

Public Concern at Work provides a variety of whistleblowing services to organisations: http://www.pcaw.org.uk/

Transparency International is a global body with an interest in corruption which offers extensive resources and research: http://www.transparency.org/ research/gcr

 ## REPRESENTATIVE BODIES

There are a small number of organisations which represent Counter Fraud Specialists and investigators.

The Institute of Counter Fraud Specialists is purely dedicated to Counter Fraud Specialists: http://www.icfs.org.uk/

The American organisation, the Association of Certified Fraud Examiners (ACFE), is the largest body in the world: http://www.acfe.com/ and also has an active UK Chapter: http://www.acfeuk.co.uk/

Insurance fraud investigators also have their own group: Insurance Fraud Investigators Group: http://www.ifig.org/

Local government fraud investigators are represented by the Local Authority Fraud Investigation Officers Group: http://www.laiog.org/

 ## FRAUD FORUMS

There are a variety of fraud forums which bring together counter fraud professionals to share best practice and knowledge to enhance the fight against fraud. Some of these are geographically based, although unfortunately not all of the

UK is covered with active forums. There are also forums which focus upon a specific type of fraud or group. All of these are listed below.

### Regional

Eastern Fraud Forum: http://www.easternfraudforum.co.uk/
London Fraud Forum: http://www.londonfraudforum.co.uk/
Midlands Fraud Forum: http://www.midlandsfraudforum.co.uk/
North East Fraud Forum: http://www.northeastfraudforum.co.uk/
South West Fraud Forum: http://www.southwestfraudforum.co.uk/
Yorkshire and Humber Fraud Forum: http://www.yhff.co.uk/
Wales Fraud Forum: http://www.walesfraudforum.com/

### Sector

Telecommunications UK Fraud Forum: http://www.tuff.co.uk/home.asp
Tenancy Fraud Forum: http://www.tenancyfraudforum.org.uk/

### Women

Fraud Women's Network: http://www.fraudwomensnetwork.com/

### Other Forum-like Bodies

Financial Fraud Action UK co-ordinates the financial services sector response to fraud: http://www.financialfraudaction.org.uk/

The National Anti-Fraud Network (NAFN) exists to support its members in protecting the public interest. It is the largest shared service in the country – managed by, and for the benefit of, its members and can provide useful access to information: www.nafn.gov.uk

The Housing Internal Audit Forum aims to share best practice in governance and control between internal audit services within the social housing sector through its best practice guides, member meetings and its discussion forum. Its membership includes both in-house and contracted-out internal audit services: www.hiaf.org.uk

 **TRAINING AND EDUCATION**

The Counter Fraud Professional Accreditation Board oversees the main counter fraud qualifications in the UK and maintains a list of approved providers: www.port.ac.uk/cfpab

The best place to look for further information about fraud is the website of the Centre for Counter Fraud Studies at University of Portsmouth: www.port.ac.uk/ccfs

The City of London Police also operates a fraud academy offering a wide range of courses: http://www.cityoflondon.police.uk/advice-and-support/fraud-and-economic-crime/fraud-training-academy/Pages/default.aspx

BDO also offer a wide range of fraud related training courses: http://www.bdo.co.uk/services/forensic-accounting/fraud-and-financial-investigations/counter-fraud-services

 ## RESEARCH ON COUNTER FRAUD

The Fraud Hub provides access to a very wide range of research publications relevant to the Counter Fraud Specialist: http://fraudhub.port.ac.uk/ but you will need to register at: http://www.port.ac.uk/centre-for-counter-fraud-studies/fraud-and-corruption-hub/register/

The Fraud Advisory Panel offers a wide range of advice and research for fraud specialists and also publishes research and guidance: https://www.fraudadvisorypanel.org/

There are also a number of publishers specialising in fraud related publications:

Wiley: http://eu.wiley.com/WileyCDA/
Gower/Ashgate: http://www.ashgate.com/default.aspx?page=295
Palgrave: http://www.palgrave.com/home/index.asp

 ## IMPORTANT ORGANISATIONS FOR INVESTIGATORS

The Information Commissioners Office (ICO) oversees data protection and there is a wide range of useful information at their website: http://ico.org.uk/

Regarding surveillance an important body is the Office of Surveillance Commissioners: https://osc.independent.gov.uk/

For all criminal investigators the College of Policing holds lots of useful information related to fraud investigation: http://www.college.police.uk/

 ## USEFUL WEBSITES

There are a wide range of websites which provide the basis to secure information for investigations and many of these are also free. The most comprehensive

list can be found at the address below where many of the following have been drawn from: http://www.uk-osint.net/favorites.html

## Companies and Directors

www.companieshouse.gov.uk – basic company information; directors; directors' information; and disqualified directors.

www.sec.gov – database of companies registered in the US.

www.icpcredit.com – international credit status reports on registered companies.

www.creditcheck.uk.com – a useful database of County Court judgments issued against companies.

## Courts and Legal Information

www.courtnewsuk.co.uk – access to a vast database; comprehensive court and tribunal diary available.

www.hmcourts-service.gov.uk – this site lists all the vexatious litigants and the date the order was made.

www.casetrack.com – access to a vast database of court and tribunal judgments.

www.courtserve.net – daily court lists available.

www.trustonline.org.uk – a database containing details of High Court judgments, magistrates' court fines defaults and tribunal awards.

## Credit Reference

www.uk.equifax.com – UK commercial and consumer credit data.

www.uk.experian.com – UK commercial and consumer credit data.

www.dbai.dnb.com – UK commercial and consumer credit data.

www.trustonline.org.uk – a database containing details of CCJs, Administration Orders and CSA Liability Orders.

www.checkmyarea.com – to search any postcode to see geo-demographic data.

www.insolvency.gov.uk – searchable register of current bankruptcies and Individual Voluntary Arrangements held by the Insolvency Service for England and Wales.

## Electoral Roll

www.192.com – name and address databases.

www.eroll.co.uk – name and address databases.

www.tracesmart.co.uk – name and address databases, with a few extra services.

www.theukelectoralroll.co.uk – name and address databases, with a few extra services.

## Image Search

www.tineye.com – a reverse image search engine, useful for linking images on social networking sites.

## Newspaper Databases

www.factiva.com – newspaper database.

www.highbeam.com – newspaper database.

www.lexisnexis.com – newspaper database.

www.allyoucanread.com – links to newspapers around the world.

www.newseum.org – newspapers from cities from around the world.

## People Search

www.yasni.co.uk – people search site, very UK focused.

www.pipl.com – a comprehensive people search engine.

www.wink.com – a search engine for individuals by name, location and interests.

www.yoname.com – check an individual against a number of the most popular social networking sites.

www.searchirc.com – check a name or nickname against a number of chat rooms and other sites.

www.123people.com – 123people is a search engine that searches just for people, checking documents, social networking groups and directories.

www.peekyou.com – PeekYou searches for people on various social networking sites, groups and directories.

www.spokeo.com – Spokeo searches for people on various social networking sites, groups and directories.

www.namechk.com – check to see if a username is used at dozens of popular social networking and social bookmarking sites.

## Property

www.voa.gov.uk – searchable database of the Valuation Office, listing all residential and business properties in England and Wales. There is also a list of certain residential rental properties.

www.landregisteronline.gov.uk – ownership database for properties in England and Wales.

## Telephone

www.infobel.com – worldwide telephone directories.

www.phonebooks.com – worldwide telephone directories.

www.btexchanges.com – BT directory enquiries in the UK.

www.ukphonebook.com – UK directory enquiries and other UK databases.

www.phonepayplus.org.uk – the premium rate services regulator, with a database for checking premium rate numbers.

www.whocallsme.com – if you received a strange call, most likely you are not the only one. Search for this phone number to see the reports of others.

www.saynoto0870.com – non-geographical alternative telephone numbers for companies.

www.numberingplans.com – some useful online tools linked to mobile phones.

www.gsmarena.com – mobile terms glossary and links to phone manufacturers, where each phones capabilities are listed.

## Vehicle

www.webuyanycar.com – if you enter a registration number it will give details of vehicle make, colour, engine size, date of first registration etc. and also a photograph of the model.

www.national.co.uk – National Tyres offer a service called 'Find My Tyres' if you enter a registration number it will give details of vehicle make, colour, engine size etc.

www.hpicheck.com – vehicle checking service.

www.mycarcheck.com – vehicle checking service, covering stolen and write-off reports which are charged for, but basic make and model details from the registration number are free.

www.rac.co.uk – basic vehicle checking service.

www.taxdisc.direct.gov.uk – click on Vehicle Enquiry and if you have the registration number and make, you can do a vehicle check and get a lot of the information from the log book apart from the keeper details.

www.ukcampsite.co.uk – stolen caravan and motor home database.

www.registerstolenplant.co.uk – stolen plant and equipment register.

www.numberplates.com – database of how different countries' vehicle registration plates are formatted.

www.frixo.com – free live road traffic reports.

## Police and Criminal Evidence Act 1984

The following link will take you to the gov.uk web page from which you can directly access the PACE Codes of Practice A–H: https://www.gov.uk/police-and-criminal-evidence-act-1984-pace-codes-of-practice

## Regulation of Investigatory Powers Act 2000

The following link will take you to the gov.uk web page from which you can directly access the RIPA Codes of Practice: https://www.gov.uk/government/collections/ripa-codes

The following link will take you to the gov.uk web page from which you can directly access the RIPA Guidance: https://www.gov.uk/government/uploads/system/uploads/attachment_data/file/270617/ripa.pdf

 ## TEMPLATES AND AIDE MEMOIRES

The remainder of the chapter presents useful templates, forms and aide memoires that the ACFS will require during the course of a counter fraud investigation.

## DATA DISCLOSURE FORM

From: _____

Address: _____

To: _____

### Data Protection Act 1998, Section 29(3)

I am making enquiries, which are concerned, with:–

* a)  the prevention or detection of crime

* b)  the apprehension or prosecution of offenders
    *(delete as appropriate)

Ref No. _____

Nature of enquiry and information requested:

_____

Summary of existing evidence (to be supplemented by copies of documentation)

_____

I confirm that the personal data requested is required for that / those purpose(s) and failure to provide the information will, in my view, be likely to prejudice that / those purpose(s).

Signed: _____

Name: (Block Capitals) _____    Date: _____

Department: _____

Signed: _____    Post: _____

(Supervisory signature where necessary)

Name: _____    Date: _____

Outcome of request and enquiry:

_____

**COPY TO BE KEPT ON FILE**

**CONFIDENTIAL**
**NATIONAL INTELLIGENCE REPORT (Form A)**

| ORGANISATION and OFFICER | XYZ Police<br>DC 3271N Joe Bloggs | | DATE/TIME OF REPORT | 0600 hours on 05/01/2007 | |
|---|---|---|---|---|---|
| INTEL SOURCE or INTEL REF No. | 0017 | | REPORT U.R.N | | |

| SOURCE EVALUATION | A<br>Always<br>Reliable | B<br>Mostly<br>Reliable | C<br>Sometimes<br>Reliable | D<br>Unreliable | E<br>Untested<br>Source |
|---|---|---|---|---|---|
| INTELLIGENCE EVALUATION | 1<br>Known to be<br>true without<br>reservation | 2<br>Known<br>personally to the<br>source but not to<br>the officer | 3<br>Not known<br>personally to the<br>source but<br>corroborated | 4<br>Cannot be<br>judged | 5<br>Suspected to be<br>false |

| | PERMISSIONS | | | RESTRICTIONS | |
|---|---|---|---|---|---|
| HANDLING CODE<br>To be completed at time of entry into an intelligence system and reviewed on disseminaion | 1<br>May be disseminated to other law enforcement and prosecuting agencies, including law enforcement within the EEA and EU compatible<br>(No Code or Conditions) | 2<br>May be disseminated to UK non-prosecuting parties (Code 3.7 conditions apply) | 3<br>May be disseminated to non-EEA law enforcement agencies<br>(Code 4.7 and/or conditions apply, specify below). | 4<br>Only disseminate within originating agency/force. Specify internal recipient(s). | 5<br>Disseminate Intelligence Receiving agency to observe conditions as specified below. |

| REPORT | | |
|---|---|---|
| SUBJECT | CRAIG RAMAGE–COMMUNITY INTELL–FEUD | |

| | | EVALUATION | | |
|---|---|---|---|---|
| | | S | I | H |
| Intelligence dated 05/01/2007 provides that<br><br>Approximately 0020 hours on Friday 5th January 2007, Craig Mitchell RAMAGE, born 05/07/1982 of 24/3 Oxland Avenue, attended at the A & E of the Royal Infirmary and was treated for injuries, which he freely stated were the result of a fight with a Jimmy DONALDSON. During treatment, RAMAGE was heard to say to an unknown male who had accompanied him to the hospital, that Jimmy DONALDSON would have his house 'torched' next week in revenge. | | A | 4 | 5 |

Sourced from: The Scottish Government (2007) Common Knowledge: Thematic Inspection of Information and Intelligence Sharing. Accessed 17 April 2014 from:

http://www.scotland.gov.uk/Publications/2007/03/13161000/8

## Investigation Plan

| | |
|---|---|
| Date allegation received: | .................................................. |
| Date complaint received by Investigator: | .................................................. |
| Date Complaint actioned by Investigator: | .................................................. |
| Details of Senior Investigating Officer in the case (investigator): | .................................................. |
| Tel: | .................................................. |
| Email: | .................................................. |
| Address: | .................................................. .................................................. |
| Location of Offence(s): | .................................................. .................................................. .................................................. |
| Date(s) of Offence(s): | .................................................. .................................................. |
| Suspect 1 Details: | |
| Name: | .................................................. |
| DoB: | .................................................. |
| Occupation: | .................................................. |
| Employment Address: | .................................................. .................................................. |
| Work Tel: | .................................................. |
| Work Email: | .................................................. |
| Employed since: | .................................................. |
| Home Address: | .................................................. |
| Home Tel: | .................................................. |
| Home Email: | .................................................. |

| | |
|---|---|
| Suspect 2 Details: | |
| Name: | .................................................................... |
| DoB: | .................................................................... |
| Occupation: | .................................................................... |
| Employment Address: | .................................................................... |
| | .................................................................... |
| Work Tel: | .................................................................... |
| Work Email: | .................................................................... |
| Employed since: | .................................................................... |
| Home Address: | .................................................................... |
| | .................................................................... |
| Home Tel: | .................................................................... |
| Home Email: | .................................................................... |
| Complainant Details (If Applicable): | |
| Name: | .................................................................... |
| DoB: | .................................................................... |
| Occupation: | .................................................................... |
| Work Address: | .................................................................... |
| | .................................................................... |
| Work Tel: | .................................................................... |
| Employed with company since (if applicable): | .................................................................... |
| Home Address: | .................................................................... |
| | .................................................................... |
| Home Tel: | .................................................................... |
| Email: | .................................................................... |

| | |
|---|---|
| Suspect 1 Name:<br>(B) ALLEGATION 1<br>   CIRCUMSTANCES – | .................................................................<br>.................................................................<br>.................................................................<br>................................................................. |
| Possible offence: | (C) Allegation 1:<br>.................................................................<br>Offences:<br>.................................................................<br>................................................................. |
| | Points to Prove:<br>.................................................................<br>.................................................................<br>................................................................. |
| Suspect 2 Name:<br>(D) ALLEGATION 1<br>   CIRCUMSTANCES – | .................................................................<br>.................................................................<br>.................................................................<br>................................................................. |
| Possible offence: | (E) Allegation 1:<br>.................................................................<br>Offences:<br>.................................................................<br>.................................................................<br>................................................................. |
| | Points to Prove:<br>Offence 1:<br>.................................................................<br>.................................................................<br>................................................................. |

## File Management/Movement Sheet

**Case reference number:**

| Referred to | Date | Referred to | Date |
|---|---|---|---|
| | | | |
| | | | |
| | | | |
| | | | |
| | | | |
| | | | |
| | | | |
| | | | |
| | | | |

**Investigation Progress Sheet**

| Record of all Events/Actions | | | |
|---|---|---|---|
| Date and Time of Action/ Event (24 hour clock) | Description of Action/Event | Recorded by (Initials and Date of Officer) | Checked by Fraud Manager (Initials and Date) |
| | | | |
| | | | |
| | | | |
| | | | |
| | | | |
| | | | |
| | | | |
| | | | |
| | | | |
| | | | |
| | | | |
| | | | |
| | | | |
| | | | |
| | | | |
| | | | |
| | | | |
| | | | |
| | | | |
| | | | |
| | | | |

**Potential Evidence Review Template**

| Description of potential evidence: | Who does the potential evidence relate to? | Significance: for example, confirms identity of suspect, supports a point to prove, corroborates evidence etc. |
|---|---|---|
| | | |
| | | |
| | | |

| Unique Reference Number | |
|---|---|

(F) PART II OF THE REGULATION OF INVESTIGATORY POWERS ACT 2000
(G) AUTHORISATION DIRECTED SURVEILLANCE

| Public Authority *(including full address)* | |
|---|---|
| | |
| (a) Name of Applicant | Unit/Branch/Division |
| Full Address | |
| Contact Details | |
| Investigation/Operation Name (if applicable) | |
| Investigating Officer (if a person other than the applicant) | |

| DETAILS OF APPLICATION |
| --- |
| 1. Give rank or position of authorising officer in accordance with the Regulation of Investigatory Powers (Directed Surveillance and Covert Human Intelligence Sources) Order 2003 No. 3171. |
| |
| 2. Describe the purpose of the specific operation or investigation. |
| |
| 3. Describe in detail the surveillance operation to be authorised and expected duration, including any premises, vehicles or equipment (for example, camera, binoculars, recorder) that may be used. |
| |
| 4. The identities, where known, of those to be the subject of the directed surveillance. |
| <ul><li>Name:</li><li>Address:</li><li>DoB:</li><li>Other information as appropriate:</li></ul> |

5. Explain the information that it is desired to obtain as a result of the directed surveillance.

6. Identify on which grounds the directed surveillance is <u>necessary</u> under section 28(3) of RIPA. *Delete those that are inapplicable. Ensure that you know which of these grounds you are entitled to rely on. (SI 2003 No. 3171)*

(b)

- In the interests of national security;

- For the purpose of preventing or detecting crime or of preventing disorder;

- In the interests of the economic well-being of the United Kingdom;

- In the interests of public safety;

- for the purpose of protecting public health;

- for the purpose of assessing or collecting any tax, duty, levy or other imposition, contribution or charge payable to a government department.

7. Explain <u>why</u> this directed surveillance is necessary on the grounds you have identified. [Code paragraph 2.4]

8. Supply details of any potential collateral intrusion and why the intrusion is unavoidable. [Bear in mind Code paragraphs 2.6 to 2.10.]

(c) Describe precautions you will take to minimise collateral intrusion.

9. Explain <u>why</u> this directed surveillance is proportionate to what it seeks to achieve. How intrusive might it be on the subject of surveillance or on others? And why is this intrusion outweighed by the need for surveillance in operational terms or can the evidence be obtained by any other means? [Code paragraph 2.5]

10. Confidential information. [Code paragraphs 3.1 to 3.12]

INDICATE THE LIKELIHOOD OF ACQUIRING ANY CONFIDENTIAL INFORMATION:

| 11. Applicant's Details | | | |
|---|---|---|---|
| Name (print) | | Tel No: | |
| Grade/Rank | | (d) Date | |
| Signature | | | |

**12. Authorising Officer's Statement. [Spell out the '5 Ws' – Who; What; Where; When; Why and HOW – in this and the following box.]**

I hereby authorise directed surveillance defined as follows: [*Why is the surveillance necessary, whom is the surveillance directed against, Where and When will it take place, What surveillance activity/equipment is sanctioned, How is it to be achieved?*]

**13. Explain <u>why</u> you believe the directed surveillance is necessary. [Code paragraph 2.4]**
   Explain why you believe the directed surveillance to be proportionate to what is sought to be achieved by carrying it out. [Code paragraph 2.5]

**14. (Confidential Information Authorisation.) Supply detail demonstrating compliance with Code paragraphs 3.1 to 3.12.**

| (e) Date of first review | |
|---|---|

Programme for subsequent reviews of this authorisation: [Code paragraph 4.22]. Only complete this box if review dates after first review are known. If not or inappropriate to set additional review dates then leave blank.

| Name (Print) | | Grade/Rank | | |
|---|---|---|---|---|
| Signature | | Date and time | | |
| Expiry date and time [for example: authorisation granted on 1 April 2005 – expires on 30 June 2005, 23.59] | | | | |

| Suspect Interview Plan | | | |
|---|---|---|---|
| Suspect: | | | |
| Date: | Interviewer 1: | Interviewer 2: | Location: |
| Potential Offences: | | | |
| Points to Prove (for example, dishonesty, intent etc.): | | | |
| Possible Defences (including portable areas of defence): | | | |

Record information disclosed to solicitor/legal representative (explain rationale):

Evidence to support allegation/suspicion(s):

| Facts already established (for example, offence occurred at a particular time, suspect was wearing particular clothing. Should include significant statement/silence and those facts that may give rise to a special warning): | Facts to be determined (for example, where was interviewee at time of the offence?): |
|---|---|

Detail Opening Question:

**Pre-interview location and equipment check:**

Interview room availability, tape recorder, sealed tapes, tape seals, obtaining a copy of tape form, aide memoire, copy PACE, refreshments, pen, paper, exhibits.

Planning Notes

**PACE INTERVIEW GUIDANCE**

### What Basics Do I Need in Place to Conduct an Interview?

**Interview Room** – You need somewhere away from other people where a private interview can take place and you will not be interrupted.

**Tape Machine** – Although interviews can be recorded by way of a contemporaneous note the consensus is that wherever possible interviews should be tape recorded. This removes any argument that the content of what was said has been changed by the interviewing officers.

**Sealed Tapes** – The tape machine used is one into which two tapes are entered. These should be sealed tapes that are unwrapped in the presence of the interviewee. Take plenty of tapes into the interview with you to make sure you have spares should you need them.

**A Copy of the PACE Code of Practice** – An up-to-date copy of the PACE Code must be available at all offices where interviews take place and the interviewee must always be offered the opportunity to consult the Code. This can be obtained from HMSO Stationers.

**Your Paperwork** – Make sure you are aware of the facts of the case and have relevant information with you to refer to in the interview, such as any witness statements you have taken and any correspondence that has been sent. Also take an interview plan in with you (see later notes on interview technique).

**Notice for the Interviewee re Accessing a Copy of the Tape** – At the end of the interview the interviewee must be given a notice explaining how they can access a copy of the tape. Have one ready to hand over and a copy for file.

### What to Consider before Starting the Interview

**If anyone appears to be under 17** – they shall be treated as a juvenile for the purposes of the Code in the absence of clear evidence that they are older. In such cases the juvenile cannot be interviewed unless an appropriate adult is present in the interview.

**If an officer has a suspicion, or is told in good faith** – that a person of any age may be mentally disordered or otherwise mentally vulnerable, in the absence of clear evidence to dispel that suspicion, the person shall be treated as such for the purposes of the Code and shall not be interviewed without an appropriate adult being present.

**If a person appears to be blind, seriously visually impaired, deaf, or unable to read or speak or has difficulty orally because of a speech**

**impediment** – they shall be treated as such for the purposes of this Code. Such persons may require the help of an interpreter or the assistance of somebody who works with the visually impaired.

**If a person informs you that they do not speak any or much English, or it appears to you that this is the case** – then it will be necessary to arrange for an interpreter to be present in interview.

**Appropriate adults** – A juvenile or person who is mentally disordered or otherwise mentally vulnerable must not be interviewed regarding their involvement or suspected involvement in a criminal offence or offences, or asked to provide or sign a written statement under caution or record of interview, in the absence of the appropriate adult.

The appropriate adult means in the case of a:

(a) Juvenile:
   ▪ The parent or guardian.
   ▪ PACE provides the alternative option of the presence of a social worker, but it also provides that the appropriate adult should not be an employee of the interviewing body.
(b) A person who is mentally disordered or vulnerable.
   ▪ A relative, guardian or other person responsible for their care or custody.
   ▪ Someone experienced in dealing with mentally disordered or mentally vulnerable people.

The appropriate adult should be somebody who has no involvement whatsoever in the investigation/proceedings that are the subject of the interview.

The appropriate adult should be present during all dealings with the interviewee and no interview should take place without the appropriate adult being present. The appropriate adult should be informed that they are not expected to act simply as an observer and the purpose of their presence is to:

▪ Advise the person being interviewed;
▪ Observe whether the interview is being conducted properly and fairly;
▪ Facilitate communication with the person being interviewed.

This should be said to them at the outset of their involvement and a written record made that this was said. They can also be reminded of this in your preamble to the taped interview.

## Interpreters

You as the interviewing officer are responsible for making sure that appropriate arrangements are in place for the provision of suitably qualified interpreters for people who do not understand English or are deaf.

A person must not be interviewed in the absence of a person capable of interpreting if:

(a) They have difficulty understanding English;
(b) The interviewer cannot speak the person's own language;
(c) The person wants an interpreter present.

If a person appears to be deaf or there is doubt about their hearing or speaking ability, they must not be interviewed in the absence of an interpreter unless they agree in writing to being interviewed without one.

Where a foreign language interpreter is used in a tape recorded interview then everything the interviewer says must be interpreted by the interpreter and the responses by the interviewee interpreted back into English by the interpreter.

Where a hand written record of interview is being taken then the language interpreter should be asked to take a written note of the interview at the time in the language of the interviewee and certify its accuracy. This should then be retained in case there is a need to call the interpreter to give evidence.

Where the interviewee is deaf or hearing impaired and the interview is being tape recorded then a written note of the interview must also be taken at the same time as the tape recording so that the person who is deaf or has impaired hearing has equivalent rights of access to the full interview as those without hearing impairment.

## Right to Legal Advice

All persons must be informed that they may at any time consult and communicate privately with a solicitor, whether in person, in writing or by telephone.

A person who asks for legal advice should be given an opportunity to consult a specific solicitor or another solicitor from that firm. An officer must not advise the suspect about any particular firm of solicitors.

Whenever a person exercises their right to legal advice by consulting or communicating with a solicitor, they must be allowed to do so in private. This right to consult or communicate in private is fundamental and this fundamental right to communicate in private should also be applied to telephone communications with the solicitor.

**Remember:**

- No officer should, at any time, do or say anything with the intention of dissuading an interviewee from obtaining legal advice.
- A person who wants legal advice should not be interviewed or continue to be interviewed until they have received such advice.
- A person who has consulted a solicitor shall be entitled on request to have the solicitor present when they are interviewed.
- A person is not obliged to give reasons for declining legal advice and should not be pressed to do so.

The solicitor can be a solicitor holding a current practice certificate, a trainee solicitor or an accredited representative. Their role is to protect and advance the legal rights of their client and on occasion this may require the solicitor to give advice that has the effect of the client avoiding giving evidence that strengthens a prosecution case. The solicitor may intervene in order to seek clarification, challenge an improper question to their client or the manner in which it was put, advise their client not to reply to particular questions, or if they wish give their client further legal advice.

## What to Do When your Interviewee First Arrives for Interview

Remind them that they are attending the interview voluntarily to assist with an investigation and may leave at will. Remind them of their right to legal advice and note their response. Make a note that you have done this.

Make your assessment of your interviewee:

- Are they or do they appear to be a juvenile?
- Does the interviewee appear mentally impaired or vulnerable?
- Do they have a proper understanding of English?
- Are they deaf or hearing impaired?

### The Interview

An interview is the questioning of a person regarding their involvement or suspected involvement in a criminal offence or offences and must be carried out under caution. Whenever a person is interviewed they must be informed of the nature of the offence that is under investigation.

**Remember:**

■ If you are interviewing more than one suspected offender they must be interviewed separately.

■ Do not discuss anything to do with the case before the formal interview, during any breaks in the interview or after the interview. All discussion about the details and facts of the case must take place and be recorded as part of the formal interview.

■ When conducting an interview do not say anything to the interviewee that can be viewed as an inducement for the interviewee to cooperate with you.

■ Do not do or say anything that is oppressive or threatening.

■ If during interview the interviewee decides they want legal advice stop the interview straightaway so that this can take place, even if this means arranging a further interview for another day.

■ Do not attempt to conduct an interview with anyone who appears to be unfit to be interviewed because they are unwell, drunk, under the influence of drugs or mentally unfit to be interviewed. Record your reasons for refusing the interview and if appropriate offer an alternative appointment.

■ If at any time during the interview the interviewee indicates that they want to stop the interview and leave, comply straightaway. The interviewee is not under arrest and is free to leave at any time and any attempt to prevent this could be viewed as false imprisonment.

## Interview Technique

### Purpose

The purpose of the interview is the questioning of a person regarding their suspected involvement in a criminal offence or offences. This must be done under caution. Remember that a suspect has a right to remain silent, but this does not prevent you from putting to them questions outlining the elements of the offence and any specific allegations.

No interviewer may try to obtain answers or elicit a statement by using oppression.

No interviewer shall indicate by word or deed (i.e. offer an inducement) the action likely to be taken by them if the interviewee cooperates with them.

The interview should cease once the interviewing officer is satisfied that:

- All the questions that they consider relevant to obtaining accurate and reliable information about the offence have been put to the suspect.
- This includes allowing the suspect to give an innocent explanation and asking questions to ascertain if the explanation is accurate and reliable.
- They have taken account of any other reliable evidence.
- The officer in the case reasonably believes there is sufficient evidence to provide a realistic prospect of conviction for the offence if that person was prosecuted for it.

In other words do not ask the same question over and over again where a suspect has given you an answer and does not shift from it. You can point out any weaknesses or inconsistencies in that answer and ask them to comment, but you must then move on. To question someone at great length by going back over the same questions repeatedly can be viewed as oppression.

## How to Conduct a Good Interview

Best practice suggests that there should be two interviewers. One as the main interviewing officer and the other making notes and raising questions about any anomalies that they spot in the interviewee's account.

Before the interview begins make sure you have a sound knowledge of the case you are interviewing about.

*Gather together all the things you need for the interview:*

- Blank tapes (including extra sets)
- Your interview guidance sheet
- Your plan for the interview
- Notice to the defendant about the tapes
- Draft statement forms
- Writing paper and pens
- All documentation/evidence that you want to put to the interviewee.

*Plan your interview:*

- Think about the elements of the offence that you need to prove and what questions you need to ask to prove it.
- Look to see what possible issues there are in the case and think about what you want to ask.

■ Look at the physical evidence you have such as witness statements and correspondence and decide in what order to produce it to the interviewee and what you want to ask.

■ If you are aware of any explanation that the interviewee is likely to give, what are your concerns about this explanation and how can you couch your concerns in a question?

■ Write down a rough draft of your interview and take it in with you and refer to it as an aide memoire.

■ If you are the second interviewer, you also need a good knowledge of the case and to have discussed with your colleague how they intend to approach the interview. Go in with a pen and paper and listen and write down any additional pointers that you can use to interject as questions at an appropriate moment or to use to pass discreet notes to your colleague.

**Remember this is your interview and you need to take control. If the interview gets out of control or you feel that nothing of any further use can be achieved, take control by bringing it to an end using the procedure on your interview guidance sheet.**

### The Caution

A person whom there are grounds to suspect of an offence must be cautioned before any questions about it are put to him/her regarding his/her involvement or suspected involvement in that offence, if his/her answers or his/her silence may be given in evidence to a court in a prosecution.

A person need not be cautioned when questions are put simply to establish identity or ownership (for example, of land)

The caution is as follows –

'You do not have to say anything, but it may harm your defence if you do not mention when questioned something which you later rely on in Court. Anything you do say may be given in evidence.'

## The Interview

An interview is the questioning of a person regarding his/her involvement in a criminal offence(s). Interview records must be maintained in accordance with

Code C – 11.5, which states –

(a)  an accurate record must be made of each interview
(b)  the record must state the place of the interview, the time it begins and ends, details of all persons present and time of the caution
(c)  the record must be made during the course of the interview.

## Tape Recorded Interviews:

- When the interviewee is brought into the interview room the interviewer shall without delay but in the interviewee's sight, take the wrapper off two new tapes and load them into the tape machine and set it to record.
- State that the interview is being tape recorded.
- Introduce themselves for the tape (if there are two interviewers both should identify themselves) giving your name and what you are, for example, Accredited Counter Fraud Specialist for......
- Ask everyone else present to identify themselves for the tape – do not identify them yourself, it is important from the point of view of voice recognition that they introduce themselves.
- State the date, time of commencement and place of the interview.
- State that the interviewee will be given a notice at the end of the interview about what will happen to the tapes.
- Remind the interviewee that they have attended the interview voluntarily and are free to leave at any time.
- Remind the interviewee of their right to obtain legal advice.
- **Caution the defendant:** 'You do not have to say anything. But it may harm your defence if you do not mention when questioned something which you later rely on in court. Anything you do say may be given in evidence.'
- Ask the interviewee whether they understand the caution and if they do not explain it until they indicate they do understand.
- Explain what the interview is about, for example, this interview is being conducted in respect of an allegation that between the dates of ....... and ....... you .....
- Again ensure the interviewee understands this.
- Again confirm the interviewee's name, address and date of birth and conduct your interview.

**Note: The caution should be given on all occasions when a person is informed they may be prosecuted.**

*End of Interview – When you have concluded your taped interview:*

- Indicate to the interviewee that you have finished your questions and give them the opportunity to add or clarify anything they want to say.
- Ask the interviewee if they wish to make a written statement and take that statement and read it back to the interviewee with the tape running.
- Indicate on the tape that you are now bringing the interview to an end and give the time and state that you are switching off the tape and then do so.
- Remove both the tapes from the machine and seal them in the presence of the interviewee. One is sealed as a master copy and the other as a working copy.
- The seals should be completed with the name of the interviewee and an identifying number. Once the seals have been placed round the tapes they should be signed by all the persons present.
- Hand to the interviewee a copy of a notice explaining how they can obtain a copy of the tape and retain a copy of that notice for your file.
- Keep your own written note of all the times for commencing and finishing the interview.

**Tapes to be handed over to the department responsible for preparation of tape summaries and accompanying statements and for retention and storage purposes.**

**Changing Tapes** – When the recorder shows that the tape only has a short time left, the interviewer should tell the interviewee that the tapes are coming to an end and round off that part of the interview. If you do need to leave the room to get fresh tapes do not leave the interviewee unattended. Remove the old tapes and seal them in the sight of the interviewee and sign them as you would at the end of the interview.

Then insert the new tapes after unwrapping them in front of the interviewee. Switch the tape on and explain that this is a continuation of a tape recorded interview with the interviewee and again outline the offence under investigation and remind the interviewee that they are still under caution and repeat the caution before recommencing the interview.

**Breaks in Interview** – Try and avoid unnecessary breaks but if it is a short break where you remain in the interview room then:

- Explain on tape why you are breaking and give the time before switching off the tape.
- When you recommence again give the time and explain the reason for the break and ask all present to confirm their agreement.
- Before recommencing the interview remind the interviewee that they are still under caution and repeat the caution.

If the break involves the suspect leaving the room then follow the same procedure of explaining the break but then follow the procedure for the end of interview and remove and seal the tapes. The interview when recommenced will have to be on new tapes. You again follow the procedure for the start of a new interview and explain that this is a continuation of the preceding interview where a break took place and again give the reason for the break and get all parties to agree.

**Failure of Recording Equipment** – If there is an equipment failure which can be rectified quickly, for example by inserting new tapes, the interviewer should follow the same procedure as when changing the tapes but explain on the old and new tapes (if possible) why this is being done. If, however, it is not possible to continue recording on the tape recorder and no replacement recorder is available my advice is that best practice would be to suspend the interview until another date when equipment is available, unless this proves totally impractical and then consider proceeding by way of a written record.

If one of the tapes snaps during interview follow the procedure for changing tapes and seal the snapped tape as the master copy and retain the unbroken tape as the working copy.

**Remember that once the master copy has been sealed this cannot be opened unless done following a set procedure in the presence of a representative of the Crown Prosecution Service.**

## Written Interview Records

This is a less satisfactory way of recording an interview as it is slow and far more open to challenge than the interview that is tape recorded. If you have to record an interview in writing remember:

- The record must state the time and place of interview and identify all persons present. You must also record all breaks and the time the interview ends.
- The interview procedure in terms of explaining the allegation to the interviewee, reminding them of their freedom to leave, right to legal advice and administering the caution are the same as in a taped interview.

- Any written record must be made and completed during the interview, unless this would not be practicable.
- Thus the written record should be a contemporaneous, verbatim account of the interview taking place.
- The interviewee should be given the opportunity, at the end of the interview, to read the record and sign it as correct or to indicate how they consider it inaccurate. If the interviewee cannot read it should be read to them and they should be then asked to sign it as correct. If they refuse to sign this should be recorded at the foot of the interview by the senior interviewer, as should any reason given for not signing.
- All other persons present should be given the opportunity to read and sign the record as being an accurate one. The interviewing officers should also sign it.
- Use words such as 'I agree this is a correct record of what was said' followed by a signature and indication of who the person signing is, for example, the interviewee Mr John Green or Mr Green's Solicitor etc. . . .
- Everything said in the interview should be recorded verbatim, even if it is an unsolicited comment.

## Written Statements Under Caution

As stated earlier, everyone who is interviewed must be offered the opportunity to make a written statement about the allegation they face and this can be done at the end of each interview and should be included on the tape or written record. This should be done in every interview, even if the interviewee has exercised their right to remain silent.

If the interview is tape recorded and the interviewee indicates that they wish to make a written statement this should be done with the tape running.

The statement can be dictated to the interviewing officer and this is preferable, but if the interviewee wishes to write their own statement this must be allowed.

If the statement is dictated to the interviewer it must be taken down as the exact words spoken by the person making the statement and must not be edited or paraphrased, although questions can be asked to make it more intelligible. These and the answers given should be included in the statement.

When the statement is completed the maker should be asked to read it (or if they cannot read it should be read to them) and make any alterations or additions (which should be signed).

At the end of the statement they should then write or have written for them:

'I have read the above statement, and I have been able to correct, alter or add anything I wish. This statement is true. I have made it of my own free will.'

## PACE INTERVIEW GUIDANCE SHEET

Unwrap new tapes in view of interviewee and insert in machine.

'This interview is being tape recorded. The date is . . . and the time is . . . and we are in an interview room at . . . '
'I am (name and job title) and my colleague is . . . '.

Second interviewer introduces themselves.
Ask everyone in the room to identify themselves for the tape.

'You will be given a notice at the end of the interview which explains what the tapes are used for and how you can access a copy of the tape.'
'I must now remind you that you have attended this interview voluntarily and that you are free to leave at any time.'
'You have the right to access legal advice and to arrange to have a legal representative present during the interview.'

If no legal representative present go on to say 'do you wish to exercise that right or are you happy for the interview to continue?'

'I am now going to caution you and it is important that you listen carefully.'

**CAUTION 'You do not have to say anything. But it may harm your defence if you do not mention when questioned something you later rely on in court. Anything you do say may be given in evidence. Do you understand?'**

If the answer to this is 'no' then explain the caution in simple terms until the interviewee intimates that they understand.

**'The purpose of today's interview is to discuss the allegation that between . . . and . . . you . . .'**

Here is where you begin the body of your interview and establish the elements of the offence and put to the interviewee any correspondence or other physical evidence, such as photographs, that you wish to produce in the interview.

> **END OF INTERVIEW** – 'I have now asked all the questions I wish to put to you. Is there anything you (the interviewee) would like to add or clarify before the interview comes to an end?'
>
> 'You may, if you wish, make a written statement about the allegations that have been put to you today. This can be dictated to us or if you prefer you can write it yourself. The tape would be left running whilst this is done. Do you wish to make a written statement?'

If the interviewee wishes to make a statement this can be dictated to you or written by the interviewee using the appropriate statement form. Leave the tape running whilst this is done and invite the interviewee to read the statement (or read to them if they cannot) and make any corrections or alterations that they wish . . . The following words must appear at the end of the statement: 'I have read/had read to me the above statement, and I have been able to correct, alter or add anything I wish. This statement is true. I have made it of my own free will.' Then get the interviewee to sign and date the statement.

'If nobody has anything they wish to add I intend to bring the interview to an end and switch off the tape. The time is now . . .' Switch off the tape recorder and remove the tapes. Seal the master tape and complete the labels on both tapes and ask everyone present to sign them.

Complete the notice re access to the tapes by filling in the relevant information, keeping a copy for your file and give a copy of the notice to the interviewee.

## List of MG Forms

| | | |
|---|---|---|
| D[1] | MG1 | File Front Sheet |
| D | MG2 | Initial Witness Assessment |
| D | MG3 | Report to Crown Prosecutor for Charging Decision |
| | MG3A | Further Report to Crown Prosecutor for Charging Decision |
| | MG4 | Charge Sheet |
| | MG4A | Conditional Bail – Grant/Variation |
| | MG4B | Request to Vary Conditional Bail |
| | MG4C | Surety/Security |
| | MG5 | Case Summary |
| D | MG6 | Case File Information |
| D | MG6B | Police Officer's Disciplinary Record |
| | MG6C | Police Schedule of Non-sensitive Unused Material |
| | MG6D | Police Schedule of Sensitive Material |
| D | MG6E | Disclosure Officer's Report |
| | MG7 | Remand Application |
| | MG8 | Breach of Bail Conditions |
| | MG9 | Witness List |
| | MG10 | Witness Non-Availability |
| D | MG11 | Witness Statement |
| | MG12 | Exhibit List |
| | MG13 | Application for Order on Conviction |
| | MG15 | Record of Interview |
| D | MG18 | Other Offences (TIC) |
| D | MG19 | Compensation Claim |
| | MG20 | Further Evidence/Information Report |
| | MG(c) | Continuation Sheet |
| D[1] | MGFSP | Submission of case for scientific examination |
| | MGNFA | No Further Action letter template |

---

[1]"D" denotes that this is a double-sided form, and care is therefore required when taking photocopies or faxing the form to other agencies.

MG 6

**RESTRICTED**
**FOR POLICE AND PROSECUTION ONLY (when complete)**

*delete as applicable

URN ☐ ☐ ☐ ☐

## CASE FILE INFORMATION

This document is for internal use only. It should be regarded as a memorandum between the police and CPS. It may well contain confidential information, and therefore must not be disclosed to the defence.

Name of Defendant: ........................................................................ Date of completion: ........................................
(Surname first)
Is the investigation complete? **Yes / No**

**The following four questions MUST be completed in all cases**

**Medical Evidence**
Are medical statements required? **Yes / No**. If **Yes**, have they been obtained? **Yes / No**
If No, target date to obtain: ..........................................
Is obtaining medical evidence a problem? **Yes / No**. If **Yes**, give brief details: ...............................................
.........................................................................................................................................................................
.........................................................................................................................................................................

**Forensic Evidence** (attach Section 13 of MGFSP)
Have items been sent for examination? **Yes / No**. If **Yes**, delivery date for receipt of report (if known): ......................
Are extra items to be sent? **Yes / No**. If **Yes**, give brief details including reasons for later submission: ......................
.........................................................................................................................................................................
.........................................................................................................................................................................

**Visually Recorded Evidence**
Has all evidence been viewed and copied? **Yes / No**. If **No**, target date for completion: ...................................
Is viewing and copying the recorded material a problem? **Yes / No**. If **Yes**, give brief details: ...............................
.........................................................................................................................................................................
.........................................................................................................................................................................

**Disclosure**
Have all MG6C, D and E Schedules been completed and signed? **Yes / No**
Are there any anticipated complications regarding unused material? **Yes / No**. If **Yes**, give brief details: ...................
.........................................................................................................................................................................
.........................................................................................................................................................................

Is there any third party material in this case? **Yes / No**. If **Yes**, give brief details: ...............................................
.........................................................................................................................................................................
.........................................................................................................................................................................

In addition to any other confidential information supplied, the following questions must be considered and, where applicable, the box ticked. Details are then to be recorded on the reverse of this form.

| | | ✓ | | | ✓ |
|---|---|---|---|---|---|
| 1 | Victim personal statement taken/to be taken? | | 10 | If no MG19 on file and compensation is an issue, enter victim's name and address | |
| 2 | Witness (including expert) statements till to be taken? | | 11 | Previous convictions / allegations against defendant with similar MO? | |
| 3 | Photographs of the injuries? (include date when available) | | 12 | Further persons to be arrested / interviewed / ID procedure? | |
| 4 | Any vulnerable or intimidated adult witness. Is a Special Measures meeting required? | | 13 | Others charged whose details do not appear on this file? | |
| 5 | Are there child witnesses / victims? | | 14 | Other person(s) yet to be charged? | |
| 6 | Have any witnesses refused to make statement (include names and evidence they could give)? | | 15 | Others receiving caution/final warning/reprimand out of the same incident? (include names, offences and reasons) | |
| 7 | Is an application required for visual link evidence? | | 16 | Matters of local / public interest? | |
| 8 | Strengths or weaknesses of evidence and / or witnesses? | | 17 | If asset recovery case, has a financial investigation commenced? | |
| 9 | Are there specific problems / needs of prosecution witnesses, eg, interpreters? | | 18 | Are there any other applications / orders required in this case? | |

2004/05 (1)

MG 6

**RESTRICTED**
**FOR POLICE AND PROSECUTION ONLY (when complete)**
*delete as applicable

## CASE FILE INFORMATION

URN | | | |

MG 9

**RESTRICTED – FOR POLICE, PROSECUTION AND THE WITNESS SERVICE ONLY (when complete).** The whole column marked ✦ must be expunged before passing to a third party.

URN ☐ ☐ ☐ ☐

## WITNESS LIST

Page No ........ of ........

Date of completion: ........................

R v .....................................................................................................

★ Tick if statement attached
◆ Previous convictions? Enter Y or N

| Wit. No. | Witness Details (In the ' Wit.No. column enter 'V' if the witness is a victim, 'Vu' if vulnerable or intimidated) | Statement Number | ★ | ◆ |
|---|---|---|---|---|
| | Name:.................................................................................................... | | | |
| | Address:................................................................................................ | | | |
| | .................................................... Post Code:........................................ | | | |
| | Occupation:........................................... Date of Birth:............................ | | | |
| | Telephone No. (Home):............................ (Work):........................... | | | |
| | Mobile/pager no:.................................... E-mail address:........................... | | | |
| | Name:.................................................................................................... | | | |
| | Address:................................................................................................ | | | |
| | .................................................... Post Code:........................................ | | | |
| | Occupation:........................................... Date of Birth:............................ | | | |
| | Telephone No. (Home):............................ (Work):........................... | | | |
| | Mobile/pager no:.................................... E-mail address:........................... | | | |
| | Name:.................................................................................................... | | | |
| | Address:................................................................................................ | | | |
| | .................................................... Post Code:........................................ | | | |
| | Occupation:........................................... Date of Birth:............................ | | | |
| | Telephone No. (Home):............................ (Work):........................... | | | |
| | Mobile/pager no:.................................... E-mail address:........................... | | | |
| | Name:.................................................................................................... | | | |
| | Address:................................................................................................ | | | |
| | .................................................... Post Code:........................................ | | | |
| | Occupation:........................................... Date of Birth:............................ | | | |
| | Telephone No. (Home):............................ (Work):........................... | | | |
| | Mobile/pager no:.................................... E-mail address:........................... | | | |

MG 10

## RESTRICTED – FOR POLICE AND PROSECUTION ONLY
### (when complete)

### WITNESS NON-AVAILABILITY

Page No ........ of ........

| URN | | | | |
| Crown Court No. | | | | |

R v ........................................................................................ at: ............................................. Magistrates/Youth/Crown Court

Witness (names)*  (  )........................................................  (  )..............................................

*Insert no.  (  )........................................................  (  )..............................................

(  )........................................................  (  )..............................................

*Mark dates when police and other witnesses are NOT available. Codes for police non-availability:*
*R = Rest day    L = Leave    C = Course    N = Night duty    S = Sickness    O = Other*

| Date | Month *Witness No | Date | Month *Witness No | Date | Month *Witness No | Date | Month *Witness No | Date | Month *Witness No | Date | Month *Witness No |
|---|---|---|---|---|---|---|---|---|---|---|---|
| 1 | | 1 | | 1 | | 1 | | 1 | | 1 | |
| 2 | | 2 | | 2 | | 2 | | 2 | | 2 | |
| 3 | | 3 | | 3 | | 3 | | 3 | | 3 | |
| 4 | | 4 | | 4 | | 4 | | 4 | | 4 | |
| 5 | | 5 | | 5 | | 5 | | 5 | | 5 | |
| 6 | | 6 | | 6 | | 6 | | 6 | | 6 | |
| 7 | | 7 | | 7 | | 7 | | 7 | | 7 | |
| 8 | | 8 | | 8 | | 8 | | 8 | | 8 | |
| 9 | | 9 | | 9 | | 9 | | 9 | | 9 | |
| 10 | | 10 | | 10 | | 10 | | 10 | | 10 | |
| 11 | | 11 | | 11 | | 11 | | 11 | | 11 | |
| 12 | | 12 | | 12 | | 12 | | 12 | | 12 | |
| 13 | | 13 | | 13 | | 13 | | 13 | | 13 | |
| 14 | | 14 | | 14 | | 14 | | 14 | | 14 | |
| 15 | | 15 | | 15 | | 15 | | 15 | | 15 | |
| 16 | | 16 | | 16 | | 16 | | 16 | | 16 | |
| 17 | | 17 | | 17 | | 17 | | 17 | | 17 | |
| 18 | | 18 | | 18 | | 18 | | 18 | | 18 | |
| 19 | | 19 | | 19 | | 19 | | 19 | | 19 | |
| 20 | | 20 | | 20 | | 20 | | 20 | | 20 | |
| 21 | | 21 | | 21 | | 21 | | 21 | | 21 | |
| 22 | | 22 | | 22 | | 22 | | 22 | | 22 | |
| 23 | | 23 | | 23 | | 23 | | 23 | | 23 | |
| 24 | | 24 | | 24 | | 24 | | 24 | | 24 | |
| 25 | | 25 | | 25 | | 25 | | 25 | | 25 | |
| 26 | | 26 | | 26 | | 26 | | 26 | | 26 | |
| 27 | | 27 | | 27 | | 27 | | 27 | | 27 | |
| 28 | | 28 | | 28 | | 28 | | 28 | | 28 | |
| 29 | | 29 | | 29 | | 29 | | 29 | | 29 | |
| 30 | | 30 | | 30 | | 30 | | 30 | | 30 | |
| 31 | | 31 | | 31 | | 31 | | 31 | | 31 | |

'O', 'C' and 'S' codes – give full details:

_____

Name of person submitting form and date

MG 11

**RESTRICTED (when complete)**

## WITNESS STATEMENT

(CJ Act 1967, s.9; MC Act 1980, ss.5A(3) (a) and 5B; MC Rules 1981, r.70)

URN

Statement of:............................................................................................................................

Age if under 18:.................................... (if over 18 insert 'over 18') Occupation:..........................................................

This statement (consisting of ............ page(s) each signed by me) is true to the best of my knowledge and belief and I make it knowing that, if it is tendered in evidence, I shall be liable to prosecution if I have wilfully stated anything in it, which I know to be false, or do not believe to be true.

Signature:.................................................................................................... Date:..........................................

Tick if witness evidence is visually recorded ☐ *(supply witness details on rear)*

..................................................................................................................................................

..................................................................................................................................................

..................................................................................................................................................

..................................................................................................................................................

..................................................................................................................................................

..................................................................................................................................................

..................................................................................................................................................

..................................................................................................................................................

..................................................................................................................................................

..................................................................................................................................................

..................................................................................................................................................

..................................................................................................................................................

..................................................................................................................................................

..................................................................................................................................................

..................................................................................................................................................

..................................................................................................................................................

..................................................................................................................................................

..................................................................................................................................................

..................................................................................................................................................

..................................................................................................................................................

Signature:........................................................... Signature witnessed by:..........................................

2004/05 (1)

MG 11

# RESTRICTED – FOR POLICE AND PROSECUTION ONLY
### (when complete)

**Witness contact details**

Home address:.........................................................................................................................................

........................................................................................................ Postcode:...........................................

Home telephone No:..................................................……... Work telephone No:...........….........................

Mobile/Pager No............................................................... E-mail address:...............................................

Preferred means of contact: .....................................................................................................................

Male / Female (delete as applicable) Date and place of birth:.............................................................

Former name:................................................... Height:............................ Ethnicity Code:........................

Dates of witness non-availability:..............................................................................................................

....................................................................................................................................................................

**Witness care**

a) Is the witness willing and likely to attend court? Yes / No. If 'No', include reason(s) on form MG6. What can be done to

ensure attendance?.................................................................................................................................

..................................................................................................................................................................

b) Does the witness require 'special measures' as a vulnerable or intimidated witness? Yes / No. If 'Yes' submit MG2 with file.

c) Does the witness have any specific care needs?     Yes / No. If 'Yes' what are they? (Healthcare, childcare, transport, disability, language
difficulties, visually impaired, restricted mobility or other concerns?)

.................................................................................................................................................................

.................................................................................................................................................................

.................................................................................................................................................................

---

**Witness Consent (for witness completion)**

a) The criminal justice process and Victim Personal Statement scheme (victims only) has been explained to me:   Yes / No

b) I have been given the leaflet 'Giving a witness statement to the police – what happens next?        Yes /No

c) I consent to police having access to my medical record(s) in relation to this matter:     Yes ☐ No ☐ N/A ☐

d) I consent to my medical record in relation to this matter being disclosed to the defence:   Yes ☐ No ☐ N/A ☐

e) I consent to the statement being disclosed for the purposes of civil proceedings       Yes ☐ No ☐ N/A ☐
   e.g. child care proceedings (if applicable):

f) The information recorded above will be disclosed to the Witness Service so that they can offer help and support, unless
   you ask them not to. Tick this box to decline their services:   ☐

Signature of witness: ...............................................................................................................................

---

Statement taken by (print name): ...................................................... Station: ...........................................

Time and place statement taken:...............................................................................................................

2004/05 (1)

MG 11 (CONT)

**RESTRICTED (when complete)**

Page No .......... of ..........

Continuation of Statement of: ........................................................................................................................................

Signature: ................................................................ Signature witnessed by: .......................................................

2004/05 (1)

MG 12

## RESTRICTED (when complete)

### EXHIBIT LIST

Page No.......... of ........

R v ................................................................................................

URN

* Tick if exhibit attached

| Police property reference | Description as per label (indicate if copy) | Exhibit reference no. | Person producing and current location of exhibit | * |
|---|---|---|---|---|
| | | | Person producing:<br><br>Current location: | |
| | | | Person producing:<br><br>Current location: | |
| | | | Person producing:<br><br>Current location: | |
| | | | Person producing:<br><br>Current location: | |
| | | | Person producing:<br><br>Current location: | |
| | | | Person producing:<br><br>Current location: | |
| | | | Person producing:<br><br>Current location: | |
| | | | Person producing:<br><br>Current location: | |
| | | | Person producing:<br><br>Current location: | |
| | | | Person producing:<br><br>Current location: | |
| | | | Person producing:<br><br>Current location: | |
| | | | Person producing:<br><br>Current location: | |

Date of completion: .................................................................................

2004/05 (1)

MG 15

**RESTRICTED (when complete)**

## RECORD OF INTERVIEW

URN ☐☐☐☐

SDN/ROTI/Contemporaneous Notes/Index of Interview with VIW/Visually recorded interview (delete as applicable)

| | |
|---|---|
| Person interviewed:............................................................ | Police Exhibit No: |
| Place of interview:............................................................ | Number of Pages: |
| ............................................................ | |
| Date of interview:............................................ | Signature of interviewer producing exhibit |

Time commenced:.................................................... Time concluded:....................................................

Duration of interview:....................................................

Audio tape reference nos. (♦):.................................... Visual image reference nos. (♦):....................................

Interviewer(s):....................................................................................................................................

Other persons present:....................................................................................................................................

| Tape counter times (♦) | Person speaking | Text |
|---|---|---|
| | | |
| | | |
| | | |
| | | |
| | | |
| | | |
| | | |
| | | |
| | | |
| | | |
| | | |
| | | |
| | | |
| | | |
| | | |
| | | |
| | | |
| | | |

Signature(s):....................................................................................................................................
(Contemporaneous notes only)                              ♦Not relevant for contemporaneous notes

2004/05 (1)

MG 15(CONT)

**RESTRICTED (when complete)**

Person interviewed: .................................................................................................................... Page No .......... of ..........

| Tape counter times (♦) | Person speaking | Text |
|---|---|---|
| | | |
| | | |
| | | |
| | | |
| | | |
| | | |
| | | |
| | | |
| | | |
| | | |
| | | |
| | | |
| | | |
| | | |
| | | |
| | | |
| | | |
| | | |
| | | |
| | | |
| | | |
| | | |
| | | |
| | | |
| | | |

Signature(s): ........................................................................................................................................................
(Contemporaneous notes only)                                                        ♦Not relevant for contemporaneous notes

2004/05 (1)

## COURTROOM GUIDANCE

### Cross-examination by the defence

The lawyer for the defence will ask questions of you, the professional witness.

**The aim is twofold:**
1. To advance their own case by:
   ■ Eliciting testimony favourable to them from you
   ■ Developing their own case theory by getting you to agree with certain propositions.
2. To undermine your case by
   ■ Limiting your testimony, area of expertise and/or length of experience,
   ■ Questioning the admissibility of evidence by discrediting your testimony, attacking methodology, investigation, basis of opinion, interpretation of facts, discrediting you as a witness (biased, inconsistent)

*Other factors to consider*

■ Don't be surprised if the questions seem repetitive, off the point or beyond your knowledge.
■ If you don't know an answer make sure you indicate that clearly to the magistrate/judge.
■ Remember the pause tactic if you need 'thinking time' and direct your answers to the magistrate/judge.
■ Keep your eyes on the magistrate/judge until you have finished your answer – despite what the lawyer is saying or doing.
■ The defence lawyer will then indicate that they have no further questions for you.

During your cross-examination you may be asked a question by the magistrate/judge if they are unclear about something you have said.

# References

Adhami, E. and Browne, D. P. (1996) *Major Crime Enquiries: Improving Expert Support for Detectives*. Home Office Police Research Group Special Interest Series Paper 9. London: Home Office.

Association of Chief Police Officers (1996) *Report on International, National and Inter-Force Crime*. London: Association of Chief Police Officers.

Association of Chief Police Officers (2005a) *Practice Advice on Core Investigative Doctrine*. Cambourne: National Centre for Policing Excellence.

Association of Chief Police Officers (2005b) *Guidance on the National Intelligence Model*. Wyboston, Bedford: National Centre for Policing Excellence.

Association of Chief Police Officers (2008) *Good Practice Guide for Computer Based Electronic Evidence* (4th edn). London: Association of Chief Police Officers and 7safe.

Atkinson, R. C. and Shiffrin, R. M. (1971) The Control of Short Term Memory. *Scientific American*, 225(2), 80–92.

Attorney General (2013) *Attorney General's Guidelines on Disclosure for investigators, prosecutors and defence practitioners*. London: Attorney General's Office.

Barker, T. and Roebuck, J. (1973) *An Empirical Typology of Police Corruption*. Springfield, IL: Bannerstone House.

Bennett, P. (1992) *Interviewing Witnesses and Victims for the Purpose of Taking Statements*. Unpublished Manuscript.

Billingsworth, R., Nemitz, T. and Bean, P. (eds) (2001) *Informers: Policing, Policy, Practice*. Cullompton: Willan Publishing.

Biondi, C. (2004) Determining Needs. In P. Carey (ed.), *Data Protection Handbook*. London: The Law Society, pp. 1–19.

Black, I. S. (2013) *The Art of Investigative Interviewing*. Waltham, MA: Butterworth-Heinemann.

Blackwell–Young, J. (2008) Witness Evidence. In G. Davies, C. Hollin and R. Bull (eds), *Forensic Psychology*. Chichester: John Wiley & Sons, pp. 209–233.

Brainerd, C. J., Reyna, V. F., Howe, M. L. and Kingma, J. (1990) The Development of Forgetting and Reminiscence. *Monographs of the Society for Research in Child Development*, 55(3–4), Serial no. 222.

British Broadcasting Corporation (2010) *Kweku Adoboli: From 'rising star' to rogue trader* Available from: www.bbc.co.uk/ news/uk-19660659 [Accessed 28 March 2014].

British Broadcasting Corporation (2013) *Ten questions posed by Vicky Pryce jury*. Available from: http://www.bbc.co.uk/news/uk-21521460 [Accessed 13 March 2014].

Brown, R. and McNeill, D. (1966) The 'Tip of the Tongue' Phenomenon. *Journal of Verbal Learning and Verbal Behavior*, 5(4), 325–337.

Bryman, A. (1986) *Leadership and Organizations*. London: Routledge and Kegan Paul.

Buckle, T. and Brown, D. (1997) *In Police Custody: Police Powers and Suspects' Rights Under the Revised PACE Codes of Practice*. Home Office Research Study 174, Home Office.

Bull, R. (1992) Obtaining Information Expertly. *Expert Evidence*, 1, 5–12.

Button, M. (2008) *Doing Security: Critical Reflections and an Agenda for Change*. Basingstoke: Palgrave.

Button, M., Johnston, L., Frimpong, K. and Smith, G. (2007) New Directions in Policing Fraud: the Emergence of the Counter Fraud Specialist in the United Kingdom. *International Journal of the Sociology of the Law*, 35, 192–208.

Button, M., Lewis, C., Shepherd, D. et al (2012) *Fraud and Punishment: Enhancing Deterrence through More Effective Sanctions*. Portsmouth: Centre for Counter Fraud Studies, University of Portsmouth.

Central Intelligence Agency (1993) *Factbook on Intelligence*. Langley, VA: Office of Public Affairs, Central Intelligence Agency.

Cheshire Constabulary (nd) *Where Will you Give your Evidence?* Available from: http://www.cheshire.police.uk/advice-information/victims-and-witnesses/witnesses/where-will-you-give-evidence.aspx [Accessed 2 July 2014].

Chitty, J. (1826) *A Practical Treatise on the Criminal Law* (2nd edn), Vol 1. Springfield: C. and G. Meriam.

CIFAS (nd) *Welcome to CIFAS*. Available from: http://www.cifas.org.uk/ [accessed 16 November 2013].

Clark, D. (2007) Covert Surveillance and Informer Handling. In T. Newburn, T. Williamson and A. Wright (eds), *Handbook of Criminal Investigation*. Cullompton: Willan Publishing, pp. 426–449.

Coleman, R. and McCahill, M. (2011) *Surveillance and Crime*. London: Sage.

College of Policing (2013a) *Investigation: Working with Suspects*. Available from: http://www.app.college.police.uk/app-content/investigations/working-with-suspects/#arrest-strategy [Accessed 7 May 2014].

College of Policing (2013b) *Intelligence Management: Intelligence Collection, Development and Dissemination*. Available from: http://www.app.college.police.uk/app-content/intelligence-management/intelligence-cycle/#collection [Accessed 7 May 2014].

Collins, R., Lincoln, R. and Frank, M. G. (2002) The Effect of Rapport in Forensic Interviewing. *Psychiatry, Psychology and Law*, 9(1), 69–78.

Cook, M. (1970) Experiments on Orientation and Proxemics. *Human Relations*, 23, 61–76.

Courts and Tribunals Judiciary (nd) *The Structure of the Courts*. Available from: http://www.judiciary.gov.uk/wp-content/uploads/JCO/Images/Layout/courts_structure.pdf [Accessed 23 June 2014].

Croall, H. (2003) Combating Financial Crime: Regulatory Versus Crime Control Approaches. *Journal of Financial Crime*, 11(1), 45–55.

Crown Prosecution Service (2012) *Making or Supplying Articles for use in Fraud*. Available from: http://www.cps.gov.uk/legal/s_to_u/sentencing_manual/making_or_supplying_articles_for_use_in_a_fraud/ [Accessed 26 March 2014].

Crown Prosecution Service (2014) *Crown Prosecution Service Disclosure Manual*. Available from:http://www.cps.gov.uk/legal/d_to_g/disclosure_manual/disclosure_manual_chapter_1/#a008, [Accessed 13 March 2014].

Crown Prosecution Service (nda) *Computer Misuse Act 1990*. Available from: https://www.cps.gov.uk/legal/a_to_c/computer_misuse_act_1990/ [Accessed 30 March 2014].

Crown Prosecution Service (ndb) *Tape Recorded Interviews*. Available from: http://www.cps.gov.uk/legal/s_to_u/tape_recorded_interviews/ [Accessed 17 October 2013].

Davis, D. and Leo, R. (2006) Strategies for Preventing False Confessions and Their Consequences. In M. R. Kebbell and G. M. Davies (eds), *Practical Psychology for Forensic Investigations and Prosecutions*. Chichester: John Wiley & Sons, pp. 121–149.

Department of Social Security (1998) *Beating Fraud is Everyone's Business: Securing the Future*, Cm 4012, London: The Stationery Office.

Farrell, S., Yeo, N. and Ladenberg, G. (2007) *Blackstone's Guide to the Fraud Act 2006*. Oxford: Oxford University Press.

Fisher, R. and Geiselman, R. (1992) *Memory-enhancing Techniques for Investigative Interviewing: The cognitive interview*. Springfield: Charles Thomas.

Fisher, R. P., Brennan, K. H. and McCauley, M. R. (2002) The Cognitive Interview Method to Enhance Eyewitness Recall. In M. L. Eisen, J. A. Quas and G. S. Goodman (eds), *Memory and Suggestibility in the Forensic Interview*. Mahwah, NJ: Lawrence Erlbaum.

Fraud Advisory Panel (2012) *Fraud Facts: An Introduction to Fraud Investigations*. Issue 16, June 2012. Available from https://www.fraudadvisorypanel.org/pdf_show_191.pdf [Accessed 13 April 2014].

General Dental Council (2013) *Dentist Struck off for Dishonesty, False Accounting and Fraud*. Available from: http://www.gdc-uk.org/Newsandpublications/Pressreleases/Pages/Dentist-struck-off-for-dishonesty,-false-accounting-and-fraud.aspx [Accessed 26 June 2014].

Gilbert, J. A. E. and Fisher, R. P. (2006) The Effects of Varied Retrieval Cues on Reminiscence in Eyewitness Memory. *Applied Cognitive Psychology*, 20, 723–739.

Goldstein, H. (1977) *Policing in a Free Society*. Cambridge, MA: Ballinger.

Griffiths, A., and Milne, R. (2006) Will it All End in Tiers? Police interviews with suspects in Britain. In T. Williamson (ed.) *Investigative Interviewing*. Cullompton: Willan Publishing, pp. 167–189.

Gudjonsson, G. H. (2003) *The Psychology of Interrogations and Confessions*. Chichester: John Wiley & Sons.

Gudjonsson, G. H. (2007) Investigative Interviewing. In T. Newburn, T. Williamson and A. Wright (Eds), *Handbook of Criminal Investigation*. Cullompton: Willan Publishing, pp. 466–492.

Hampshire and Isle of Wight Counter Fraud Service (2010) *Fraud Matters*. Issue 26, December 2010.

Hampson, R. (2011) *Forensic Accounting*. London: The Association of Accounting Technicians.

Haslers Chartered Accountants and Business Advisors (2013) *Vet Convicted of Fraud Struck off*. Available from: http://www.haslers.com/3047-vet-convicted-of-fraud-struck-off/ [Accessed 26 June 2014].

Holmberg, U. (2004) *Police Interviews with Victims and Suspects of Violent and Sexual Crimes: Interviewees' Experiences and Interview Outcomes*. Doctoral Dissertation. Stockholm: Stockholm University.

Holmberg, U. and Christianson, S. A. (2002) Murderers' and Sexual Offenders' Experiences of Police Interviews and Their Inclination to Admit and Deny Crimes. *Behavioural Sciences and the Law*, 20, 31–45.

Home Office (2007) *Achieving Best Evidence in Criminal Proceedings: Guidance on Interviewing Victims and Witnesses, and using Special Measures*. London: Home Office.

Home Office (2010a) *Covert Surveillance and Property Interference: Revised Code of Practice*. Norwich: The Stationery Office.

Home Office (2010b) *Covert Human Intelligence Sources: Code of Practice*. Norwich: The Stationery Office.

House of Lords (2009) *Bribery Bill: Explanatory Notes*. Available from: http://www.publications.parliament.uk/pa/ld200910/ldbills/003/en/10003x–.htm [Accessed 29 March 2014].

Information Commissioner's Office (2008) *CCTV Code of Practice, Revised Edition 2008*, Wilmslow: Information Commissioner's Office.

Information Commissioner's Office (2011) *Employment Practices Data Protection Code*, 2011, Wilmslow: Information Commissioner's Office.

Information Commissioners Office (2012) *Protection for Whistle-blowers Disclosing Information to the ICO*. Available from: http://ico.org.uk/concerns/~/media/documents/library/Corporate/Practical_application/protection_for_whistle_blowers.ashx [Accessed 1 May 2014]

Innes, M. (2007) Investigation Order and Major Crime Inquiries. In T. Newburn, T. Williamson and A. Wright (eds), *Handbook of Criminal Investigation*. Cullompton: Willan Publishing, pp. 255–276.

John, T. and Maguire, M. (2004) *The National Intelligence Model: Early Implementation Experience in Three Police Force Areas*. Working Paper Series, Paper 50. Cardiff: School of Social Sciences, Cardiff University.

Johnson, L. K. (2007) Introduction. In L. K. Johnson (ed.), *Handbook of Intelligence Studies*. Oxford: Routledge, pp. 1–14.

Johnson, M. and Rogers, K. M. (2007) The Fraud Act 2006: The E-Crime Prosecutor's Champion or the Creator of a New Inchoate Offence? *International Review of Law Computers*, 21(3), 295–304.

Kember, D., Jones, A., Loke, A. Y. et al (2001) *Reflective Teaching and Learning in the Health Professions*. Oxford: Blackwell Science.

Kendon, A. (1967) Some Functions of Gaze Direction in Social Interaction. *Acta Psychologica*, 2, 1–47.

Landry, J. and St-Yves, M. (2004) La Pratique de l'interrogatoire de police. In J. Landry and M. St-Yves (eds) *Psychologie des entrevues d'enquête: de la recherche à la pratique*. Cowansville: Éditions Yvon Blais.

Larson, M. S. (1977) *The Rise of Professionalism: A Sociological Analysis*. Berkeley: University of California Press.

Law Commission (2002) *Fraud: Report on a reference under section 3(1) (e) of the Law Commissions Act 1965*. Cm5560. London: The Law Commission.

Lea, J. and Young, J. (1993) *What is to be done about Law and Order?* London: Pluto Press.

Legislation.gov.uk (2010) *Bribery Act 2010: Explanatory Notes–Commentary on Sections–Section 6*. Available from: http://www.legislation.gov.uk/ukpga/2010/23/notes/division/5/6 [Accessed 29 March 2014].

Lennon, J. (2009) A Defence Perspective. In R. Billingsley (ed.) *Covert Human Intelligence Sources*. Hook: Waterside Press, pp. 29–41.

Leo, R. A. (1992) From Coercion to Deception: The Changing Nature of Police Interrogation in America. *Crime, Law and Social Change*, 18, 33–59.

Lichfield Live (2014) *Lichfield woman ordered to pay back £50,000 given to her by mistake*. Available from: http://lichfieldlive.co.uk/2014/06/25/lichfield-woman-ordered-to-pay-back-50000-given-to-her-by-mistake/ [Accessed 7 July 2014].

Lipton, J. (1977) On the Psychology of Eyewitness Testimony. *Journal of Applied Psychology*, 62, 90–93.

Lord, V. B. and Cowan, A. D. (2011) *Interviewing in Criminal Justice: Victims, Witnesses, Clients and Suspects*. Sudbury, MA: Jones and Bartlett.

Mackinnons (2011) *Bribery Act 2010–First Conviction*. Available from: http://www.mackinnons.com/expertise/business-law/news/bribery-act-2010-first-conviction/ [Accessed 7 July 2014].

Macrory, R. B. (2006) *Regulatory Justice: Making Sanctions Effective*. London: Cabinet Office.

Maguire, M. (2000) Policing by Risks and Targets: Some Dimensions and Implications of Intelligence-Led Crime Control. *Policing and Society*, 9, 315–336.

Maguire, M. (2008) Criminal Investigation and Crime Control. In T. Newburn (ed.) *Handbook of Policing* (2nd edn). Cullompton: Willan, pp. 430–464.

Manunta, G. (1996) The Case Against: Security Management is Not a Profession. *International Journal of Risk, Security and Crime Prevention*, 1, 233–240.

McConville, M. and Hodgson, J. (1993) Custodial Legal Advice and the Right to Silence. *Royal Commission on Criminal Justice Research, Research Study no 16*. London: HMSO.

McGurk, B. J., Carr, M. J. and McGurk, D. (1993) *Investigative Interviewing Courses for Police Officers: An Evaluation*. Police Research Series Paper 4. London: Home Office.

McKenzie, I. and Milne, R. (1997) *Memory and Interviewing Skills*. Psychology and Policing Course Unit Three (BSC (Hons) Policing and Police Studies). Portsmouth: Institute of Police and Criminological Studies, University of Portsmouth.

Melton, A. W. (1963) Implications of Short-Term Memory for a General Theory of Memory. *Journal of Verbal Learning and Verbal Behaviour*, 2, 1–21.

Metro (2012) '*Professional fraudster' jailed for Britain's biggest Ponzi scheme*. Available from: http://metro.co.uk/2012/03/08/professional-fraudster-kautilya-nandan-pruthi-jailed-for-britains-biggest-ponzi-scheme-344895/ [Accessed 27 June 2014].

Metropolitan Police (2002) *Decision Making*. London: Metropolitan Police Recruit Training School.

Metropolitan Police (2012) *Woman was Sentenced to 27 Months Imprisonment for Abuse of Position*. Available from: http://content.met.police.uk/News/Woman-was-sentenced-to-27-months-imprisonment-for-Fraud-by-Abuse-of-Position/1400010953932/1257246745756 [Accessed 27 June 2014].

Metropolitan Police (2014) *Cyber Crime Gang Behind Major Bank Fraud Jailed*. Available from: http://content.met.police.uk/News/Cyber-crime-gang-behind-major-bank-fraud-jailed/1400023721922/1257246745756 [Accessed 27 June 2014].

Milne, R. (2004) *The Enhanced Cognitive Interview: a step by step guide*. Unpublished training document.

Milne, R. and Bull, R. (1999) *Investigative Interviewing: Psychology and Practice*. Chichester: John Wiley & Sons.

Milne, R. and Bull, R. (2001) Interviewing Witnesses with Learning Disabilities for Legal Purposes. *British Journal of Learning Disabilities*, 29, 93–97.

Morgan, R. and Newburn, T. (1997) *The Future of Policing*. Oxford: Clarendon Press.

Moston, S., and Stephenson, G. M. (1992) Predictors of Suspect and Interviewer Behaviour During Police Questioning. In F. Lösel, D. Bender and T. Bliesener (eds), *Psychology and Law: International Perspectives*. Berlin: de Gruyter, pp. 212–219.

Mullock, J. and Leigh-Pollitt, P. (1999) *The Data Protection Act Explained*. London: The Stationery Office.

National Police Improvement Agency (2009) *National Investigative Interviewing Strategy 2009. Briefing Paper*. Wyboston: National Police Improvement Agency. Available from: http://www.acpo.police.uk/documents/crime/2009/200901CRINSI01.pdf [Accessed 20 April 2014].

National Prosecution Team (2011) *The Prosecution Team Manual of Guidance: For the Preparation, Processing and Submission of Prosecution Files*. Available from: http://library.college.police.uk/docs/appref/MoG-final-2011-july.pdf [Accessed 23 April 2014].

Newham London (2013) *Bent Registrar Jailed for Five Years Over Birth Certificate Scam*. Available from: http://www.newham.gov.uk/Pages/News/Bent-registrar-jailed-for-five-years-over-birth-certificate-scam.aspx [Accessed 27 June 2014].

Neyroud, P. and Disley, E. (2007) The Management, Supervision and Oversight of Criminal Investigations. In T. Newburn, T. Williamson and A. Wright (eds), *Handbook of Criminal Investigation*. Cullompton: Willan Publishing, pp. 549–571.

NHS Business Services Authority (2010) *Sisters Jailed for £123K NHS Fraud*. Available from: http://www.nhsbsa.nhs.uk/3127.aspx [Accessed 26 June 2014].

NHS Counter Fraud Service (2007) *Applying Appropriate Sanctions Consistently*. London: NHS Counter Fraud Service.

NHS Protect (2013) *Applying Appropriate Sanctions Consistently: Policy Statement– April 2013*. London: NHS Protect.

Office of the Surveillance Commissioner (2013) *Annual Report of the Chief Surveillance Commissioner to the Prime Minister and to Scottish Ministers for 2012–2013*. London: The Stationery Office.

Ormerod, D. (2007) Criminalising Lying. *Criminal Law Review*, March, pp. 193–219.

O'Shea, E. (2011) *The Bribery Act 2010: A Practical Guide*. Bristol: Jordan Publishing.

Oxford, K. (1986) The Power to Police Effectively. In J. Benyon and C. Bourn (eds) *Police Powers, Proprieties and Procedures*. Oxford: Pergamon Press, pp. 61–74.

PACE Code of Practice B (2010) *Code of Practice for Searches of Premises by Police Officers and the Seizure of Property Found by Police Officers on Persons or Premises*. Norwich: The Stationery Office.

PACE Code of Practice C (2012) *Code of Practice for the Detention, Treatment and Questioning of Persons by Police Officers*. Norwich: The Stationery Office.

Palfrey, C., Thomas, P. and Phillips, C. (2004) *Effective Healthcare Management*. Oxford: Blackwell.

Pepper, I. K. and Pepper, H. (2009) *Keywords in Policing*. Maidenhead: McGraw Hill.

Phillips, E. (1978) *The Social Skills Base of Psychopathology*. New York: Grune and Stratton.

Police and Criminal Evidence Act 1984 (2010). *CODE E. Code of Practice on Audio Recording Interviews with Suspects*. Available from: https://www.gov.uk/government/uploads/system/uploads/attachment_data/file/117585/pace-code-e.pdf [Accessed 23 April 2014].

Police and Criminal Evidence Act 1984 (2012) *CODE C. Revised. Code of Practice for the Detention, Treatment and Questioning of Persons by Police Officers.* Available from: https://www.gov.uk/government/uploads/system/uploads/attachment_data/file/117589/pace-code-c-2012.pdf [Accessed 23 April 2014].

Powell, M. B. and Snow, P. C. (2007) Guide to Questioning Children During the Free-narrative Phase of an Investigative Interview, *Australian Psychologist*, 42(1), 57–65.

Punch, M. (1985) *Conduct Unbecoming: The Social Construction of Police Deviance and Control.* New York: Tavistock.

Punch, M. (2009) *Police Corruption: Deviance, Accountability and Reform in Policing.* Cullompton: Willan Publishing.

Reiner, R. (2000) *The Politics of the Police* (3rd edn). Oxford: Oxford University Press.

Roberts, P. (2007) Law and Criminal Investigation. In T. Newburn, T. Williamson and A. Wright (eds) *Handbook of Criminal Investigation.* Cullompton: Willan Publishing, pp. 92–145.

Room, S. (2007) *Data Protection and Compliance in Context.* Swindon: British Computer Society.

Roy, R. (2006) Investigative Interviewing: Suspects' and Victims' Rights in Balance. In T. Williamson (ed.), *Investigative Interviewing: Rights, Research, Regulation.* Cullompton: Willan Publishing, pp. 292–317.

Rye and Battle Observer (2012) *Man faces court over alleged £17k fraud.* Available from: http://www.ryeandbattleobserver.co.uk/news/local/man-faces-court-over-alleged-17k-fraud-1-3833437 [Accessed 27 June 2014].

Scarman, Lord. (1982) *The Scarman Report: The Brixton Disorder, 10–12 April 1981.* Hardmondsworth: Pelican.

Schön, D. (1983) *The Reflective Practitioner: How Professionals Think in Action.* New York: Basic Books.

Shepherd, E. (1984) Values into Practice: The Implementation and Implications of Human Awareness Training. *Police Journal*, 57, 286–300.

Shepherd, E. (1986) Conversational Core of Policing. *Policing*, 2, 294–303.

Simonsen, C. E. (1996) The Case For: Security Management is a Profession. *International Journal of Risk, Security and Crime Prevention*, 1, 229–232.

Smith, N. and Flanagan, C. (2000) *The Effective Detective: Identifying the Skills of an Effective SIO.* Police Research Series Paper 122. London: Home Office.

Sommer, P. and Becker, F. D. (1969) Territorial Defence and the Good Neighbour. *Journal of Personality and Social Psychology*, 11, 85–92.

Sperry, L. (2003) *Becoming an Effective Healthcare Manager*. Baltimore: Health Professions Press.

Stelfox, P. (2009) *Criminal Investigation: An Introduction to Principles and Practice*. Cullompton: Willan Publishing.

St-Yves, M. (2006) The Psychology of Rapport: Five Basic Rules. In T. Williamson (ed.), *Investigative Interviewing: Rights, Research, Regulation*. Cullompton: Willan Publishing, pp. 87–106.

Tulving, E. (1974) Cue Dependent Forgetting. *American Scientist*, 62, 74–82.

Tulving, E. (2001) Episodic Memory and Common Sense: How far apart? *Philosophical Transactions of the Royal Society of London. Series B: Biological Sciences*, 356(1413), 1505–1515.

Tweney, R. D. and Chitwood, S. (1995) Scientific Reasoning. In S. E. Newstead and J. St. B. T. Evans (eds), *Perspectives on Thinking and Reasoning*. Hove: Laurence Erlbaum Associates Limited, pp. 241–260.

United Nations Office on Drugs and Crime (2010) *Criminal Intelligence: Manual for Front Line Law Enforcement*. Vienna: United Nations Office on Drugs and Crime.

Villiers, P. and Adlam, R. (2003) Introduction. In R. Adlam and P. Villiers (eds), *Police Leadership in the Twenty-first Century*. Winchester: Waterside, p xii.

Wadham, J. and Griffiths, J. (2005) *Blackstone's Guide to the Freedom of Information Act 2000* (2nd edn). Oxford: Oxford University Press.

Wadham, J. and Mountfield, H. (1999) *Blackstone's Guide to the Human Rights Act 1998*. London: Blackstone Press Limited.

Walkley, J. (1987) *Police Interrogations: A Handbook for Investigators*. London: Police Review Publication.

Whetten, D. and Cameron, K. (2002) *Developing Management Skills*. Upper Saddle River, NJ: Prentice Hall.

Wright, A. (2007) Ethics and Corruption. In T. Newburn, T. Williamson and A. Wright (eds), *Handbook of Criminal Investigation*. Cullompton: Willan Publishing, pp. 586–609.

# Index